Succeed in
IELTS

9

Practice Tests

GlobalELT

English Language Teaching Books

Succeed in IELTS

Introduction

IELTS is the International English Language Testing System. It tests all four language skills: listening, reading, writing and speaking. It is intended for people who want to study or work in an English-speaking country.

There are **two** versions of the test, the **Academic** version and the **General Training** version. The Academic version is for those who want to study or train in an English-speaking university. University admission to undergraduate and postgraduate courses is based on the results of the Academic test.

The General Training version is mainly for those who are going to English-speaking countries to do secondary education or get a job and focuses on basic survival skills in social and workplace environments.

All candidates have to take the Listening & Speaking Modules. There are different versions for the Reading and the Writing Modules, depending on whether candidates are taking the Academic or the General Training version of the test.

The 9 complete IELTS Practice Tests included in this book are for the Academic version of the test.

Published by GLOBAL ELT LTD
www.globalelt.co.uk
Copyright © **GLOBAL ELT LTD, 2011**

Contributors:
Sean Haughton, Christina Oliver and Linda Collins

Every effort has been made to trace the copyright holders and we apologize in advance for any unintentional omission. We will be happy to insert the appropriate acknowledgements in any subsequent editions.

British Library Cataloguing-in-Publication Data

A catalogue record of this book is available from the British Library.

● Succeed in IELTS - 9 Practice Tests - Student's Book - ISBN: 978-1-904663-33-1
● Succeed in IELTS - 9 Practice Tests - Teacher's Book - ISBN: 978-1-904663-34-8

The authors and publishers wish to acknowledge the following use of material:
The photos in the reading section of the Test 1 - 9, 10 © Ingram Publishing Image Library

Contents

Succeed in IELTS

IELTS FORMAT

Academic	**General Training**
For entry to undergraduate or postgraduate studies or for professional reasons.	For entry to vocational or training programmes not at degree level, for admission to secondary school and for immigration purposes.

The test Modules are taken in the following order:

MODULE	QUESTIONS	TIME	QUESTION TYPES
Listening	4 sections, 40 items	*approximately 30 minutes*	multiple choice, short-answer questions, sentence completion, notes, form, table, summary, flow-chart completion, labelling a diagram/map/plan, classification, matching
Academic Reading	3 Sections, 40 items	*60 minutes*	multiple choice, short-answer questions, sentence completion, notes, form, table, summary, flow-chart completion, labelling a diagram/map/plan, classification, matching, choosing suitable paragraph headings, identification of author's views, -yes, no, not given, -true, false, not given questions
General Training Reading	3 sections, 40 items	*60 minutes*	
Academic Writing	2 tasks	*60 minutes*	**Task 1** (150 Words - 20 minutes) Candidates have to look at a diagram, chart, or graph and present the information in their own words. **Task 2** (250 Words - 40 minutes) Candidates have to present a solution to a problem or present and justify an opinion.
General Training Writing	2 tasks	*60 minutes*	**Task 1** (150 Words - 20 minutes) Candidates have to respond to a problem with a letter asking for information. **Task 2** (250 Words - 40 minutes) Candidates have to present a solution to a problem or present and justify an opinion.
Speaking		*11 to 14 minutes*	It consists of three parts; **Part 1** - Introduction and interview, **Part 2** - Long turn, **Part 3** - Discussion.
		Total Test Time *2 hours 44 minutes*	

IELTS

LISTENING SECTION

EXAM GUIDE

This section contains a detailed analysis of the Listening section of the exam with Exam Tips and Guidance for all the different Listening tasks that students will encounter taking the IELTS exam, with reference to the tasks included in the Practice Tests.

Listening Section Format

Section	No. of Questions	Text Type	Context	Task Types
1	10 (usually1 / 2 tasks)	a conversation / interview between two speakers	giving or exchanging information on an everyday topic	note completion form completion
2	10 (usually 2 tasks)	a monologue (occasionally introduced by a second speaker)	giving information on an everyday topic e.g. on a talk show	table completion sentence completion flow-chart completion
3	10 (up to 3 tasks)	a conversation between 2/3/4 speakers	an educational or training context	map labelling diagram labelling
4	10 (up to 3 tasks)	a monologue	an academic setting e.g. a lecture / presentation / talk / speech	matching multiple choice

Time: **40 minutes** (including 10 minutes to transfer your answers onto the answer sheet)

Marking: 1 mark for each correct answer

SECTION 1

is...
- a face-to-face or telephone conversation
- about a topic of general interest
- usually comprised of one or two tasks (there is a pause between tasks)
- ten questions long WITH an example at the beginning

tests...
- your understanding of specific information (i.e. dates, everyday objects, places etc.)
- spelling (all words must be spelt correctly)

spelling:
- if you are asked to write the name of a street, person, company etc., it will be spelt for you
- you should be very familiar with the names of the letters of the alphabet to aid you in spelling what you hear

numbers:
- you may have to write down a year, phone number, part of an address etc.
- remember that '0' can be pronounced 'oh' or 'zero' when saying a phone number
- when talking about money, we typically say amounts in the same way as in the examples below:
    - £4.50 = four pound(s) fifty / four fifty
    - $31.85 = thirty-one dollar(s) and eighty-five cents / thirty-one eighty-five
- most years are pronounced in the same way as in the examples below:
    - 1985 = nineteen eighty-five
    - 2015 = twenty fifteen
  (we put the first two numbers together and then the second two)
    - except for the years 2000 - 2009, example:
    - 2000 = two thousand
    - 2009 = two thousand and nine or two thousand nine
  (we say the year as we would a number)
- you can write dates in different ways and still get full marks:
  3rd March, March 3rd, March 3 and 3 March are all considered the same two-word answer
- for measurements, you can write either the whole thing or an abbreviation, for example:
    - 25m = 25 metres = 25 meters

SECTION 2

is...
- a talk / speech / announcement / recorded message / radio excerpt with one speaker talking (possibly introduced by another speaker)
- about a topic of general interest
- usually comprised of two tasks (there is a pause between tasks)
- 10 questions long - there is NO example

tests...
- your understanding of factual information
- your ability to select relevant information from what you hear

SECTION 3

is...
- a discussion between two to four speakers (e.g. between two students and a university lecturer)
- concerned with some aspect of academic life
- up to three tasks (there is a pause between tasks)
- 10 questions long - there is NO example

tests...
- your ability to identify key facts and ideas and how they relate to each other
- your ability to identify speakers' attitudes and opinions

SECTION 4

is...
- a lecture / talk / presentation / speech, often in front of an audience
- concerned with a topic of academic interest, like a scientific subject for example
- up to three tasks (there is no pause between tasks)
- 10 questions long - there is NO example

tests...
- your ability to follow the speaker's opinion
- your ability to spell accurately
- your ability to understand and distinguish between different ideas (e.g. causes, reasons, effects, consequences)
- your ability to follow the way the ideas are organised (e.g. main ideas, specific information and attitude)

TASK TYPES: (1) NOTE COMPLETION

Remember...

1. Always check the word limit in the instructions.
2. Use the time before the recording starts to look at the heading and read through the notes.
3. Look at each gap individually and think about what kind of word(s) would fill it i.e. numbers, a date, an address, a noun, a verb etc.
4. Follow the introduction carefully when the recording starts; the narrator will tell you what the section is about.
5. Focus on each question in turn as you listen to the recording. Keep up with the recording as it moves from one question to the next and do not dwell on gaps you have missed; there isn't time and this will possibly cost you the answer to the next gap as well.

If you don't know an answer, guess it at the end when you are filling in your answer sheet; you have nothing to lose!

EXAMPLE:
TEST 1 - SECTION 1

There will always be an example in Section 1. While this is being played you have an opportunity to establish a context for what you would expect to hear in the rest of the recording. Also use the point in the recording where the example finishes as a cue to listen carefully for your first answer.

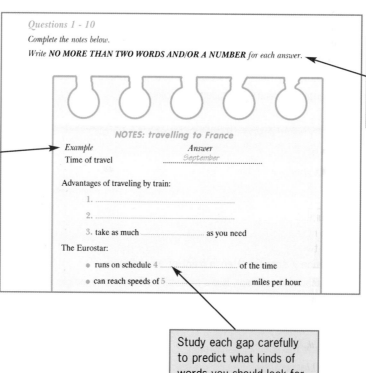

Questions 1 - 10

Complete the notes below.

Write **NO MORE THAN TWO WORDS AND/OR A NUMBER** for each answer.

NOTES: travelling to France

Example	Answer
Time of travel	September

Advantages of traveling by train:

1. ....
2. ....
3. take as much .... as you need

The Eurostar:

• runs on schedule 4 .... of the time
• can reach speeds of 5 .... miles per hour

Always stick to the word limit; you can write one, two or three words for each answer in this case.

Study each gap carefully to predict what kinds of words you should look for. In 4, for example, we might need to listen out for a percentage (a number).

TASK TYPES: (2) MULTIPLE CHOICE

Remember...

1. The questions will follow the order of the recording.
2. You will be told either to choose ONE option from A, B and C, or TWO options from A, B, C, D and E.
3. Always read the questions before you start. This will give you an idea of what the recording is about and what to listen for.
4. Listen carefully to the narrator's introduction to find out what the recording is about.
5. As soon as you've finished one question, listen out for the answer to the next (do not dwell on questions you aren't sure of as you only hear the recording once; quickly move on or risk missing another answer).

EXAMPLE: TEST 3 - SECTION 2

Read the instructions carefully to see whether you have to select one or two of the options. The most common MCQ question is the select-one-option type.

Although the questions will be in the order they appear on the recording, the options, A, B and C, will not necessarily be in the order they are heard.

As with all tasks, do not always expect the questions to be worded in the exact same way as the information on the recording. Often, the correct answer will be paraphrased.

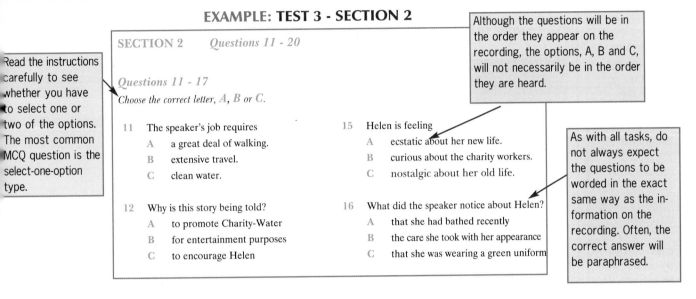

SECTION 2   *Questions 11 - 20*

Questions 11 - 17
Choose the correct letter, A, B or C.

11 The speaker's job requires
   A a great deal of walking.
   B extensive travel.
   C clean water.

12 Why is this story being told?
   A to promote Charity-Water
   B for entertainment purposes
   C to encourage Helen

15 Helen is feeling
   A ecstatic about her new life.
   B curious about the charity workers.
   C nostalgic about her old life.

16 What did the speaker notice about Helen?
   A that she had bathed recently
   B the care she took with her appearance
   C that she was wearing a green uniform

TASK TYPES: (3) FORM COMPLETION

N.B. Form completion tasks are very similar to note completion exercises.

EXAMPLE: TEST 3 - SECTION 1

You don't have to write the same number of words in each space; you can write up to the maximum number of words allowed, so, in this case, one, two or three.

The importance of not going over the word limit cannot be stressed enough. If you write too many words you will not receive any marks for that question.

Do not expect the information around the gap to appear in exactly the way it is heard on the recording; it may be paraphrased, or the word order may be modified. However, the missing word(s) itself will always be found on listening to the recording.

Look how we can predict what type of word to write:
5 = noun
6 = number
7 = noun

Remember that your spelling must be accurate. For names, places etc. you will hear the missing word(s) spelt on the recording.

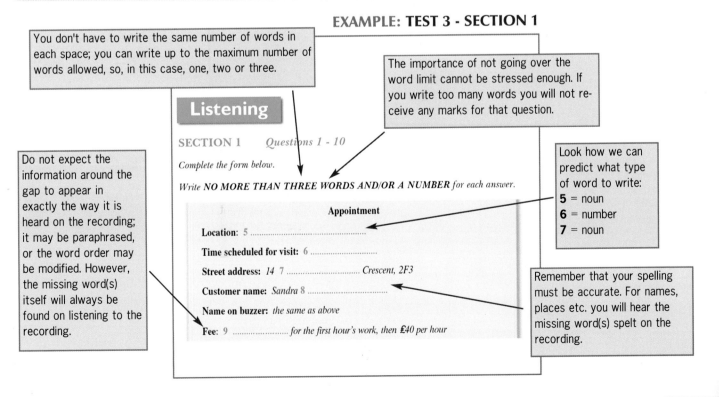

Listening

SECTION 1   *Questions 1 - 10*

Complete the form below.

*Write **NO MORE THAN THREE WORDS AND/OR A NUMBER** for each answer.*

Appointment

Location: 5 ....

Time scheduled for visit: 6 ....

Street address: *14* 7 .... *Crescent, 2F3*

Customer name: *Sandra* 8 ....

Name on buzzer: *the same as above*

Fee: 9 .... *for the first hour's work, then £40 per hour*

TASK TYPES: (4) TABLE COMPLETION

N.B. Table completion tasks are very similar to note completion exercises.

EXAMPLE: TEST 5 - SECTION 3

You will hear the exact word you need to write, though the information around it may be phrased differently.

The questions are in the same order as the information on the recording, so, if they go across the table row-by-row, then the information on the recording follows in the same way, with each row being discussed in turn. If they go down column-by-column, then the recording will discuss each column in turn.

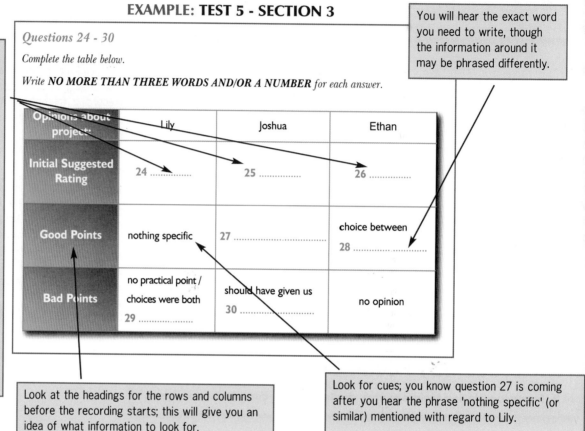

Questions 24 - 30

Complete the table below.

Write **NO MORE THAN THREE WORDS AND/OR A NUMBER** *for each answer.*

Opinions about project:	Lily	Joshua	Ethan
Initial Suggested Rating	24	25	26 ....
Good Points	nothing specific	27	choice between 28 ....
Bad Points	no practical point / choices were both 29	should have given us 30	no opinion

Look at the headings for the rows and columns before the recording starts; this will give you an idea of what information to look for.

Look for cues; you know question 27 is coming after you hear the phrase 'nothing specific' (or similar) mentioned with regard to Lily.

ASK TYPES: (5) FLOW-CHART COMPLETION

Remember...

1. Flow-charts require you to follow the development of a discussion.
2. The steps in the flow-chart will be in the same order as what you hear.
3. Listen carefully to the part of the discussion to which the task relates because you will only hear it once.
4. There are two types of flow-chart task; A and B (see below). A requires you to choose an option (A, B, C etc.) from the box to complete each space. B requires you to write the exact word(s) you hear in the space.

EXAMPLE (TYPE A) TEST 4 - SECTION 3

There will usually be more op-tions than there are spaces, so there are some options you will not need. Do not use any option more than once.

Look for cues; the answer to question 26 will come shortly after you hear 'labo-ratory supervisor reviews the applica-tion' (or similar).

The questions are in the order that you will hear them, so follow the flow-chart in the direction the questions lead you.

Questions 26 - 30

Complete the flow chart below.

Choose **SIX** answers from the box and write the correct letter, A - G, next to questions 26 - 30.

Experimental Design Procedure For Final Year Projects in Chemistry

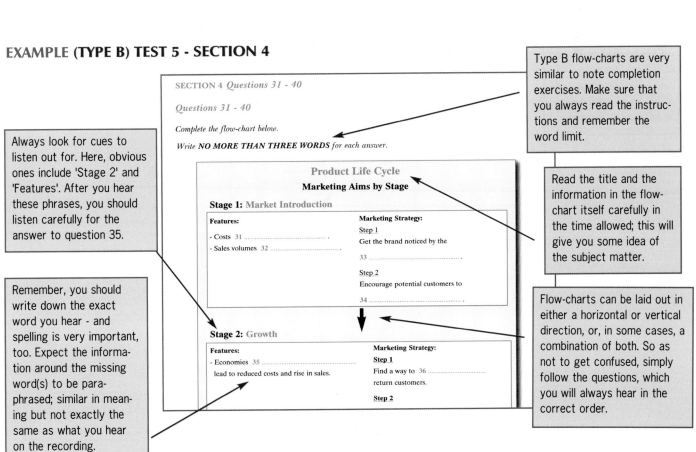

EXAMPLE (TYPE B) TEST 5 - SECTION 4

Type B flow-charts are very similar to note completion exercises. Make sure that you always read the instruc-tions and remember the word limit.

Always look for cues to listen out for. Here, obvious ones include 'Stage 2' and 'Features'. After you hear these phrases, you should listen carefully for the answer to question 35.

Read the title and the information in the flow-chart itself carefully in the time allowed; this will give you some idea of the subject matter.

Remember, you should write down the exact word you hear - and spelling is very important, too. Expect the informa-tion around the missing word(s) to be para-phrased; similar in mean-ing but not exactly the same as what you hear on the recording.

Flow-charts can be laid out in either a horizontal or vertical direction, or, in some cases, a combination of both. So as not to get confused, simply follow the questions, which you will always hear in the correct order.

SECTION 4 *Questions 31 - 40*

Questions 31 - 40

Complete the flow-chart below.

Write **NO MORE THAN THREE WORDS** for each answer.

Product Life Cycle
Marketing Aims by Stage

Stage 1: Market Introduction

Features:
- Costs 31 ....
- Sales volumes 32 ....

Marketing Strategy:
Step 1
Get the brand noticed by the
33 ....

Step 2
Encourage potential customers to
34 ....

Stage 2: Growth

Features:
- Economies 35 ....
  lead to reduced costs and rise in sales.

Marketing Strategy:
Step 1
Find a way to 36 ....
return customers.

Step 2

TASK TYPES: (6) DIAGRAM LABELLING

Remember...

1. You will have to transfer the information you hear to a simple picture or plan of some kind.
2. You will need to be familiar with the kind of language used to express where things are.
3. Listen carefully to the part of the discussion to which this task relates because you will only hear it once.
4. There are three types of diagram labelling tasks. See below for details.

EXAMPLE (TYPE A) TEST 2 - SECTION 2

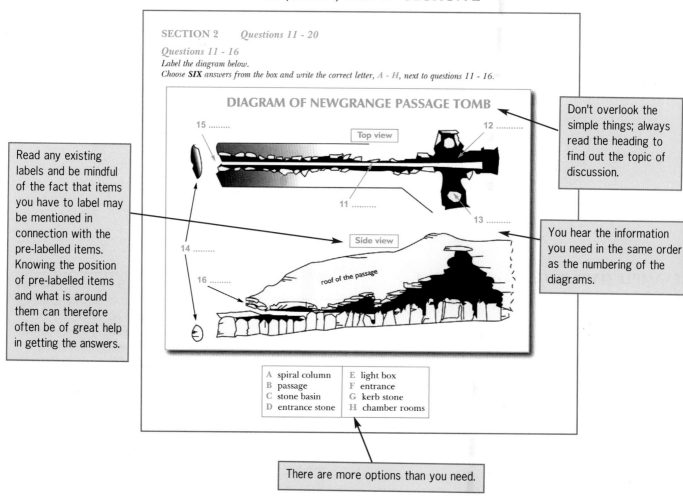

SECTION 2   Questions 11 - 20

Questions 11 - 16
Label the diagram below.
Choose **SIX** answers from the box and write the correct letter, A - H, next to questions 11 - 16.

DIAGRAM OF NEWGRANGE PASSAGE TOMB

15 ....   Top view   12 ....

11 ....

13 ....

14 ....   Side view

16 ....   roof of the passage

A spiral column	E light box
B passage	F entrance
C stone basin	G kerb stone
D entrance stone	H chamber rooms

Read any existing labels and be mindful of the fact that items you have to label may be mentioned in connection with the pre-labelled items. Knowing the position of pre-labelled items and what is around them can therefore often be of great help in getting the answers.

Don't overlook the simple things; always read the heading to find out the topic of discussion.

You hear the information you need in the same order as the numbering of the diagrams.

There are more options than you need.

EXAMPLE (Type B) TEST 1 - SECTION 2

Questions 16 - 20

Label the floor plan below.
Write the correct letter A - G next to the questions below.

FLOOR PLAN OF THE CUBE, BIRMINGHAM

16	restaurant with view	
17	hotel	
18	office space	
19	exlusive shops	
20	waterside restaurant	

The letters A-G are not in the order they will be discussed in the recording. The information in the recording will follow the same order as questions 16-20.

Not all the letters will be used.

As always, listen out for cues and use them to help you locate the items you are looking for. Areas such as the rooftop, canal and atrium are great reference points.

EXAMPLE (Type C) TEST 6 - SECTION 2

Questions 16 - 20

Label the diagram below. Write **NO MORE THAN TWO WORDS** *for each answer.*

The third type of diagram labelling is similar to note completion. Listen out for the exact word(s) you need, adhere to the word limit for each space and ensure that you spell your answers correctly.

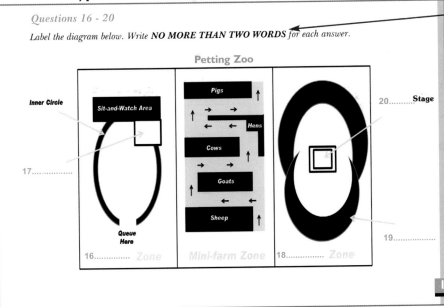

Petting Zoo

Inner Circle

Sit-and-Watch Area

Pigs

Hens

Cows

Goats

Sheep

Queue Here

20........... Stage

17.................

19.................

16.............. Zone

Mini-farm Zone

18............... Zone

141

TASK TYPES: (7) MAP LABELLING

N. B. Map labelling is very similar to diagram labelling. There are three types of map questions and they follow the format of types A, B and C above.

Remember...
1. Read the instructions so you know what to write (e.g. a word or letter).
2. Look at the map and try to understand what it shows and how each location might be described.
3. Use the places already marked on the map to help you follow the recording.

EXAMPLE (MAP 1) TEST 6 - SECTION 2

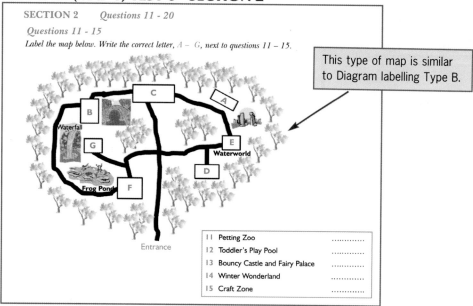

SECTION 2   Questions 11 - 20

Questions 11 - 15

Label the map below. Write the correct letter, A – G, next to questions 11 – 15.

This type of map is similar to Diagram labelling Type B.

11	Petting Zoo	....
12	Toddler's Play Pool	....
13	Bouncy Castle and Fairy Palace	....
14	Winter Wonderland	....
15	Craft Zone	....

EXAMPLE (MAP 2) TEST 9 - SECTION 2

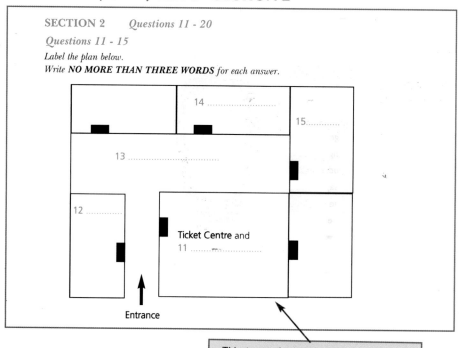

SECTION 2   Questions 11 - 20

Questions 11 - 15

Label the plan below.
Write **NO MORE THAN THREE WORDS** for each answer.

14 ....

15 ....

13 ....

12 ....

Ticket Centre and
11 ....

Entrance

This type of map is similar to Diagram labelling Type C.

TASK TYPES: (8) MATCHING

Remember...
1. Matching requires you to listen to detailed information and connect it to a number of places, people, groups etc.
2. You will only hear the part of the recording related to the matching task ONCE.
3. Match ONE piece of information from the box to each question.

EXAMPLE (Type 1) TEST 9 - SECTION 2

In this matching task you can choose the options more than once.

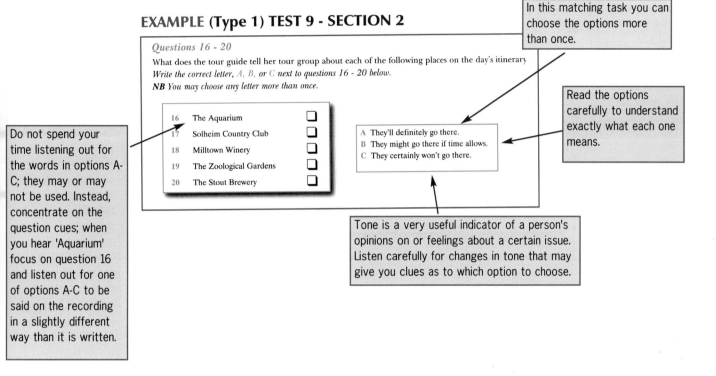

Questions 16 - 20

What does the tour guide tell her tour group about each of the following places on the day's itinerary
Write the correct letter, A, B, or C next to questions 16 - 20 below.
NB *You may choose any letter more than once.*

16	The Aquarium	☐
17	Solheim Country Club	☐
18	Milltown Winery	☐
19	The Zoological Gardens	☐
20	The Stout Brewery	☐

A They'll definitely go there.
B They might go there if time allows.
C They certainly won't go there.

Read the options carefully to understand exactly what each one means.

Do not spend your time listening out for the words in options A-C; they may or may not be used. Instead, concentrate on the question cues; when you hear 'Aquarium' focus on question 16 and listen out for one of options A-C to be said on the recording in a slightly different way than it is written.

Tone is a very useful indicator of a person's opinions on or feelings about a certain issue. Listen carefully for changes in tone that may give you clues as to which option to choose.

EXAMPLE (Type 2) TEST 5 - SECTION 3

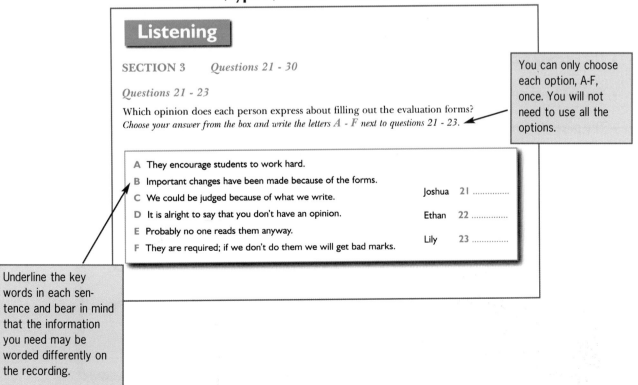

Listening

SECTION 3   *Questions 21 - 30*

Questions 21 - 23

Which opinion does each person express about filling out the evaluation forms?
Choose your answer from the box and write the letters A - F next to questions 21 - 23.

You can only choose each option, A-F, once. You will not need to use all the options.

A They encourage students to work hard.
B Important changes have been made because of the forms.
C We could be judged because of what we write.
D It is alright to say that you don't have an opinion.
E Probably no one reads them anyway.
F They are required; if we don't do them we will get bad marks.

Joshua   21 ....
Ethan   22 ....
Lily   23 ....

Underline the key words in each sentence and bear in mind that the information you need may be worded differently on the recording.

TASK TYPES: (9) SENTENCE COMPLETION

N.B. Sentence completion is similar to note completion.

EXAMPLE: TEST 9 - SECTION 3

Note that for all 'completion' tasks, hyphenated words are counted as one word and contracted words are never tested.

As with all 'completion' tasks, adhere to the word limit for each space.

Identify the key words to listen out for, e.g. 'consumer' and 'laser devices' in question 21. Use these as your cues to tell you when to get ready to hear the answer. Try to pick key words that aren't easily paraphrased (e.g. laser devices) or just think of key concepts, e.g. the concept of movement or motion for question 23.

SECTION 3   Questions 21 - 30

Questions 21 - 25

Complete the sentences below.
Write **NO MORE THAN TWO WORDS** for each answer.

Gyroscopes are used in laser devices and are found in many consumer 21 ....

The purpose of the project is to design a functional, 22 .... and beneficial consumer product.

The gyroscopic exercise ball can be set in motion by movement of the 23 .... and wrist together in synch.

The gyroscopic ball could help people in 24 .... who have lower-arm injuries.

The product could also be aimed at 25 .... for whom lower-arm strength is very important.

General Listening Tips

- The listening paper lasts 30 minutes.

- You will be given ten minutes at the end to transfer your answers to your answer sheet.

- The paper is common to both the academic and general modules of the IELTS.

- The level of difficulty increases from Section 1 to Section 4.

- Each section is heard ONCE only.

- The instructions for each task are written on the paper.

- There is a short pause before each section and a short pause before each separate task.

- A brief introduction is heard before each section, outlining the context of the recording. This introduction is not written on the paper itself.

- Correct spelling is absolutely essential.

IELTS

READING SECTION

EXAM GUIDE

This section contains a detailed analysis of the **Reading** section of the exam with Exam Tips and Guidance for all the different Reading tasks that students will encounter taking the IELTS exam, with reference to the tasks included in the Practice Tests.

Reading Section Format

Passage	No. of Questions	Text Type	Task Types
1	13 (2 or 3 tasks)	Texts may be sourced from books, journals, magazines, newspapers or websites. They are suitable for under-graduate and postgraduate level reading, but are general-interest not specialist-interest.	multiple choice matching short-answer choosing True/False/Not given choosing Yes/No/Not given diagram labelling summary completion sentence completion note/table/flow-chart completion locating information
2	13 (2 or 3 tasks)		
3	14 (2 or 3 tasks)		

Time: 60 minutes (including time to transfer your answers onto the answer sheet)

Marking: 1 mark for each correct question

READING PASSAGE 1

is...
- a text of up to 900 words (usually factual or descriptive)
- made up of two or three tasks and 13 questions in total
- usually slightly easier than passages 2 and 3

tests...
- your understanding of texts which could be included in an academic course
- your ability to follow an argument and/or opinions and/or a series of facts or ideas
- a range of reading skills including **reading for main ideas** and **reading for detail**, as well as understanding the structure of a text at both sentence and paragraph level

READING PASSAGE 2

is...
- a text of up to 900 words
- made up of two or three different tasks and 13 or 14 questions in total
- usually slightly harder than passage 1

for what it tests refer to Passage 1 guidelines

READING PASSAGE 3

is...
- a text of up to 950 words (so can be slightly longer than 1 and 2)
- made up of two or three different tasks and 13 or 14 questions in total
- usually more difficult than passages 1 and 2

for what it tests refer to Passage 1 guidelines

READING TIPS

- there are **40 questions** in total on the reading paper
- no one passage will have more than **14 questions** attached to it
- only answers found in or implied from the information in the texts are correct; you are not required to use your background knowledge
- attempt all questions; you have nothing to lose by guessing

TASK TYPE: (1) TRUE/FALSE/NOT GIVEN

Task: Compare the information given in each statement with the information found in the text to decide whether or not the information is the same in both.

You must...
1. Read the statements carefully (they will be in the same order as the information in the passage).
2. Scan the text to find the information you need (and read the section carefully if necessary).
3. Decide if the idea expressed in each statement agrees with the text (TRUE) or contradicts the text (FALSE), or, if there is no information about the statement in the text (NOT GIVEN).

EXAMPLE: TEST 1 - PASSAGE 1

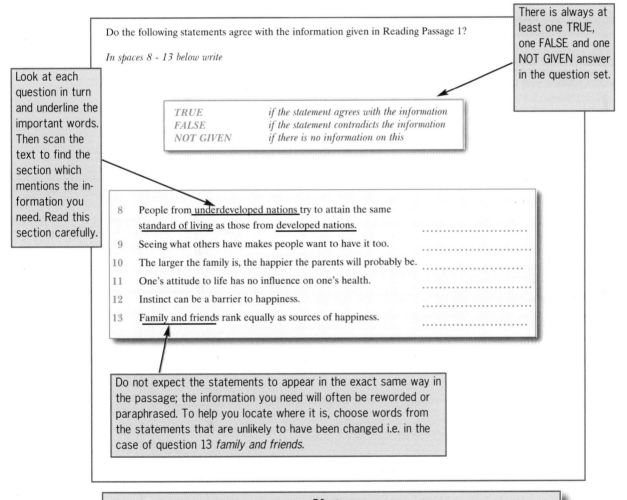

Do the following statements agree with the information given in Reading Passage 1?

In spaces 8 - 13 below write

There is always at least one TRUE, one FALSE and one NOT GIVEN answer in the question set.

TRUE	*if the statement agrees with the information*
FALSE	*if the statement contradicts the information*
NOT GIVEN	*if there is no information on this*

Look at each question in turn and underline the important words. Then scan the text to find the section which mentions the information you need. Read this section carefully.

8 People from <u>underdeveloped nations</u> try to attain the same <u>standard of living</u> as those from <u>developed nations</u>. ....

9 Seeing what others have makes people want to have it too. ....

10 The larger the family is, the happier the parents will probably be. ....

11 One's attitude to life has no influence on one's health. ....

12 Instinct can be a barrier to happiness. ....

13 <u>Family and friends</u> rank equally as sources of happiness. ....

Do not expect the statements to appear in the exact same way in the passage; the information you need will often be reworded or paraphrased. To help you locate where it is, choose words from the statements that are unlikely to have been changed i.e. in the case of question 13 *family and friends*.

Note:

- Remember the questions are in the order the information appears in the text. If you have found 8 and 10, but cannot find the answer to 9, you can therefore narrow your search down to the text between where you found those answers.

- The information you need to find will not necessarily be evenly spaced in the passage. There may even be some paragraphs which do not relate to the questions.

- Always look at the title and the information in the opening few lines of the text before you do anything else. This will give you an idea of what the text might be about.

- Next, read the text quickly (gist-read) in order to get a general understanding of what is being discussed.

TASK TYPE: (2) YES/NO/NOT GIVEN

Task: Compare the information given in each statement with the information found in the text to decide whether or not the information is the same in both. You have to be able to understand the different opinions, ideas and/or attitudes expressed.

You must...

1. Read the statements carefully (they will be in the same order as the information in the passage).

2. Scan the text to find the information you need (and read the relevant section carefully if necessary).

3. Decide if the ideas expressed in each statement agree with the opinions/ideas of the writer (YES) or contradict them (NO), or, if there is no information about the opinion/idea in the text (NOT GIVEN).

Read the instructions very carefully. Here it talks about the claims in the article generally. If it said 'do the following statements agree with the writer's views?', then it would only be the writer's views you should concern yourself with, even if other views are mentioned in the text.

EXAMPLE: TEST 9 - PASSAGE 3

Questions 34 - 40

Do the following statements agree with the information given in Reading Passage 3?
In spaces 154 - 40 below, write

This task-type is very similar to Type 1.
Remember all three options: YES, NO and NO GIVEN, must be used at least once.

YES	*if the statement agrees with the information*
NO	*if the statement contradicts the information*
NOT GIVEN	*if there is no information on this*

Underline the key word(s) in the statements and scan the passage for them. Be mindful of the fact that the passage may not contain the exact word(s) you are looking for, but a synonym instead.

34   Banks demand larger deposits from first-time property investors.   _____

35   By making a larger deposit, investors can limit their personal financial risk.   _____

36   There are a lot of long-term costs to take into consideration before purchasing a rental property.   _____

37   Banks require you to hold a lot of money in reserve to meet your long-term property maintenance costs.   _____

38   Many investors are tempted to pay more than they should for their investment properties.   _____

39   At the moment, house prices are extremely high in general.   _____

40   There are a lot of urban renewal projects that have been earmarked by the government.   _____

TASK TYPE: (3) DIAGRAM LABELLING

Task: To understand a detailed description, and relate it to information in a diagram. The section of the passage related to the diagram will often be concerned with a process or a description of something.

You must...
1. Scan the text to find specific information.
2. Find the word(s) or number in the text which fits each space and copy it into the gap.

EXAMPLE: TEST 3 - PASSAGE 1

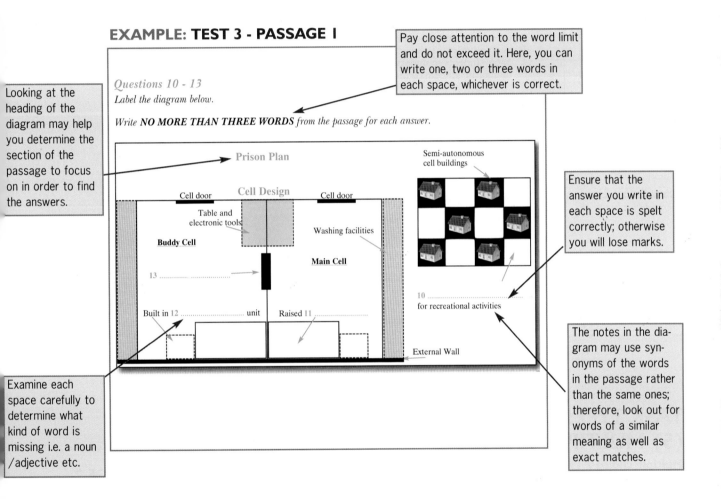

Looking at the heading of the diagram may help you determine the section of the passage to focus on in order to find the answers.

Questions 10 - 13
Label the diagram below.

Write **NO MORE THAN THREE WORDS** *from the passage for each answer.*

Pay close attention to the word limit and do not exceed it. Here, you can write one, two or three words in each space, whichever is correct.

Ensure that the answer you write in each space is spelt correctly; otherwise you will lose marks.

Examine each space carefully to determine what kind of word is missing i.e. a noun /adjective etc.

The notes in the diagram may use synonyms of the words in the passage rather than the same ones; therefore, look out for words of a similar meaning as well as exact matches.

Note:

You must use words copied directly from the passage. The form of the words copied should not be altered. The information in the diagram will not always be numbered/displayed in the same order as it is written about in the passage.

TASK TYPE: (4) MULTIPLE CHOICE

Task: To develop a general and detailed understanding of the text.

You must...

1. Read questions or incomplete sentences which focus on ideas and information in the text.
2. Choose the correct option A, B, C or D to answer the question or complete the statement.

EXAMPLE: TEST 6 - PASSAGE 2

In four-option multiple choice questions, there will never be more than one correct option.

Multiple choice questions do follow the order of the text, so the answer to 20 will come before 21.

Questions 19 - 22

Choose the correct letter A, B, C or D.

19   One purpose of the summer school is to

A   encourage students to work individually.
B   enable students to be assessed directly.
C   allow students to undertake simple experiments.
D   familiarise students with laboratory equipment.

20   Instructional designers advise faculty on the

A   course content.
B   support services for students.
C   suitability of library material.
D   visual display of coursework.

21   Staff tutors are responsible for the

A   monitoring of students' progress.
B   suitability of courses for students' needs.
C   appointment of certain teaching staff.
D   training of all teaching staff.

Note:
The questions may relate to a small part of the passage, a large section or, occasionally, questions may refer to the passage as a whole.

Careful! Often the incorrect options will use similar words to those in the text to act as a distraction and focus your attention away from the correct answer.

Make sure you read far enough to cover all four options; then you can make an informed decision as to the right answer.

TASK TYPE: (5) MULTIPLE CHOICE

Multiple choice 2 - select more than one option

1 always read the instructions for every question very carefully

2 don't assume because it is multiple choice that you only have to select one answer

3 for multiple choice questions containing MORE THAN FOUR OPTIONS you will be required to select AT LEAST TWO of them

EXAMPLE: TEST 9 - PASSAGE 2

Questions 20 - 21

*Choose **TWO** letters, A - E*

Which **TWO** of the following are hazards that surfers face?

A being held underwater by reefs.

B the potential for shark attacks.

C frequent encounters with jellyfish.

D demanding water conditions.

E hazardous rescue attempts.

TASK TYPE: (6) MATCHING SENTENCE ENDINGS

Task: To understand a number of significant ideas expressed in the text.

You must...

1. Read the first halves of the sentences.
2. Choose the ending for each half sentence from a number of options so that the complete sentence correctly reflects an idea or opinion that is expressed in the passage.

EXAMPLE: TEST 4 - PASSAGE 2

Questions 14 - 20

Complete each sentence with the correct ending A - K from the box below.

Write the correct letter A - K in spaces 14 - 20 below.

The questions are laid out in the order the information appears in the text.

14	Colour blindness can be caused by a birth defect, or	....
15	Surprisingly, some people who are colour blind	....
16	People with hereditary colour blindness	....
17	Because of our genetic make-up, colour blindness	....
18	Red-green genetic photoreceptor disorders mean that people	....
19	People with <u>monochromacy</u>	....
20	The inability to see certain lights	....

Look out for words/ideas that are hard to rephrase and scan for these in the text.

Make sure that the option you select for the gap fits grammatically (i.e. the sentence makes sense) as well as reflecting the information expressed in the text.

A	can see better at night than during the day.
B	cannot be treated by surgery.
C	can affect men much more easily than women.
D	can affect their sensitivity to bright lights.
E	can see no colour at all, other than shades of black, grey and white.
F	can see things that people with normal vision cannot.
G	can have very dangerous consequences for colour blind people.
H	can be acquired or inherited.
I	can mean having to wear contact lenses.
J	cannot distinguish certain colours if they stand alone.
K	can match all colours of the spectrum.

There are always more options than needed.
Read carefully as some may have similar meanings but differ on important points.

Note:

As always, start by reading the passage for gist (to get a general idea of what it is about). Then look at the questions, underline the key words and scan for where they appear in the text. Read the section around the key words carefully.

TASK TYPE: (7) SENTENCE COMPLETION

Task: To understand key points in the text.

You must...

1. Read each sentence and identify where in the text the information to fill the gap is located.
2. Complete each gap by choosing a word or words from the text.

REMEMBER, FOR ALL COMPLETION EXERCISES...

1 there is a maximum number of words you can use to fill each gap, which is stated in the instructions

2 the information is not necessarily displayed in the order that it appears in the passage

3 you must copy the words from the text exactly as they appear - do not alter their form

EXAMPLE: TEST 5 - PASSAGE 2

Questions 21 - 23

Stick to the word limit in the instructions.

Complete the sentences.

Choose **NO MORE THAN THREE WORDS** *from the passage for each answer.*

The order of the questions or gaps does not necessarily reflect the order in which the information will be found in the text.

Highlight technical terms such as the one underlined here. These terms are very difficult to paraphrase so you can usually locate the same term in the text quite quickly by scanning for it.

21 One aspect of cognitive behavioural treatment includes the preparation of .... by offenders.

22 The treatment requires offenders to consider the .... that lead to a crime being committed.

23 Treatment programmes encourage offenders to recognise .... before they happen, and know what to do in case they do happen.

Make sure that the words you choose are:
(i) copied exactly as they appear in the text
(ii) spelt correctly
(iii) a grammatically correct fit - if they are not, do not be tempted to change the form of the words - look again for the correct answer which will fit without being altered in any way.

If you don't know the answer for a particular gap, at least guess what it is and ensure that your guess is a word lifted from the text.

TASK TYPE: (8) NOTE COMPLETION

EXAMPLE: TEST 5 - PASSAGE 2

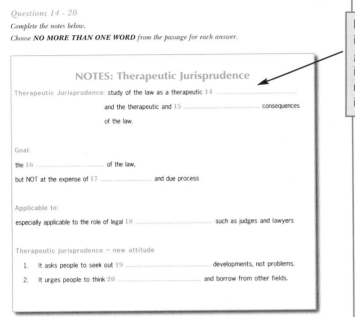

Questions 14 - 20

Complete the notes below.

Choose NO MORE THAN ONE WORD from the passage for each answer.

NOTES: Therapeutic Jurisprudence

Therapeutic Jurisprudence: study of the law as a therapeutic 14 ....

and the therapeutic and 15 .... consequences

of the law.

Goal:

the 16 .... of the law,

but NOT at the expense of 17 .... and due process

Applicable to:

especially applicable to the role of legal 18 .... such as judges and lawyers

Therapeutic jurisprudence = new attitude

1. It asks people to seek out 19 .... developments, not problems.

2. It urges people to think 20 .... and borrow from other fields.

> If a notes/table completion or summary type task is the first type of task you must answer for a given passage, it may be helpful to skim over the information in the notes/table/summary before reading the passage as this will give you a good idea of what the passage is about.

> **NOTE**
> - all completion tasks are similar: sentence/note/flow-chart/table
> - but for note, flow-chart and table completion you must understand a whole section(s) of the text not just key points

TASK TYPE: (9) FLOW-CHART COMPLETION

Task: To understand the description of a process or sequence of events.

You must...

1. Scan the text to find specific information using the key words in the flow-chart to help you locate where the relevant information is in the passage.

2. Find the word(s) or number in the text which fits each space and copy it into the gap.

EXAMPLE: TEST 1 - PASSAGE 3

Reading

Always pay attention to the word limit in the instructions.

The parts of the chart that don't contain a gap can act as guides; pointing you to the correct place in the passage to start looking for the next piece of information.

Questions 27 - 32

Complete the flow-chart below.

Write NO MORE THAN THREE WORDS for each answer.

> **Reading Tip:**
> Pay attention to how many words are required for an answer.

> **Note**
> The questions do not necessarily appear in the same order as the information will be found in the passage.

Scan the passage looking for the key words.

productive land

degradation proceeds at 27 ....

multiple causes

DESERTIFICATION

28 .... **a climate trend**

29 .... **a change in climate**

resulting in greater 30 ....

depletion of 31 ....

depletion of 32 ....

TASK TYPE: (10) SUMMARY COMPLETION

Task: To understand the main points of part (or occasionally all) of the text.

You must...

1. Locate the parts of the text to which the summary refers and find the answer to the questions.

There is another type of **SUMMARY COMPLETION** that does not require you to write words in the gaps; this is outlined below:

Note:
Be aware that the answers might **NOT** be in the same order that they appear in the text. However, the correct answers will be the **exact words** that you find in the text.

EXAMPLE: TEST 5 - PASSAGE 3

Questions 36 - 40

Complete the summary.
*Choose **NO MORE THAN TWO WORDS** from the passage for each answer.*

Sleep is so essential to a person that he can actually go longer without food than without sleep. During sleep, the brain has the chance to close down and do some repair work on neuronal connections which could otherwise 36 .... in a state of inactivity. Sleep also gives the brain the opportunity to organise data, especially newly-learned information.

During this rest period, the 37 .... drops and energy consumption goes down. At the same time, the cardiovascular system has a much-needed rest. While they go into a deep sleep, humans don't fall into 38 .... , unlike some small animals such as rodents. A 39 .... of 24 hours is described as a person's 40 .... , and this greatly influences a person's amount of sleep, and the type of sleep he gets.

Try to predict from context what part of speech the missing word is: e.g. Question **37** must be a noun because of the article 'the' that precedes it.

TASK TYPE: (11) SUMMARY COMPLETION 2

EXAMPLE: TEST 1 - PASSAGE 1

Questions 4 - 7

Complete the summary using the list of words, A - I, below.

Write the correct letter, A - I, in the spaces below.

Reading Tip:
When reading, remember to scan for key words and practise scanning for paraphrases of key words.

Note:
The words in the box are **NOT** always **exactly** as you will find them in the text. They may be paraphrased or in a different form.

Money can buy you just about anything, but not, it seems, happiness. Whether on a personal or national 4 .... , your bank balance won't make you happier. Once the basic criteria of a roof over your head and food on the table have been met, money ceases to play a part. One of the most important factors in achieving happiness is the extent of our social 5 .... - our relationships with family, friends, colleagues and so on. Equally important is the amount of 6 .... we have, either in our personal life, working life, or even in our ability to influence the political 7 .... that our country embarks on.

A episode	B interaction	C cooperation
D control	E number	F level
G course	H conflict	I limit

There are always more options than you need.

Think of it as a multiple choice question where you have nine possible options for each answer and must select one.

TASK TYPE: (12) TABLE COMPLETION

Task: To understand the sequence and find specific information in a text.

You must...

1. Locate the part of the text where the answer can be found.
2. Find and copy the exact words from the text which correctly fill the gap.

Use the column and row headings to give you a clue for where you should look in the passage to find the missing information.

EXAMPLE: TEST 2 - PASSAGE 1

Questions 6 - 9

Complete the table below.

Write *NO MORE THAN THREE WORDS* from the passage for each answer.

Disorder	Personality Trait Exhibited by Sufferer
Autism Spectrum Disorder	May excel in activities of a 6 .... nature.
Attention Deficit Disorder	May appear 7 ....
Schizophrenia	May respond to experiencing episodes of the disease by behaving in very 8 ....
Depression	May experience feelings of futility that lead to thoughts of 9 ....
Obsessive Compulsive Disorder	May frequently experience feelings of doubt and anxiety.

TASK TYPE: (13) MATCHING

(A) Matching Names

Task: To relate ideas, information or opinions in the text to a number of people, places, dates etc.

You must...

1. Read a list of statements and match them to a list of options by finding the information in the text.
2. Write the letter of the matching statement in the gap for each question.

(B) Matching Headings

Task: To select an appropriate title for some or all of the paragraphs

You must...

1. Read a list of headings and match them to the lettered paragraphs of the original passage.
2. Write the letter of the matching heading in the gap for each question.

EXAMPLE: (TYPE A) TEST 2 - PASSAGE 1

Remember, the statements are likely to be paraphrased so try to identify key words or concepts.

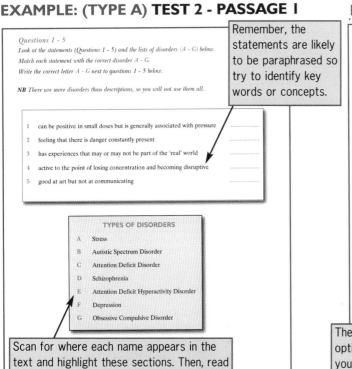

EXAMPLE: (TYPE B) TEST 6 - PASSAGE 1

The heading should reflect the overall content of the paragraph not just one or two sentences in it.

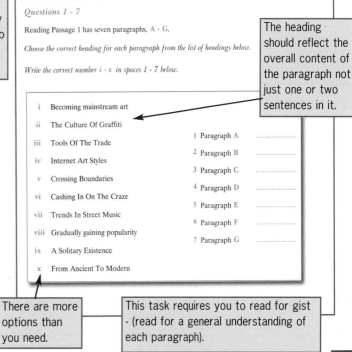

There are more options than you need.

This task requires you to read for gist - (read for a general understanding of each paragraph).

Scan for where each name appears in the text and highlight these sections. Then, read carefully and see which statements match.

TASK TYPE: (14) LOCATING INFORMATION

Task: Scan the passage to find specific information in different paragraphs.

You must...
1. Read a text divided into labelled paragraphs.
2. Read statements which focus on details from individual paragraphs.
3. Find which paragraph contains the information in the statement.

EXAMPLE: TEST 2 - PASSAGE 3

Questions 27 - 31

Reading Passage 3 has eight paragraphs, A - H.

Which paragraph contains the following information?

Write the correct letter A - H in spaces 27 - 31 below.

> Some sections may contain the answers to more than one question.

27	possible health hazards associated with the use of biometrics	....
28	convicted criminals were not the first to be identified by the use of biometrics	....
29	the application of mathematics in assessing biometric data	....
30	despite its limitations, biometrics has become a commercial field of activity	....
31	some biometric methods are useful only in conjunction with others	....

Note:
You should scan the passage for key words/concepts contained in each statement then read related sections carefully to confirm your answer.

General Reading Tips

1. start each reading section by scanning over the first task (this will give you an idea of what the passage is about)

2. then read the passage for gist (read it to get a general understanding of what is being discussed)

3. finally, adopt the strategy required for each task as outlined in this guide; generally:
   (i) scan the passage for key words in the question
   (ii) read the section you have identified carefully to confirm the correct answer

IELTS

WRITING SECTION

EXAM GUIDE

This section contains a detailed analysis of the Writing section of the exam with Exam Tips and Guidance with examples from writing tasks included in the Practice Tests.

Writing Section Format

Task	Suggested time and marks	Text type and number of words
1	**20 minutes** one-third of the marks for the writing paper	**a summary of the information shown on the graph, chart, table or diagram** 150 words minimum
2	**40 minutes** two-thirds of the marks for the writing paper	**a discursive essay in response to a statement of opinions or ideas** 250 words minimum

TASK 1

is...
- a writing task based on data which is presented in the form of a graph, bar chart or diagram

tests.....
- your ability to write about the information shown in an accurate and concise manner
- your ability to use an appropriate register i.e. formal / neutral
- your ability to write using accurate grammar, spelling and punctuation
- your ability to organise ideas clearly and cohesively

requires you to...
- recognise and select important and relevant data from the graph/chart/diagram
- summarise the data shown in at least 150 words
- plan, write and revise your answer in approximately 20 minutes
- write about the most important parts of the data
- compare and contrast features of the data as appropriate
- draw attention to and interpret any significant or unusual features of the data

TASK 2

is...
- a formal discursive essay

tests...
- how well you can express and evaluate ideas
- whether or not you can use an appropriate style
- your use of grammar and vocabulary, as well as your spelling
- your ability to organise your thoughts into paragraphs which form a cohesive whole

requires you to...
- present arguments in a clear and organised way
- discuss the idea or subject outlined in the task
- write at least 250 words in approximately 40 minutes
- give your opinion and use examples to support it
- conclude your writing with a brief statement making clear your final opinion on the idea/subject being written about

STRATEGY

always...
- read the task (1 or 2 min)
- highlight the key words in the question
- try to understand exactly what is being asked
- make a note of all the points you have to cover in your answer
- [task 1 only] take some time to study the graph/chart/diagram and the kind of data it is presenting (1 min)
- plan your answer (3 or 5 min) and decide what you want to say/put in each paragraph
- review your work for mistakes at the end (1 min)

TASK ANALYSIS (UNDERSTANDING THE QUESTION)

TASK I WRITING TEST 7

1
Read the first part of the question carefully. It tells you what information is represented on the chart.

2
Identify what you are being asked to do in the question. (For Task 1, this is usually the same three things every time.)
(i) summarise
(ii) report main features
(iii) compare

3
Look at the chart itself:
▸ read the main title
▸ read the axis titles

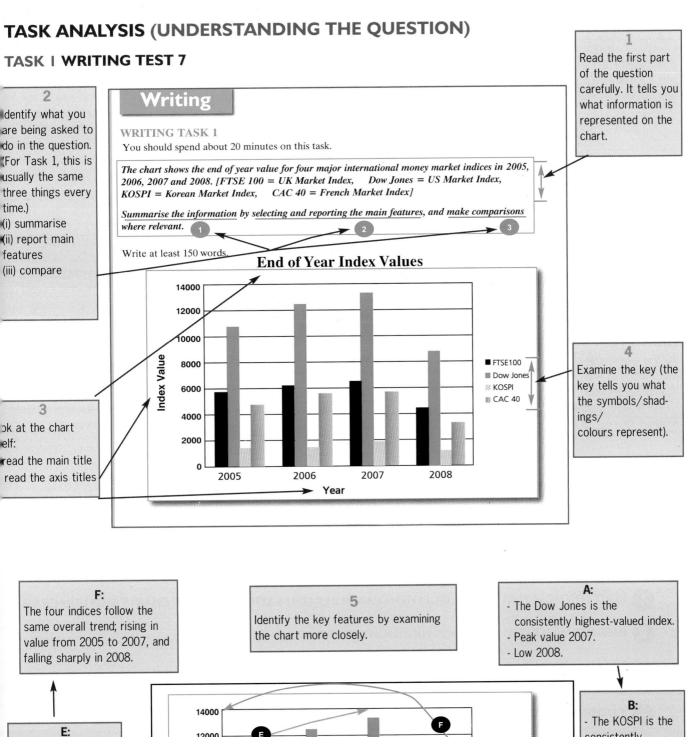

Writing

WRITING TASK 1
You should spend about 20 minutes on this task.

The chart shows the end of year value for four major international money market indices in 2005, 2006, 2007 and 2008. [FTSE 100 = UK Market Index,   Dow Jones = US Market Index, KOSPI = Korean Market Index,   CAC 40 = French Market Index]

Summarise the information by selecting and reporting the main features, and make comparisons where relevant. ① ② ③

Write at least 150 words.

End of Year Index Values

4
Examine the key (the key tells you what the symbols/shadings/colours represent).

F:
The four indices follow the same overall trend; rising in value from 2005 to 2007, and falling sharply in 2008.

5
Identify the key features by examining the chart more closely.

A:
- The Dow Jones is the consistently highest-valued index.
- Peak value 2007.
- Low 2008.

E:
- From 2005 until 2007, there was an upward trend in the values of the indices.

B:
- The KOSPI is the consistently lowest-valued index.
- same high and low pattern as Dow.

D:
- 2008 was the year in which the four indices had their worst performance.

C:
- 2007 was the year in which all four indices performed best.

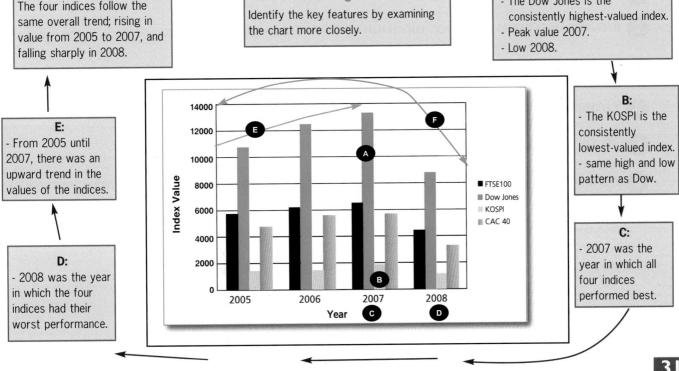

F:
The KOSPI is the least volatile index, making the smallest gains and losses.

7
Compare the data.

A:
All four indices have performed in a very similar way to one another; they rose in value from 2005 - 2007, peaked in value at end of 2007 and reached their lowest values in 2008.

E:
The Dow Jones is the most volatile index, registering the largest increases and decreases in value.

D:
The KOSPI is by far the lowest-valued index. It is less than half the value of the next-biggest index.

B:
The Dow Jones is a very strong index; it is twice the value of the next-strongest one, the FTSE.

C:
The FTSE and CAC 40 are similar-sized indices.

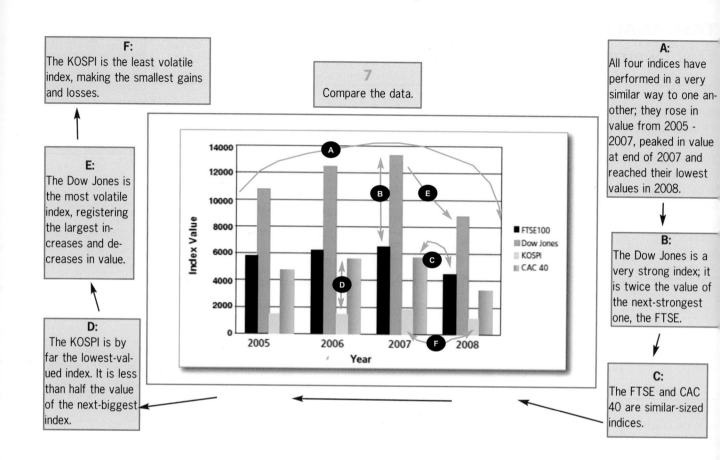

TASK ANALYSIS : SUMMARY OF STEPS

1 READ THE FIRST PART OF THE QUESTION CAREFULLY (TELLS YOU ABOUT THE CHART/GRAPH/DIAGRAM)

2 IDENTIFY WHAT YOU MUST DO - HIGHLIGHT KEY POINTS IN QUESTION

3 STUDY CHART/GRAPH/DIAGRAM; READ MAIN TITLE AND AXIS TITLES (OR LABELS)

4 EXAMINE KEY; UNDERSTAND WHAT EACH SYMBOL/COLOUR/SHADE REPRESENTS

5 STUDY CHART/DIAGRAM/GRAPH CLOSELY AND IDENTIFY KEY FEATURES

6 COMPARE THE DATA ; NOTE PATTERNS IN DATA AND SIMILARITIES/DIFFERENCES BETWEEN INDIVIDUAL DATA SETS

FORMULATING YOUR ANSWER

Plan:
A simple plan is all that is required for this task-type. You are writing a basic summary, which will typically have three or four paragraphs.

Opening Paragraph: State what is being shown in the chart/diagram/graph. You could also make a general statement of the main overall point.

Main body: This may be one paragraph summarising the main points shown in more detail. However, if the diagram involves more than one main idea, it is fine to make two or more paragraphs - one addressing each main idea.

Conclusion: Briefly state the overall point of the diagram, and if you wish to speculate about reasons for the trends shown, or draw conclusions about what is shown, this is the place to do it.

SAMPLE PLAN

P1: The chart shows ... the value of four international money markets .....

P2: The American index was the strongest....
The British market index was the second-most valuable....
The French and British markets are closely aligned.....
Korean market was the lowest-valued.....

Concluding paragraph: From 2005 until 2007, the graph suggests that .....

SAMPLE ANSWER

Open by explaining what information the chart illustrates.

This chart follows the value of four international money markets over four years. *All four of the market indices rose steadily in value from 2005 to 2007 inclusive, registering a sharp drop in value at the end of 2008.* The four markets seem to mirror each other's performance, suggesting that there is a strong correlation in market trends; a rise or fall in one index is reflected in the other indices.

The American index was the strongest in each of the four years, peaking in value at around 13,000 points in 2007, before dropping off to its lowest level at around 9,000 points in 2008. The British market index was the second-most valuable throughout the four years, peaking in 2007 at about 6,500 points before registering a 2,000 point drop in value by the end of 2008. The French and British markets are closely aligned in terms of value and performance, suggesting their economies may be of similar size, while the Korean market was the lowest-valued in each of the four years, though it exhibited a similar performance trend.

From 2005 until 2007, the graph suggests that the global economy may have been performing strongly since all four markets registered steady increases in value. It is also clear that in 2008, the economy contracted, both locally and globally, as is reflected in the significant fall in market value registered across the four indices.

Be familiar with the kind of language used to describe changes in values.

Show that you can read the data by quoting some relevant figures.

Mention obvious features / patterns / trends.

The section in Italics is known as the main idea; a general summary of the chart's main features.

After opening and stating main idea, compare features in more detail in the second paragraph.

State the overall point of the diagram and draw conclusions about what is shown.

USEFUL LANGUAGE

downward trend

volatile / unstable performance

upward trend

steady / stable performance

(register a) sharp/steep drop/fall (in value)

(register a) sharp/steep rise/increase (in value)

Note:
Briefly check spelling, grammar and length (150+ words) at the end of the task.

MORE USEFUL LANGUAGE

The Language of Contrast:

On the one hand… + On the other hand…
It is clear that… + whereas/while…
We can see that… + however…
It is clear that… + By contrast,

Describing what you see:
It is clear that…
It can be seen that…
The chart shows…
The chart illustrates…
The chart represents…

Describing numbers and amounts as they get bigger/smaller:

to rise / to fall
to increase / to decrease
to grow / to shrink
to double / to halve
to go up / to go down
to expand / to contract

The language of similarity
It is clear that… + similarly,…
We can see that… + likewise,…

Percentages and proportions:

90%	10%
ninety percent (of)	ten percent (of)
a large/high percentage (of)	a small/low percentage (of)
most (of)	few (of)
the (vast) majority (of)	a (small) minority (of)
nine out of ten	one out of ten
nine in every ten	one in every ten
nine-tenths (of)	one-tenth (of)
nearly all (of)	barely any (of)

TASK ANALYSIS (UNDERSTANDING THE QUESTION)
TASK 2 WRITING TEST I

1
The first bold section will inform you about the subject matter of your composition. Highlight the key words before going any further.

2
The second bold section tells you what you must write i.e. in this case you must express your personal view on the subject.

WRITING TASK 2

You should spend about 40 minutes on this task.

Write about the following topic:

Schools concentrate far too much on traditional subjects which do not adequately prepare students for the realistic demands of the modern working world.

To what extent do you agree or disagree?

Give reasons for your answer and include any relevant examples from your own knowledge or experience.

Write at least 250 words.

4
Before proceeding any further, think of ways you can paraphrase the statement in bold in order to introduce the subject of your composition in paragraph 1.

NOTE
In Task 1 you were given a lot of input material to write about. This is not the case in Task 2. You must come up with your own ideas and justify them; therefore, planning is very important in the context of this question.

3
The second-to-last sentence tells you what you must include in your answer. It is important to provide both reasons for your views and examples to explain them. Failing to do so will result in the loss of a significant amount of marks.

TASK ANALYSIS : SUMMARY OF STEPS

1 READ THE FIRST BOLD SECTION OF THE QUESTION TO FIND OUT THE SUBJECT AND HIGHLIGHT KEY WORDS TO SIMPLIFY WHAT YOU ARE BEING ASKED TO WRITE ABOUT.

↓↓↓

2 READ THE SECOND BOLD SECTION TO CONFIRM THE REASON FOR WRITING I.E. TO GIVE YOUR OPINION.

↓↓↓

3 READ THE SECOND-TO-LAST SENTENCE TO CONFIRM THE INFORMATION YOU MUST INCLUDE I.E. REASONS FOR YOUR VIEWS AND EXAMPLES TO JUSTIFY THEM.

↓↓↓

4 PARAPHRASE THE QUESTION FOR YOUR INTRODUCTION.

FOCUS ON PLANNING

- The first thing you need to do is 'brainstorm'; basically think of as many points/ideas for and against the opinion expressed in the question statement as you can and write these down in note form.

- You then need to select the points you want to use in your composition and think of examples and reasons to justify them.

- Next, fit the ideas you wish to write about into your composition plan to help you focus on what points need to be discussed where in the composition.

SAMPLE BRAINSTORM

Paraphrase the question statement now - never repeat the question statement word-for-word in your introduction or you will lose marks.

When brainstorming, write down as many ideas as you can come up with quickly. Don't worry about whether they are good or bad, or the order they come in; this can be decided when you fill in your plan.

Always start by looking at both sides of the argument. This will help you formulate a well-balanced discussion.

Having considered both sides of the argument, decide where you stand. You do not have to agree or disagree with the question statement, you can choose to partially agree if you wish, though sometimes it is easier to take sides.

Topic:

the school curriculum's focus on academic subjects leads to a failure to prepare students for the challenges of the real world of work

Agree:
True ... school overly focused on academic subjects ... disadvantageous for two reasons ... many students are not academically-minded so school does not cater for them or equip them with skills to help them find a job in future ... school doesn't teach life skills - doesn't show students how to cope with life problems i.e. dealing with people, managing stress etc. ... moreover, most subjects we learn at school we never make use of in day-to-day lives

Disagree:
School doesn't have to officially 'teach' life skills ; it's where we learn them naturally ... learn how to communicate and make friends ... cope with stress (exams) ... organise our workload (study) ... teaches us value of respect, discipline and hard work ... moreover, academic subjects are vital ... broaden perspective ... history might not seem that useful, but we learn from the mistakes of the past and have a better understanding of who we are and who other people are ... besides, traditional subjects are key - English for communication and literacy, Maths for basic numerical skills ... fundamental skills needed in almost any job

My view?
School prepares us well, but does let those who are not academically minded down ... broaden curriculum ... include more practical courses ... possibly life skills courses too

PLANNING
Here are two of the most common paragraph plan outlines.

Option 1

Paragraph 1 - Introduction
Rephrase the question and express your opinion (in agreement or disagreement with the statement).

Paragraph 2 - Main body
Give one reason that supports your opinion. Use facts, observations and examples to support this statement.

Paragraph 3 - Main body
Give another reason that supports your opinion and justify.

Paragraph 4 - Conclusion
Summarise the reasons for your opinion and state again what you believe. Don't use the same words that you used in the introduction and main body; paraphrase.

Option 2

Paragraph 1 - Introduction
Introduce the topic by restating the question statement (in your own words) and giving your reaction to it.

Paragraph 2 - Main body
Discuss the points in favour of the question statement citing examples where relevant.

Paragraph 3 - Main body
Discuss the points against the question statement citing examples where relevant.

Paragraph 4 - Conclusion
State your opinion and give reasons why you hold this view.

SAMPLE PLAN

Intro: people often say... school doesn't adequately prepare students for real world ... is it true?

P2: True that many students aren't academic ... fail at school ... example; might be poor at maths and English, get bad grades ... skilful and good at making things ... pointless going to school ... wasted talent ... also no practical life skills classes ... doesn't teach us how to deal with office politics, communicating with people, working in team, managing stress

P3: School offers all-round education ... teaches life skills indirectly ... discipline ... coping with stress - exams ... working with other people - sports class and projects ... communicating - making friends and school politics ... like a microcosm of real world ... also academic subjects crucial ... broaden mind ... teach us key skills like numeracy and literacy ... help us to develop analytical minds

Conclusion: true school is imperfect ... but a lot of value in getting good education ... maybe needs to cater more for those who are not academic and could give students more advice on dealing with real-life situations ... overall though, the failures are far outnumbered by successes and school is very productive and relevant learning environment

SAMPLE ANSWER

Generalising the statement and then asking an open-ended question is a very effective way of opening the discussion / introducing the topic.

It is very important to use linking words/phrases to help your ideas flow smoothly from one to the next and improve the flow of the composition generally.

Note:
Marks will be lost if you fail to structure your composition well. Good paragraphing is essential, therefore. As a general rule, use four paragraphs; an introduction, two for the main body, and a concluding paragraph.

People often say that school's greatest failure is that it focuses too intently on academic subjects and fails to equip students with the real-life skills necessary to cope in the world of work. But is it fair to criticise the education system in this way?

Certainly not all students have the attributes necessary to excel in an academic environment, so, if the focus of school is solely on the traditional academic subjects, then it would seem to be failing the more practically- and technically-minded children. A teenager with a talent for crafting things with his hands, for example, is letting his talent go to waste if he does not hone his skills during adolescence. School is also failing children if it does not equip them with life skills - in the real world, knowing how to deal with office politics, communicate with people, manage stress, and work in a team is far more important than being academically-minded.

On the other hand, it could be argued that school does not need to offer formal classes in life skills because it is a lesson in life skills from the start to the very end. School life indirectly teaches students self-discipline and how to motivate themselves to work hard. It also teaches them how to cope with the stress of exams and deadlines. Finally, they learn how to work with other people, such as their classmates and teachers, and even how to make friends. Basically, what happens inside the school building is a microcosm of what is happening outside in the real world. And not only that, but it is also teaching students numeracy and literacy - the two most vital skills of all.

No one would argue that school is perfect; however, a good education is still invaluable. While school could perhaps cater for the non-academic student more fairly and should work on developing programmes suited to the more technically-minded, the strengths of the school system far outnumber its failings. School is still a very productive and relevant learning environment today; one that does prepare students for the 'big bad world' of work.

Paragraph 2 examines the points which support the question statement.

Use examples to illustrate points.

Paragraph 3 examines the other side of the argument.

Using examples adds credibility to the points you are making.

In the final paragraph you present your opinion. It is not necessary to take a clear stance in total agreement or disagreement with the question statement if you don't want to - here the writer agrees that school has some failings, but believes it prepares students well overall.

Useful Language

Positive comments:

The first advantage of ... is...
Among the many advantages of ... is/are...
The benefits of ... include/are ...
... is (extremely) beneficial on account of the fact that...
Another positive result of ... is ...
One of the major pros / plus points of ... is ...
A positive aspect of ... is ...
One of the advantages of ... is ...
... is advantageous in the sense that ...
The benefits of ... far outweigh the drawbacks.

Negative comments:

One of the (major) drawbacks of ... is ...
A negative aspect of ... is ...
... is disadvantageous in the sense that ...
Among the many drawbacks of ... is/are ...
One of the disadvantages of ... is ...
The benefits of ... are far outweighed by the drawbacks.
There is a long list of disadvantages / drawbacks including ...
... is disadvantageous on account of the fact that ...
The first drawback of ... is ...

General Notes / Summary

1 There are two tasks. **Task 1** requires you to summarise a chart/graph/diagram.
Task 2 is a discursive essay.

2 You should spend around 20 minutes on task 1. Summarise the input material by:
(i) describing what the chart/graph/diagram is about
(ii) explaining the main idea (the main trend or feature)
(iii) comparing the chart/graph/diagram data in greater detail

3 You should spend around 40 minutes on task 2. There is little input material. You must
(i) paraphrase the question statement in an introduction and state your opinion
(ii) support your opinion
(iii) re-state your view and paraphrase the reasons that support it and reach a conclusion

4 Do:
- Highlight key information in the task question.
- Plan your answer.
- Structure your answer into paragraphs.
- Use linking words to connect your ideas and points and improve the flow of the essay/summary as a whole.
- Check your answer for minor errors at the end.

IELTS

SPEAKING SECTION

EXAM GUIDE

This section contains a detailed analysis of the
Speaking section of the exam with Exam Tips,
Guidance and Useful Vocabulary for the three
parts of the IELTS Speaking section.

Speaking Section Format

Section	Time	Task Type
1	4-5 minutes	giving personal information and talking about everyday subjects
2	1 minute preparation, 2 minutes talking	giving a prepared talk on a subject the examiner has given to you and answering one or two follow-up questions
3	4-5 minutes	a discussion with the examiner based on the topic in Part 2, offering the opportunity to discuss more complex and abstract issues and ideas

PART 1

is...
- a short introductory conversation lasting between 4 and 5 minutes
- testing your ability to talk about personal experiences and interests

you must...
- be able to answer questions about everyday topics such as *family and friends, home life, studies / work, leisure, pastimes* etc.
- answer each question in at least one or two sentences

DEVELOPING YOUR ANSWERS

A simple question like *Where do you live?* can be replied to with a simple, yet detailed response. Always show off what you know! For example:

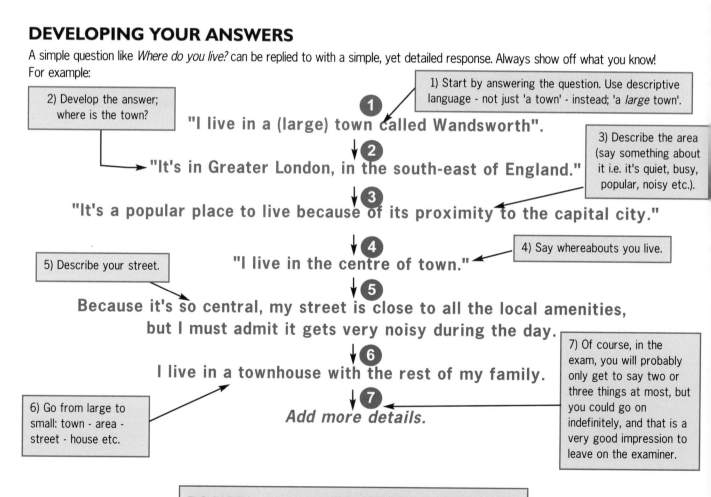

2) Develop the answer; where is the town?

1) Start by answering the question. Use descriptive language - not just 'a town' - instead; 'a *large* town'.

"I live in a (large) town called Wandsworth". ①

"It's in Greater London, in the south-east of England." ②

3) Describe the area (say something about it i.e. it's quiet, busy, popular, noisy etc.).

"It's a popular place to live because of its proximity to the capital city." ③

"I live in the centre of town." ④

4) Say whereabouts you live.

5) Describe your street.

Because it's so central, my street is close to all the local amenities, but I must admit it gets very noisy during the day. ⑤

I live in a townhouse with the rest of my family. ⑥

6) Go from large to small: town - area - street - house etc.

Add more details. ⑦

7) Of course, in the exam, you will probably only get to say two or three things at most, but you could go on indefinitely, and that is a very good impression to leave on the examiner.

DO NOT be tempted to **MEMORISE** answers though, just practise often saying as much as you can in relation to the different subjects you might get asked about.

SPEAKING PART I - EXAM TIPS

DO:
- avoid yes/no answers
- avoid one-word answers
- show off your English
- this is a relatively easy section, so continue expanding each answer until prompted to move on to the next question

PREPARE:
- you know the general topics that come up in this section, so prepare for them in advance
- practise talking about your family, friends, hobbies, work, pastimes, study etc. and try to say as much as you can about each topic
- Be prepared to talk about your likes and dislikes in general, too, for example:
  Where you like to travel/eat out.   What types of food/books/films/music/sports you like.
  Whether you prefer the cinema or DVDs / fast food or home-cooked food / public or private transport etc.

And finally, remember...

- **Part I** is not graded separately; marks are awarded across all three parts (an overall mark).
- If the examiner asks you to stop before you have finished what you are saying, don't worry; he/she is constrained by time and may simply have to move on. It is not a reflection on how well you have answered the last question.
- The speaking will be recorded, but this is for administrative purposes only; don't let that distract you.
- Listen carefully to the tense in the question, and respond using the right one in your answer.

EXAMPLE QUESTIONS FOR YOU TO PRACTISE:

Home / local area / travel	Studies / work	Leisure time	Family / friends
Where are you from? What's the area where you live like? What is there to do near where you live? If you could live anywhere, where would it be? What are the advantages/disadvantages of living in your town/city/country? What would you change about the area where you live, if you could? Have you always lived in your home town? Do you like living there? Do you think your home town is likely to change much in the future? Do many tourists visit your area? What do they come to see? Have you ever been abroad? Where would you like to go on holiday? Would you prefer to live in the city, countryside or by the sea? Where did you go on holiday last year? Where are you planning to go on holiday this year?	How do you get to school/college/work every day? Are you a full-time student at the moment? Where do you study? How long have you studied there? What job would you like to have in the future? What work do you do? How long have you been working there? What job did you want to do when you were a child? What would you regard as the perfect job? How long have you been learning English? Have you studied any other languages? Why is it important to get a good education?	Do you have a lot of free time? What do you like to do to relax when you are at home? Where do you go when you go out? Do you try to keep fit? Why is it important for young people to keep fit? Do you play any sports/have any hobbies? What is the value of having hobbies? How often do you watch T.V./go to the movies/go to the theatre? What kind of music/sport/entertainment do you like? Do you ever go to concerts? Do you play or would you like to play a musical instrument? Do you enjoy reading or do you prefer watching T.V.? Given the choice, would you sooner go to the cinema or watch a DVD? Are there any hobbies/sports you would like to try?	Are your friends interested in the same kind of music as you? Do you spend more time with your family or friends? Who do you confide in when you have a problem? With whom in your family do you have the best relationship? Do you have / would you like to have any siblings? Who are more important; your family or friends? Where do you and your friends hang out at the weekend? What likes and interests do you share with your friends? Tell me about your best friend. Do you think you will stay friends for life with the friends you have now?

PART 2

is...
- a short talk
- testing your ability to speak continuously for about 2 minutes
- testing your ability to organise your ideas and speak fluently and cohesively

you must...
- prepare and talk about a topic given to you during the test by the examiner

DO:
- read the card with the task on it
- make notes on each of the separate parts of the task
- talk about the topic in the task, answering the questions on the card
- stop talking once the examiner indicates that you should
- answer the follow-up questions the examiner puts to you

EXAMPLE TASK

Describe a person you admire.
    You should say:
    - who the person is
    - what kind of person they are
    - what they have achieved in life
and explain the reasons you admire them.

Instructions:
The examiner will give you a topic on a card like this one. You will then have one minute to think about what you are going to say. You will be provided with some paper and a pencil so you can make notes if you want to.

Remember:
- you will be told when to begin your talk
- the examiner may ask you some questions during or after your talk
- don't worry if you haven't finished when the examiner tells you to stop; this is never an indication of having done well or badly.

WEB DIAGRAM
One of the most effective methods of note-making is to use what is called a *Web* or *Spider* diagram. The main idea goes in the middle and the items to discuss branch out on different threads.

This is only an outline of a Web Diagram. A detailed example is shown on the next page. Note-making is a very important part of this section of the speaking exam. It is highly recommended that you **DO** make notes as this will help you to focus your mind clearly and order your thoughts. It will also provide you with something on which to fall back if you get stuck as you can refer back to your notes during the talk.

TAKING NOTES

Practise note-making as much as possible. You should not be writing full sentences but rather key words or ideas which you can link together in a logical way.

Use the points on the card as the themes of each of your four threads.

TAKING NOTES

Completed Web Diagram

Use short, simple phrases - these will function as cues when you begin your talk.

Where possible, use what you know; that is far easier than trying to think up new ideas on the spot. Don't say you admire someone for the sake of it. Say who you really admire because then it will be easier to think of why.

Bono - frontman of the rock band U2 - world-famous rock star

Artistic and creative - writes great lyrics and songs - passionate - loves his work - caring

Explain what you say - give reasons or use examples. Why is Bono creative and artistic? Because he writes great lyrics and songs...

Person I admire

his lyrics are very powerful - also not just a star - campaigns for charity - headed the LIVE 8 campaign - meets world leaders - encourages them to write off loans poor countries owe them

Focus on the points (like this one) you have the most to talk about. Don't dwell on a point if you have little to say.

Sold millions of records - written beautiful songs - helped his band become biggest on the planet - a living legend of rock

Structure your talk around the points on the card to make it easier for you. Start by talking about point 1, then point 2 and so on. Your web diagram should reflect this structure.

SPEAKING PART 2 - EXAM TIPS

1 Use Stock or Opening phrases for each new point you make to give you some time to think. For example (based on the question and diagram above):

Box (i): <u>I admire many people, but I think the person most worthy of my admiration is</u> Bono....
Box (ii): <u>Bono has all the qualities you would look for in a great person.</u> He is...
Box (iii): <u>Bono has done quite an amazing amount in his life so far;</u> he has
Box (iv): <u>The list of reasons why I admire him is very long; here are just a few</u> ....

You are not giving any detail when you use these opening or stock phrases; you are talking in general terms but staying on-topic. This gives you a chance to order your thoughts and compose yourself.

2 Stock phrases can also be used to buy you thinking time when the examiner asks you a question. Examples of useful stock phrases include:

(i) That's a difficult question to answer...   (ii) Interesting question...
(iii) That's a very good question...   (iv) I need to think about this for a moment; hmm, let me see...

PART 3

is...
- a discussion of general and abstract ideas lasting 4-5 minutes
- testing your ability to analyse and discuss ideas in depth

you must...
- answer questions which are broadly related to the topic in part 2
- express your opinions and justify them

Stock phrases : Responding when someone gives their opinion.

Agree	Strongly Agree	Disagree	Strongly disagree
With a person: I see what you're saying... I see where you're coming from... What you say is true... I agree with you... We're in agreement... I feel the same way... I think so, too... **With an idea** I agree with the idea that... I support the idea that... I'm in favour of... I'm behind the idea that... I applaud the idea that...	**With a person** I completely agree... I couldn't agree more... You're absolutely right... I'm totally behind you... We're in complete agreement... I couldn't have said it better myself... **With an idea** I'm totally for the idea that... I'm completely behind the idea that... I'm totally in favour of... I'm very much in favour of the idea that... I completely agree with the notion that...	**With a person** I see what you're saying, but... We don't quite see eye to eye... I see where you're coming from, but... I know what you mean, but... I disagree because... I can't say I feel exactly the same way... I'm inclined to disagree with you... I'm not so sure about that... **With an idea** I'm against the idea of... I'm not in favour of... I don't support the idea that... I'm not behind the idea that... I don't agree that...	**With a person** I couldn't disagree more with what you're saying... I completely disagree with you... I feel the exact opposite... We're poles apart in our views... **With an idea** I'm totally against the idea that... I'm absolutely not in favour of... I am not at all behind the idea that... I'm not at all in favour of... There's no way I would agree with that...

Expressing your opinion...

- If you ask me....
- In my view...
- I'm of the belief that...
- I'm of the view that...
- I'm inclined to believe...
- It's my firm belief that...
- As far as I see it...
- As far as I'm concerned...
- The way I see it...
- In my opinion...

SPEAKING PART 3 - EXAM TIPS

- MAKE SURE YOU INTRODUCE THE TOPIC

- COVER ALL THE POINTS ON THE CARD *(THEY DO NOT HAVE TO BE IN THE ORDER THEY APPEAR, BUT THIS IS THE SIMPLEST METHOD)*

- CONNECT YOUR SENTENCES AND IDEAS TOGETHER USING LINKING WORDS.

- TRY TO USE A RANGE OF VOCABULARY

- STAY ON-TOPIC AND ANSWER THE QUESTION DIRECTLY

- IF YOU DON'T HEAR A QUESTION THE EXAMINER CAN REPEAT IT FOR YOU.

- AVOID GIVING REHEARSED OR OFF-BY-HEART ANSWERS; THIS WILL REFLECT NEGATIVELY ON YOUR SCORE.

EXAMPLE TASK (QUESTIONS 1-11)

Describe a person you admire.
You should say:
- who the person is
- what kind of person they are
- what they have achieved in life
and explain the reasons you admire them.

Subject matter:
This is the topic card used in Part 2.
Part 3 is a series of questions related to the theme of Part Two which, in this case, is people we admire.

1 **What makes a person popular or admirable?**

2 **Do you have to be popular to be admired?**

The questions will be more difficult than Part in 1. You might be asked for your opinion, as in this question.

3 **Do you admire a lot of famous people or look up to them?**

4 **Do you regard celebrities as good role models?**

5 **What are the qualities we should look for in someone to admire?**

6 **Would you like to be the object of other people's admiration?**

7 **Are you influenced by the way people you look up to behave?**

You might be asked about hypothetical situations.

8 **Have you ever tried to copy another person; perhaps their behaviour or style?**

9 **Why do you think so many people want to be like celebrities?**

10 **Why are famous and rich people the object of so much admiration?**

You might be asked to speculate on the cause of something or why something is.

11 **Do you think celebrities of the future will be better role models?**
[Example answer] I think it is highly unlikely that....

You might also be asked: to comment on what might happen in the future or to predict the possible consequences of something

Stock phrases : Talking about the Future	
Probable	**Improbable**
It is (highly) likely that....	I (highly) doubt that...
It seems (quite/very) probable that...	It's doubtful whether...
I would expect that...	I can't imagine that...
It seems (quite/very) likely that...	I think it is unlikely that...
I would imagine that...	It's highly unlikely that...
In all likelihood, ...	It's highly improbable that...
In all probability...	It seems unlikely that...
I'm quite sure that...	
I'm fairly certain that...	

Stock phrases: Making general statements

Before giving our own opinion, we often make a general statement. A general statement describes what most people believe, what is popularly believed or what is usually true. For example:

Q: *Do you think people today are too concerned about their appearance?*
A: *Most people would say that looking good is extremely important, but, in my experience,* whether a person looks good or not is no indication of their character and I think people should learn to look beyond appearances. We are definitely too concerned with the way we look and not concerned enough with other more important qualities.

The underlined section is an example of a general statement, which is followed by a personal statement.

Here are some more STOCK PHRASES to help you make GENERAL STATEMENTS:

(i) For the most part....
(ii) In general,...
(iii) Most people believe that...
(iv) It's widely acknowledged that...

(v) Most people are of the view that...
(vi) Generally speaking,...
(vii) It's widely believed that...
(viii) According to popular belief...

Example Question: *Do you think people will live longer lives in the future?*

Example Answer:
I think it is highly likely that life expectancy will improve over the coming years because of the *advances we are seeing in medical science.* New cures are being discovered all the time, and many diseases considered deadly today will no doubt be treatable in a few years' time. *Moreover,* as the wealth of the world increases, more people have access to clean water, good sanitation and nutrition. This will improve the average life expectancy across the developing world.

Stock phrase for expressing probability.

Reason for / justification of your opinion.

The use of linking words is very important to connect your ideas and make them flow.

Stock phrases: Where the correct answer / your opinion can change

Some questions are not easy to answer 'yes' or 'no' to; sometimes there is a situation where, in some cases, we would say yes, or agree, and, in other cases, we would say no, or disagree. For example;

Q: *Do you think television has a negative impact on children?*
A: *<u>That depends.</u> Certainly, watching too much television is harmful because it promotes a sedentary and anti-social lifestyle. Having said that, television in small doses can be quite educational.*

The underlined section is an example of a phrase used to indicate that the answer changes depending on the situation.

Here are some more stock phrases to help you express this notion:

(i) In some circumstance.... In others....   (v) In some cases... In other cases...
(ii) To some extent... but...   (vi) Sometimes... Having said that...
(iii) Some believe... while others...   (vii) For some people... For others...
(iv) Some would say... while others...   (viii) That can vary according to the situation.

Stock phrases: Contrasting your opinion with what most people think

Here are some more stock phrases to help you express the idea that you disagree with other people:

(i) For many people... but I believe...   (v) A lot of people think... but I beg to differ.
(ii) To some people... but to me...   (vi) For some people... but for me...
(iii) Some believe... but I...   (vii) I differ from a lot of people in that I believe...
(iv) Some would say... but I...   (viii) You might expect me to say ... but actually...

Example Question: *How do you feel about nuclear energy?*

Example Answer:
<u>Most people believe that</u> nuclear energy is quite dangerous and, for that reason, they are against it, but, <u>if you ask me</u>, I think nuclear energy is a clean fuel source; therefore, <u>I am strongly in favour of</u> it. Energy sources such as oil and coal have been polluting the atmosphere for a very long time now, and scientists think <u>this could lead to global warming</u>. Perhaps clean energy sources like nuclear fuel are the answer to the problem.

Stock phrase for making a general statement.

Stock phrase for giving your opinion.

Always give examples or evidence to support your points.

Stock phrase for expressing your agreement with an idea.

Speaking Tips

- The speaking section of the exam lasts approximately 11-13 minutes in total.

- It is common to both the General and Academic modules.

- It is a face-to-face interview and it will be recorded.

- You receive one grade for the entire speaking exam; the individual parts are not graded separately.

- You will be provided with a pen and some note paper for Section 2.

- Avoid yes/no answers and always respond as fully as possible to questions posed to you by the examiner.

- If the examiner interrupts you, this is not a sign you have done badly; he/she is working to strict guidelines on timing.

- Remember to bring your passport or I.D. card with you on the day.

IELTS

Practice Tests

Test 1

Listening

SECTION 1   *Questions 1 - 10*

Listening - Section 1
...... **(1)** It's much faster, **(2)** more affordable
(3) and you can take as much luggage as you need,
there aren't limits.
Check the **Audioscript** in the **Self-Study Guide**
for the **Justification of the Answers** for
ALL the Sections of the Listening Test

Questions 1 - 10

Complete the notes below.

Write **NO MORE THAN TWO WORDS AND/OR A NUMBER** *for each answer.*

NOTES: travelling to France

Example	*Answer*
Time of travel	September

Advantages of traveling by train:

1. faster

2. more affordable

3. take as much luggage as you need

The Eurostar:

- runs on schedule **4** 92.4 percent of the time

- can reach speeds of **5** 186 miles per hour

Two options from Paris to Nice:

1. Catch the TGV train at **6** 11:46

2. Catch the TGV train at **7** 22:25 and travel **8** overnight

Single tickets cost approximately **9** half (of) the return fare.

Flying from London to Nice takes **10** 2 hours

SECTION 2   Questions 11 - 20

Questions 11 - 15

Complete the table below.

*Write **NO MORE THAN THREE WORDS AND/OR A NUMBER** for each answer.*

PROJECT DEVELOPMENT SCHEDULE		
Project name: **The Cube**	Length of project: **11** .... **142 weeks**	Current stage of project: .... **halfway through** ....

ACTIVITY	TIME FRAME
Completion of each floor	**12** .... **2-3 weeks** ....
Installation of exterior	Beginning in **13** .... **February** ....
"Topping out" of frame	Towards the end of **14** .... **summer** ....
Installation of fretwork screen	Coming together in **15** .... **early autumn** ....

Questions 16 - 20

Label the floor plan below.

*Write the correct letter **A - G** next to the questions below.*

16 restaurant with view	C
17 hotel	E
18 office space	F
19 exlusive shops	B
20 waterside restaurant	A

FLOOR PLAN OF THE CUBE, BIRMINGHAM

Listening

Listening Tip:
Use any extra time given to look through the questions and think about the topic of the exercise.

SECTION 3 Questions 21 - 30

Questions 21 - 25

Which student expresses each of the opinions about their tutor?
*Choose your answer from the box and write the letters **A - D** next to questions 21 - 25.*

> **A David**
>
> **B Thomas**
>
> **C Sophie**
>
> **D Lynn**

When things don't make sense I think it's my mistake at first.	21	D
I find the tutor's mistakes entertaining.	22	B
I think it's unfortunate when tutors confuse people.	23	C
I don't believe the situation is so serious.	24	A
The professor should be aware of his tutor's abilities.	25	D

Questions 26 - 30

Complete the sentences below.

*Write **NO MORE THAN TWO WORDS** for each answer.*

RECOMMENDATIONS FOR SURVIVING THE CONFUSING LAB CLASS

♦ Remember that English is not Marlena's first language. She doesn't understand when you're joking around, so don't **26** ......**tease**.......... her so much.

♦ If you pick on her, you will make her **27** ....**so nervous**...... that she can't think clearly.

♦ If you need help, make an appointment to meet with her **28** ......**individually**.......... and you might see a **29** ......**different side**...... of her.

♦ Remember that tutors are not old academics; she is not yet experienced as a **30** ......**teacher**........ .

SECTION 4 *Questions 31 - 40*

Questions 31 - 40

Complete the notes below.

Write **NO MORE THAN THREE WORDS AND/OR A NUMBER** *for each answer.*

COURSE: *Epidemiology 101*   **DATE:** *23 May*

Tuberculosis (also called TB)

- *Tuberculosis is closely associated with the 31* .... AIDS epidemic ....

In the UK:

- *common in the 19th century*
- *since then better living conditions, 32* .... better nutrition .... ,
  immunisation and effective treatments have made it uncommon

Globally:

- *still common in 33* ..... developing countries ..... *and parts of 34* ..... Eastern Europe .....
- *causes 35* ..... three million ..... *deaths per year; more than any other infectious disease*
- *overall, 36* ..... one third ... *of the world's population is infected but not everyone gets sick*

Risk factors

- *a weakened immune system - due to HIV infection, immune-suppressing treatment, or alcohol or 37* ..... drug addiction .....
- *age - babies and the elderly are more likely to become sick*
- *certain environments - more common among homeless people, among prisoners, and people in 38* ..... large cities ..... *and in more impoverished areas*

Treatment

- *50 years ago, a way 39* ..... to cure ..... *TB was found*
- *The most recent form of tuberculosis, XDR-TB, poses a 40* ... (serious) threat ...
  to general TB control.

Reading

READING PASSAGE 1

*You should spend about 20 minutes on **Questions 1 - 13**, which are based on Reading Passage 1 below.*

Hello Happiness!

Ask 100 people what would make them happy, and a sizeable majority would say "winning the lottery." Yet, if they won a vast fortune, within a year they would be back to their previous level of happiness. The fact is that money has many uses, but more money does not mean more happiness. Surveys carried out in recent years by leading psychologists and sociologists all confirm that while individuals may increase their material wealth during the course of their lifetime, this has no bearing on their well-being. And what is true for individuals can be applied on a larger scale to the world population. Statistically, wealthier nations do not achieve higher scores on the happiness-ometer than developing or underdeveloped nations. Once the basic criteria of adequate shelter and nutrition are satisfied, increased wealth plays no significant role. So why the obsession with getting rich? The answer, say researchers, is simple. Call it jealousy, competitiveness, or just keeping up with the Joneses, however well we are doing, there is always someone else who is doing better. Just as we acquire a new $25,000 car, our neighbour parks his brand spanking new $40,000 set of wheels in his drive, causing us much consternation, but fuelling us with new aspirations in the process. And so the cycle continues. Money, or material wealth, may be a prime mover, but it is not the foundation of our well-being.

If money isn't the key to happiness, then, what is? In all 44 countries surveyed by a prominent research centre, family life provided the greatest source of satisfaction. Married people live on average three years longer and enjoy greater physical and psychological health than the unmarried and, surprisingly, couples in a cohabitational relationship. Having a family enhances well-being, and spending more time with one's family helps even more. Social interaction among families, neighbourhoods, workplaces, communities and religious groups correlates strongly with subjective well-being. In fact, the degree of individuals' social connections is the best benchmark of their happiness.

Friendship is another major factor. Indeed, to return to the dollar-equals-happiness equation, in one survey, having a friend converted into $50,000 worth of happiness, and confirms the well-known phenomenon that loneliness can lead to depression. Work is another area central to well-being, and certain features correlate highly with happiness. These include autonomy over how, where, and at what pace work is done, trust between employer and employee, fair treatment, and active participation in the making of decisions. Occupationally, happiness tends to be more common among professionals and managers, that is, people who are in control of the work they do, rather than subservient to their bosses. Inequality implies less control for those who are in the weaker position, although there are more risks of losing their privileges for those in the stronger position.

Control of one's life in general is also key. Happiness is clearly correlated with the presence of favourable events such as promotion or marriage, and the absence of troubles or bad luck such as accidents, being laid off or conflicts. These events on their own signal the success or failure to reach one's goals, and therefore the control one has. On a national level, the more that governments recognise individual preferences, the happier their citizens will be. Choice, and citizens' belief that they can affect the political process, increase subjective well-being. Furthermore, evidence exists for an association between unhappiness and poor health: people from the former Soviet Union are among the unhappiest in the world, and their life expectancy has been falling steadily. People are more satisfied in societies which minimally restrict their freedom of action, in other words, where they are in control rather than being controlled. Happy people are characterised by the belief that they are able to control their situation, whereas unhappy people tend to believe that they are a victim of fate. Happy people are also more psychologically resilient, assertive and open to experience.

But how good is the evidence for this alternative viewpoint then - that happiness, and not financial status, contributes to good health, and long life? A study of nuns, spanning seven decades, supports this theory. Autobiographies written by the nuns in their early 1920s were scored for positive and negative emotions. Nuns expressing the most positive emotions lived on average ten years longer than those expressing the least positive emotions. Happy people, it seems, are much less likely to fall ill and die than unhappy people.

But what must we do to be happy? Experts cite the old maxim "be happy with what you've got." Look around you, they say, and identify the positive factors in your life. Concentrating on the negative aspects of one's life is a no-no, and so is worrying. Worrying is a negative thinking habit that is nearly always about something that lies in the future. It stems, apparently, from our cave dwelling days, when we had to think on a day-to-day basis about how and where to find food and warmth, for example. But in the modern world, worrying simply undermines our ability to enjoy life in the present. More often than not, the things we worry about never come to pass anyway. Just as important is not to dwell on the past - past mistakes, bad experiences, missed opportunities and so on.

What else can we do? Well, engage in a loving relationship with another adult, and work hard to sustain it. Try to plan frequent interactions with your family, friends and neighbours (in that order). Make sure you're not working so hard that you've no time left for personal relationships and leisure. If you are, leave your job voluntarily to become self-employed, but don't get sacked— that's more damaging to well-being than the loss of a spouse, and its effects last longer. In your spare time, join a club, volunteer for community service, or take up religion.

If none of the above works, then vote for a political party with the same agenda as the King of Bhutan, who announced that his nation's objective is national happiness.

Reading

Questions 1 - 3

*Choose **THREE** letters **A - H**.*

*Circle the correct letters, **A - H**, below.*

NB *Your answers may be given in any order.*

Which **THREE** of the following statements are true, according to the text?

A	Money can bring misery.
B	Wealthier nations place more emphasis on happiness than poorer ones.
(C)	Securing a place to live is a basic human need.
D	The desire for social status is a global phenomenon.
(E)	An unmarried couple living together is less likely to be happy than a married couple.
F	The less responsibility one has, the happier one is.
(G)	Involvement in policy making can increase well-being.
H	Our prehistoric ancestors were happier than we are.

Questions 4 - 7

*Complete the summary using the list of words, **A - I**, below.*

*Write the correct letter, **A - I**, in the spaces below.*

> **Reading Tip:**
> When reading, remember to scan for key words and practise scanning for paraphrases of key words.

Money can buy you just about anything, but not, it seems, happiness. Whether on a personal or national **4** ....**F**........ , your bank balance won't make you happier. Once the basic criteria of a roof over your head and food on the table have been met, money ceases to play a part. One of the most important factors in achieving happiness is the extent of our social **5** ....**B**........ - our relationships with family, friends, colleagues and so on. Equally important is the amount of **6** ....**D**........ we have, either in our personal life, working life, or even in our ability to influence the political **7** ....**G**........ that our country embarks on.

A episode	**B** interaction	**C** cooperation
D control	**E** number	**F** level
G course	**H** conflict	**I** limit

Questions 8 - 13

Do the following statements agree with the information given in Reading Passage 1?

In spaces 8 - 13 below write

TRUE	*if the statement agrees with the information*
FALSE	*if the statement contradicts the information*
NOT GIVEN	*if there is no information on this*

8 People from underdeveloped nations try to attain the same standard of living as those from developed nations. .... NOT GIVEN

9 Seeing what others have makes people want to have it too. .... TRUE

10 The larger the family is, the happier the parents will probably be. .... NOT GIVEN

11 One's attitude to life has no influence on one's health. .... FALSE

12 Instinct can be a barrier to happiness. .... TRUE

13 Family and friends rank equally as sources of happiness. .... FALSE

Reading Passage 1
Justification of the Answers

1. C is **True** because the text states that 'Once the basic criteria of adequate shelter and nutrition are satisfied...'

2. E is **True** because a married couple 'live on average three years longer and enjoy greater physical and psychological health than ...... couples in a cohabitational relationship'.

3. G is **True** because the text says that 'certain features correlate highly with happiness. These include autonomy over how, where and at what pace work is done'. 'Control of one's life in general is also key'.

4. Paragraph 1: 'And what is true for individuals can be applied on a larger **scale (level)** to the world population.'

5. Paragraph 2: 'Social **interaction** among families, neighbourhoods, workplaces, communities and religious groups correlates strongly with subjective well-being.'

6. Paragraph 3: '... people who are in control of the work they do... ' '**Control** of one's life in general is also key. '

7. Paragraph 4: 'Choice, and citizens' belief that they can affect the **political process**, increase subjective well-being' - Paraphrased: if you can affect the political process you change the **course** of politics.

8. NOT GIVEN as although the text implies that underdeveloped nations are not concerned with achieving material wealth, it is not stated in the text that they do or do not try to attain the same standard of living as developed countries.

9. TRUE as the first paragraph explains how the 'obsession with getting rich' is down to 'jealousy, competitiveness or just keeping up with the Joneses'.

10. NOT GIVEN as although the text mentions that 'family life provided the greatest source of satisfaction', it does

not say that this increased with the size of the family.

11. FALSE as the text states that poor health **is** determined by one's attitude to life in the fourth paragraph, where it states that 'evidence exists for an association between unhappiness and poor health'. 'Happy people, it seems, are much less likely to fall ill and die than unhappy people'.

12. TRUE as worrying is instinctive and causes unnecessary stress in the modern world. The fifth paragraph details how this 'stems from our cave-dwelling days'.

13. FALSE because both the second and the seventh paragraph state that family is more important than friends in ensuring happiness.

Reading

READING PASSAGE 2

You should spend about 20 minutes on **Questions 14 - 26**, *which are based on Reading Passage 2 below*

One Who Hopes

A

Language lovers, just like music lovers, enjoy variety. For the latter there's Mozart, The Rolling Stones and Beyonce. For the former there's English, French, Swahili, Urdu... the list is endless. But what about those poor overworked students who find learning difficult, confusing languages a drudge? Wouldn't it put a smile on their faces if there were just one simple, easy-to-learn tongue that would cut their study time by years? Well, of course, it exists. It's called Esperanto, and it's been around for more than 120 years. Esperanto is the most widely spoken artificially constructed international language. The name derives from Doktoro Esperanto, the pseudonym under which L. L. Zamenhof first published his *Unua Libro* in 1887. The phrase itself means 'one who hopes'. Zamenhof's goal was to create an easy and flexible language as a universal second language to promote peace and international understanding.

B

Zamenhof, after ten years of developing his brainchild from the late 1870s to the early 1880s, had the first Esperanto grammar published in Warsaw in July 1887. The number of speakers grew rapidly over the next few decades, at first primarily in the Russian empire and Eastern Europe, then in Western Europe and the Americas, China, and Japan. In the early years speakers of Esperanto kept in contact primarily through correspondence and periodicals, but since 1905 world congresses have been held on five continents every year except during the two World Wars. Latest estimates for the numbers of Esperanto speakers are around 2 million. Put in percentage terms, that's about 0.03% of the world's population - no staggering figure, comparatively speaking. One reason is that Esperanto has no official status in any country, but it is an optional subject on the curriculum of several state education systems. It is widely estimated that it can be learned in anywhere between a quarter to a twentieth of the time required for other languages.

C

As a constructed language, Esperanto is not genealogically related to any ethnic language. Whilst it is described as 'a language lexically predominantly Romanic', the phonology, grammar, vocabulary, and semantics are based on the western Indo-European languages. For those of us who are not naturally predisposed to tucking languages under our belts, it is an easy language to learn. It has 5 vowels and 23 consonants. It has one simple way of conjugating all of its verbs. Words are often made from many other roots, making the number of words which one must memorise much smaller. The language is phonetic, and the rules of pronunciation are very simple, so that everyone knows how to pronounce a written word and vice-versa, and word order follows a standard, logical pattern. Through prefixing and suffixing, Esperanto makes it easy to identify words as nouns, verbs, adjectives, adverbs, direct objects and so on, by means of easy-to-spot endings. All this makes for easy language learning. What's more, several research studies demonstrate that studying Esperanto before another foreign language speeds up and improves the learning of the other language. This is presumably because learning subsequent foreign languages is easier than learning one's first, while the use of a grammatically simple and culturally flexible language like Esperanto softens the blow of learning one's first foreign language. In one study, a group of European high school students studied Esperanto for one year, then French for three years, and ended up with a significantly better command of French than a control group who had studied French for all four years.

D

Needless to say, the language has its critics. Some point to the Eastern European features of the language as being harsh and difficult to pronounce, and argue that Esperanto has an artificial feel to it, without the flow of a natural tongue, and that by nature of its artificiality, it is impossible to become emotionally involved with the language. Others cite its lack of cultural history, indigenous literature - "no one has ever written a novel straight into Esperanto" - together with its minimal vocabulary and its inability to express all the necessary philosophical, emotional and psychological concepts.

E

The champions of Esperanto - *Esperantists* - disagree. They claim that it is a language in which a great body of world literature has appeared in translation: in poetry, novels, literary journals, and, to rebut the accusation that it is not a 'real' language, point out that it is frequently used at international meetings which draw hundreds and thousands of participants. Moreover, on an international scale, it is most useful - and fair - for neutral communication. That means that communication through Esperanto does not give advantages to the members of any particular people or culture, but provides an ethos of equality of rights, tolerance and true internationalism.

F

Esperantists further claim that Esperanto has the potential – were it universally taught for a year or two throughout the world – to empower ordinary people to communicate effectively worldwide on a scale that far exceeds that which is attainable today by only the most linguistically brilliant among us. It offers the opportunity to improve communication in business, diplomacy, scholarship and other fields so that those who speak many different native languages will be able to participate fluently in international conferences and chat comfortably with each other after the formal presentations are made. Nowadays that privilege is often restricted to native speakers of English and those who have special talents and opportunities for learning English as a foreign language.

G

What Esperanto does offer in concrete terms is the potential of saving billions of dollars which are now being spent on translators and interpreters, billions which would be freed up to serve the purposes of governments and organisations that spend so much of their resources to change words from one language into the words of others. Take, for example, the enormously costly conferences, meetings and documentation involved in the European Union parliamentary and administrative procedures - all funded, essentially, by tax payers. And instead of the World Health Organisation, and all NGOs for that matter, devoting enormous sums to provide interpreters and translations, they would be able to devote those huge amounts of money to improving the health of stricken populations throughout the world.

Reading

Questions 14 - 19

Reading Passage 2 has seven paragraphs, **A** - **G**.

Choose the correct heading for paragraphs **B** - **G** *from the list of headings below.*

Write the correct number **i** - **ix** *in spaces 14 - 19 below.*

i	A non-exclusive language			
ii	Fewer languages, more results	*Example*	Paragraph **A**	*Answer* **vii**
iii	Language is personal		14 Paragraph **B**	...........v..........
iv	What's fashionable in language		15 Paragraph **C**	..........viii.........
v	From the written word to the spoken word		16 Paragraph **D**	...........iii.........
vi	A real language		17 Paragraph **E**	...........vi..........
vii	Harmony through language		18 Paragraph **F**	............i..........
viii	The mechanics of a language		19 Paragraph **G**	...........ii..........
ix	Lost in translation			

Questions 20 - 22

Choose the correct letter **A, B, C** *or* **D**.

20   What advantage is there to learning Esperanto as one's first foreign language?
   A   Its pronunciation rules follow that of most European languages.
   B   There are no grammar rules to learn.
   (C)   It can make the learning of other foreign languages less complicated.
   D   Its verbs are not conjugated.

21   What do its critics say of Esperanto?
   A   It is only used in artificial situations.
   B   It requires emotional involvement.
   C   It cannot translate works of literature.
   (D)   It lacks depth of expression.

22   How could Esperanto help on a global level?
   A   It would eliminate the need for conferences.
   (B)   More aid money would reach those who need it.
   C   The world population would be speaking only one language.
   D   More funds could be made available for learning foreign languages.

Questions 23 - 26

Do the following statements agree with the information given in Reading Passage 2?

In spaces 23 - 26 below, write

YES	*if the statement agrees with the information*
NO	*if the statement contradicts the information*
NOT GIVEN	*if there is no information on this*

23   Supporters of Esperanto say it gives everyone an equal voice.   **YES**

24   Esperanto is the only artificially constructed language.   **NO**

25   Esperanto can be learned as part of a self-study course.   **NOT GIVEN**

26   Esperanto can be used equally in formal and casual situations.   **YES**

Reading Passage 2
Justification of the Answers

14. Paragraph B is **v** as it outlines how the written work that Zamenhof published became a spoken language.

15. Paragraph C is **viii** as the paragraph discusses the basic structural details of Esperanto and the way that it functions as a language.

16. Paragraph D is **iii** as it explains that some people can not identify with Esperanto and find it 'artificial'.

17. Paragraph E is **vi** as it says 'to rebut the accusation that it is not a 'real' language, point out that it is frequently used at international meetings.'

18. Paragraph F is **i** as it builds on the previous paragraph and argues that Esperanto allows everyone to learn the language given its structure.

19. Paragraph G is **ii** as this paragraph describes how so many languages are used at the moment and this prevents the optimum results being achieved. Having just the one second language would increase productivity, effectiveness and efficiency immensely.

20. C because paragraph C details how research has been done into this.

21. D - 'Esperanto has an artificial feel' and 'by nature of its artificiality it is impossible to become emotionally involved with that language'.

22. B because speaking just Esperanto would save 'billions of dollars which are now being spent on translators and interpreters', which could be spent on 'improving the health of stricken populations of the world'.

23. YES because 'Esperanto does not give advantages to the members of any particular people or culture, but provides an ethos of equality of rights, tolerance and true internationalism'

24. NO because the first paragraph states that it is the 'most widely spoken artificial language', which means that there must be others.

25. NOT GIVEN because the text does not mention self-study courses.

26. YES. Paragraph F describes how Esperanto can be used to make formal presentations and can be used in informal conversations.

Reading

READING PASSAGE 3

*You should spend about 20 minutes on **Questions 27 - 40**, which are based on Reading Passage 3 below*

LONG-TERM FORECAST: HOT AND DRY

A

Melting land ice in the Arctic is set to cause a global rise in sea levels, leading to disastrous effects for both man and wildlife. Many species worldwide are threatened with extinction, and low-lying islands and land masses will disappear entirely. But the havoc wreaked by the effect of greenhouse gases won't be confined to just too much water, but the absence of it, as well. In other words, desertification. A decrease in the total amount of rainfall in arid and semi-arid areas could increase the total area of dry-lands worldwide, and thus the total amount of land potentially at risk from desertification.

B

Desertification is officially recognised as 'land degradation in arid, semi-arid and dry sub-humid areas resulting from various factors including climatic variations and human activities'. This degradation of for-merly productive land is a complex process. It involves multiple causes, and it proceeds at varying rates in different climates. Desertification may intensify a general climatic trend, or initiate a change in local climate, both leading towards greater aridity. The more arid conditions associated with desertifica-tion accelerate the depletion of vegetation and soils. Land degradation occurs all over the world, but it is only referred to as desertification when it takes place in drylands. This is because these areas are especially prone to more permanent damage as different areas of degraded land spread and merge together to form desert-like conditions.

C

Global warming brought about by increasing greenhouse gas levels in the atmosphere is expected to increase the variability of weather conditions and extreme events. Many dryland areas face increasingly low and erratic rainfalls, coupled with soil erosion by wind and the drying-up of water resources through increased regional temperatures. Deforestation can also reduce rainfall in certain areas, increasing the threat of desertification. It is not yet possible, despite sophisticated technology, to identi-fy with an acceptable degree of reliability those parts of the Earth where desertification will occur. Existing drylands, which cover over 40% of the total land area of the world, most significantly in Africa and Asia, will probably be most at risk from climate change. These areas already experience low rain-fall, and any that falls is usually in the form of short, erratic, high-intensity storms. In addition, such areas also suffer from land degradation due to over-cultivation, overgrazing, deforestation and poor irri-gation practices.

D

It is a misconception that droughts cause desertification. Droughts are common in arid and semi-arid lands. Well-managed lands can recover from drought when the rains return. Continued land abuse dur-ing droughts, however, increases land degradation. Nor does desertification occur in linear, easily definable patterns. Deserts advance erratically, forming patches on their borders. Areas far from natural deserts can degrade quickly to barren soil, rock, or sand through poor land management. The pres-ence of a nearby desert has no direct relationship to desertification. Unfortunately, an area undergoing desertification is brought to public attention only after the process is well underway. Often little or no data are available to indicate the previous state of the ecosystem or the rate of degradation. Scientists still question whether desertification, as a process of global change, is permanent or how and when it can be halted or reversed.

E

But desertification will not be limited to the drylands of Africa and Asia. According to the environmental organisation Greenpeace, the Mediterranean will suffer substantially, too. If current trends in emissions of greenhouse gases continue, global temperatures are expected to rise faster over the next century than over any time during the last 10,000 years. Significant uncertainties surround predictions of regional climate changes, but it is likely that the Mediterranean region will also warm significantly, increasing the frequency and severity of droughts across the region. As the world warms, global sea levels will rise as oceans expand and glaciers melt. Around much of the Mediterranean basin, sea levels could rise by close to 1m by 2100. As a result, some low-lying coastal areas would be lost through flooding or erosion, while rivers and coastal aquifers would become more salty. The worst affected areas will be the Nile Delta, Venice in Italy and Thessaloniki in Greece, two major cities where local subsidence means that sea levels could rise by at least one-and-a-half times as much as elsewhere.

F

The consequences of all this, says Greenpeace, are far-reaching, and the picture is a gloomy one. Livestock production would suffer due to a deterioration in the quality of rangeland. Yields of grains and other crops could decrease substantially across the Mediterranean region due to increased frequency of drought. Crop production would be further threatened by increases in competition for water and the prevalence of pests and diseases and land loss through desertification and sea-level rise. The combination of heat and pollution would lead to an upsurge in respiratory illness among urban populations, while extreme weather events could increase death and injury rates. Water shortages and damaged infrastructure would increase the risk of cholera and dysentery, while higher temperatures would increase the incidence of infectious diseases, such as malaria and dengue fever. Serious social disruption could occur as millions are forced from their homelands as a result of desertification, poor harvests and sea-level rise, while international disputes over shared water resources could turn into conflict.

G

Future climate change could critically undermine efforts for sustainable development in the Mediterranean region through its impacts on the environment and social and economic well-being. While in many respects climate change exacerbates existing problems instead of creating new ones, the sheer magnitude of the potential problem means it cannot be ignored. There is some scope for adaptation, but the fact that many measures would be beneficial irrespective of climate change suggests that radical changes in our policies and practices will be needed. It is also vital that developed countries meet their obligations to assist adaptation in developing countries through access to know-how and financial assistance. Ultimately, however, the long-term sustainability of the Mediterranean region requires keeping climate change within tolerable bounds. Current understanding of safe limits points to the need for prompt international agreement - and action - to make the drastic cuts in emissions of greenhouse gases required to stabilise atmospheric concentrations of these gases.

Reading

Reading Tip:
Pay attention to how many words are required for an answer.

Questions 27 - 32
Complete the flow-chart below.

*Write **NO MORE THAN THREE WORDS** for each answer.*

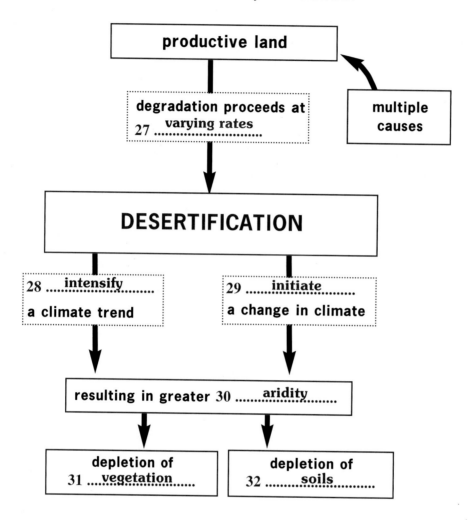

```
                    productive land
                          |
                          v
       degradation proceeds at          multiple
   27 ....varying rates.........          causes
                          |
                          v
                  DESERTIFICATION
                    |          |
                    v          v
   28 ...intensify...    29 ....initiate....
   a climate trend       a change in climate
                    |          |
                    v          v
         resulting in greater 30 .....aridity.....
                    |          |
                    v          v
       depletion of          depletion of
   31 ...vegetation...     32 ......soils......
```

Questions 33 - 36

Reading Passage 3 has seven paragraphs, **A - G**.

Which paragraph contains the following information?

*Write the correct letter **A - G** in spaces 33 - 36 below.*

33	Human intervention is a potential solution to potential disaster.	......G......
34	The rate of climate change is set to accelerate dramatically.	......E......
35	There is seldom enough information available in some areas to track how fast the effects of climate change have happened in the past.	......D......
36	Desertification is attributable to a number of factors.	......B......

Questions 37 - 40

*Complete the summary with the list of words **A - I** below.*

*Write the correct letter **A - I** in spaces 37 - 40 below.*

Climate change may have catastrophic effects on the human and animal world. As glaciers melt, sea levels will rise, causing extensive flooding and land **37** ....E............... .

Another consequence of global warming is **38** ....G..............., which affects areas known as **39** ....C............... . These areas are subject to irregular weather patterns, but also suffer from human intervention or neglect, such as inadequate or inefficient **40** ....A............... systems.

A irrigation	**B** cooling	**C** drylands
D cause	**E** loss	**F** abuse
G desertification	**H** deserts	**I** emission

Reading Passage 3
Justification of the Answers

27. 'varying rates' - **Paragraph 2:** *This degradation of formerly productive land is a complex process. It involves multiple causes, and it proceeds at **varying rates** in different climates.*

28. 'intensify' - **Paragraph 2:** *'Desertification may **intensify** a general climatic trend, or initiate a change in local climate, both leading towards greater aridity.'*

29. 'initiate' - **Paragraph 2:** *'Desertification may ..... **initiate** a change in local climate, both leading towards greater aridity.'*

30. 'aridity' - **Paragraph 2:** *'Desertification may ..... initiate a change in local climate, both leading towards greater **aridity**.'*

31. 'vegetation' - **Paragraph 2:** *'The more arid conditions associated with desertification accelerates the depletion of **vegetation** and soils.'*

32. 'soils' - **Paragraph 2:** *'The more arid conditions associated with desertification accelerates the depletion of vegetation and **soils**.'*

33. G - The paragraph suggests that 'drastic cuts in emissions of greenhouse gases is required to stabilize atmospheric concentrations of these gases.'

34. E - 'if current trends in emissions of greenhouse gases continue, global temperatures are expected to rise faster over the next century than over any time in the last 10,000 years.'

35. D - 'Often little or no data is available to indicate the previous state of the ecosystem or the rate of degradation'.

36. B - as the paragraph details how desertification results 'from various factors including climatic variations and human activities'.

37. loss - **Paragraph F** - *'Crop production would be further threatened by increases in competition for water and the prevalence of pests and diseases and **land loss** through desertification and sea-level rise.'*

38. desertification - **Paragraph B** -*'Land degradation occurs all over the world, but it is only referred to as **desertification** when it takes place in drylands.'*

39. drylands - **Paragraph B** - *'...... but it is only referred to as desertification when it takes place in **drylands**.'*

40. irrigation - **Paragraph C** - *'In addition, such areas also suffer from land degradation due to over-cultivation, overgrazing, deforestation and poor **irrigation** practices.'*

Writing

WRITING TASK 1

You should spend about 20 minutes on this task.

> *The graph below shows the weekday volume of passenger activity on the Toronto Metro system for July, 2007.*
>
> *Summarise the information by selecting and reporting the main features, and make comparisons where necessary.*

Write at least 150 words.

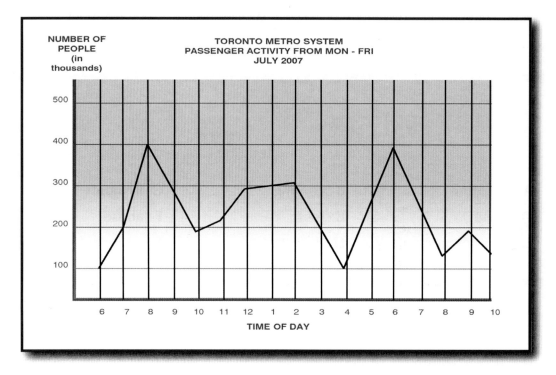

WRITING TASK 2

You should spend about 40 minutes on this task.

Write about the following topic:

> *Schools concentrate far too much on traditional subjects which do not adequately prepare students for the realistic demands of the modern working world.*
>
> *To what extent do you agree or disagree?*

Give reasons for your answer and include any relevant examples from your own knowledge or experience.

Write at least 250 words.

Speaking

PART 1   (4-5 minutes)

The examiner asks the candidate about him/herself, his/her home, work or studies and other familiar topics.

Language

* What language do you speak at home?
* Do you speak any other languages?
* What is the best way to learn a foreign language?
* What is your opinion about English as an international language?

PART 2   (2 minutes)

You will have to talk about the topic for one to two minutes. You have one minute to think about what you are going to say. You can make some notes to help you if you wish.

Describe a celebration that is important in your country.

You should say:
* **when the celebration takes place**
* **what people do during the celebration**
* **what you like or dislike about it**
    and explain why this celebration is important.

PART 3   (4-5 minutes)

Discussion topics:

Customs and Traditions

* How important do you think customs and traditions are for a country?

* Do you think that a country's customs and traditions are just as important to younger people as older people? Why (not)?

* Are there any traditions in your culture that you would like to see disappear?

International Customs

* What influence have cultures from other countries had on your country?

* Should people who immigrate to a new country keep the customs of their home country?

* Are movies, TV and the internet making customs the same all over the world?

    Do you think this is a good or bad thing?

Test 2

Listening

SECTION 1   *Questions 1 - 10*

Questions 1 - 7

Listening - Section 1
L: **(1)** Well, I have a class at college in the morning until 11.15. Wait, no, 11.30, so any time after then.   **J: (2)** I have a lecture until about 12.15.
Check the **Audioscript in the Self-Study Guide** for the **Justification of the Answers for ALL the Sections of the Listening Test**

Complete the notes below.

Write **NO MORE THAN TWO WORDS AND/OR A NUMBER** *for each answer.*

Visiting Gaudi's Exhibition

Example   *Answer*

Day of visit: .... *tomorrow*

Laurel's schedule:
- Class at college until: **1** .... 11.30 ....

Jason's schedule:
- He says that his lecture finishes at: **2** ...... 12.15 ......

- Gallery's name: **Tate**

- Jason suggests they meet at the **3** .... tube .... at 12.30

- Laurel suggests they meet at the gallery's **4** ...... ticket office ....

Tickets prices:
- Jason does not get a concession so he will pay **5** ...... £15 ....

- Laurel will pay **6** ...... £10 ...... because she gets a concession.

- They will get there in Jason's **7** .... van ....

Questions 8 - 10

Complete the sentences below.

Write **NO MORE THAN THREE WORDS AND/OR A NUMBER** *for each answer.*

Address:

8   **Flat:** .... 6   9   **Number:** .... 83 ....

10   **Street:** ...... Alexandra ...... Avenue, West Hampstead

SECTION 2   *Questions 11 - 20*

Questions 11 - 16
Label the diagram below.
*Choose **SIX** answers from the box and write the correct letter, **A - H**, next to questions 11 - 16.*

DIAGRAM OF NEWGRANGE PASSAGE TOMB

15 .....F.....

Top view

12 ..H.....

11 ..B.....

13 ..C.....

14 ...D....

Side view

roof of the passage

16 ...E.....

A spiral column	**E** light box
B passage	**F** entrance
C stone basin	**G** kerb stone
D entrance stone	**H** chamber rooms

Questions 17 - 20
Complete the sentences below.
*Write **ONLY ONE WORD** for each answer.*

The Winter Solstice at Newgrange

17   Anyone may join the gathering of people at Newgrange for the Solstice sunrise; however, access to the chamber itself is ......**limited**........ .

18   Access to the chamber is decided in advance by ......**lottery**......... .

19   The winners of the draw will be notified by the middle of ......**October**...... .

20   Each winner may bring a ......**guest**......... .

Practice Test 2

Practice Test 2 *(side margin)*

Listening

SECTION 3   *Questions 21 - 30*

Questions 21 - 24

Choose the best answer A, B, C, or D.

21   What is the doctor's name?

    A   Dr Garrison
    B   Dr Peters
    (C) Dr Smith

22   The patient is looking for a remedy for his

    A   obesity.
    B   lack of exercise.
    (C) stomach complaint.

23   How often does the patient exercise?

    (A) about once a month
    B   every five days
    C   every hour

24   What does the doctor think?

    A   that the patient should make a list of what he likes to eat
    (B) that the patient should change his lifestyle
    C   that there is no point in the patient going on exercising hard

Questions 25 - 30

Complete the summary below.

Write **NO MORE THAN THREE WORDS AND/OR A NUMBER** *for each answer.*

Patient's Diet:

Breakfast is to consist of hot water with squeezed lemon juice, which should be followed 25 ....**20/twenty minutes**........ later by juice and cereal or toast. Organic honey or jam is permitted, but no 26 ....**butter**................., salt, or sugar is allowed. Lunch is to be a sandwich with salad and, for dinner 27 ....**100 grammes/a small quantity**........... of brown rice or pasta with vegetables and fish.

For dessert you can have a piece of fruit or 28 ....**organic yogurt**.... that can be bought from the shop opposite the 29 ....**town hall**........ in the High Street. The patient must also absolutely abstain from 30 ....**alcohol, coffee**.... and cigarettes.

SECTION 4 *Questions 31 - 40*

Questions 31 - 40

Complete the notes below.

Write **NO MORE THAN TWO WORDS** *for each answer.*

Notes from Photography Lecture 2

✦ *Exposure = the amount of light you let strike your 31* ......film......

✦ *A good photographer must know:* *1. how much light is required*
                                    2. how to control light reaching film

   1. how much light is required:
      Usually determined by camera's 32 .....inbuilt..... *light metre*

   2. how to control light reaching film:
      Usually taken care of by aperture and shutter 33 .....settings.....

✦ *An aperture is simply a 34* .....hole..... *that lets light pass through.*
   - aperture size is 35 .....described..... *in f-numbers*
   - a smaller f-number allows more light in

✦ *The shutter has a 36* .....crucial..... *role.*
   - prevents light from reaching film until the 37 .....instant..... *of exposure*
   - opens for a predetermined amount of time
   - shutter 38 .....speed..... *is expressed in fractions of a second*

✦ *Overexposure = 39* .....more light..... *than necessary to capture image*
   - pale shades and poor, washed-out colours

✦ *Underexposure = not enough light to capture image*
   - dark image, poor details and 40 .....shadows.....

Practice Test 2

Reading

READING PASSAGE 1

*You should spend about 20 minutes on **Questions 1 - 13**, which are based on Reading Passage 1 below.*

DISORDERS: AN OVERVIEW

Autistic Spectrum Disorder

Children with Autistic Spectrum Disorder have difficulty understanding what other people are saying, need help to play with other children, enjoy routines and find unfamiliar situations difficult. People with Autistic Spectrum Disorder can be good at creative activities like art, music and poetry. They can concentrate on one thing for a long time so they can become very good at something that they like doing.

ADHD - Attention Deficit Hyperactivity Disorder

People with ADHD have three types of problems. Overactive behaviour (hyperactivity), impulsive behaviour and difficulty paying attention. Children with ADHD are not just very active but have a wide range of problem behaviours which can make them very difficult to care for and control. Those who have ADHD often find it difficult to fit in at school. They may also have problems getting on with other children. Some children have significant problems with concentration and attention, but are not necessarily overactive or impulsive. These children are sometimes described as having Attention Deficit Disorder (ADD) rather than ADHD. ADD can easily be missed because the child is quiet and dreamy rather than disruptive. ADHD is not related to intelligence. Children with all levels of ability can have ADHD.

Stress

Stress can be defined as the way you feel when you're under abnormal pressure. All sorts of situations can cause stress. The most common, however, involve work, money matters and relationships with partners, children or other family members. Stress may be caused either by major upheavals and life events such as divorce, unemployment, moving house and bereavement, or by a series of minor irritations such as feeling undervalued at work or dealing with difficult children. Some stress can be positive and research has suggested that a moderate level of stress makes us perform better. It also makes us more alert and can help us in challenging situations such as job interviews or public speaking. Stressful situations can also be exhilarating and some people actually thrive on the excitement that comes with dangerous sports or other 'high-risk' activities.

Schizophrenia

Schizophrenia is a diagnosis given to some people who have severely disrupted beliefs and experiences. During an episode of schizophrenia, a person's experience and interpretation of the outside world is disrupted - they may lose touch with reality, see or hear things that are not there and act in unusual ways in response to these 'hallucinations'. An episode of schizophrenia can last for several weeks and can be very frightening. The causes are unknown but episodes of schizophrenia appear to be associated with changes in some brain chemicals. Stressful experiences and some recreational drugs are sometimes thought to trigger an episode.

Depression

Depression describes a range of moods, from the low spirits that we all experience, to a severe problem that interferes with everyday life. The latter type, sometimes referred to as 'clinical depression', is defined as 'a persistent exaggeration of the everyday feelings that accompany sadness'. If you have severe depression you may experience low mood, loss of interest and pleasure as well as feelings of worthlessness and guilt. You may also experience tearfulness, poor concentration, reduced energy, reduced or increased appetite, changes in weight, sleep problems and anxiety. You may even feel that life is not worth living, and plan or attempt suicide.

Practice Test 2

Obsessive Compulsive Disorder in Adults

Imagine you are getting up in the morning. You know you will need to go to the bathroom, but the thought of accidentally touching the doorknob is frightening. There may be dangerous bacteria on it. Of course you cleaned the entire bathroom yesterday, including the usual series of spraying disinfectant, washing and rinsing. As usual it took a couple of hours to do it the right way. Even then you weren't sure whether you had missed an area, so you had to re-wash the floor. Naturally the doorknob was sprayed and rubbed three times with a bactericidal spray. Now the thought that you could have missed a spot on the doorknob makes you very nervous.

This description might give you some sense of the tormented and anxious world that people with Obsessive Compulsive Disorder (OCD) live in. It is a world filled with dangers from outside and from within. Often elaborate rituals and thoughts are used to ward off feared events, but no amount of mental or physical activity seems adequate, so doubt and anxiety are often present.

People who do not have OCD may perform behaviours in a ritualistic way, repeating, checking, or washing things out of habit or concern. Generally this is done without much, if any, worry. What distinguishes OCD as a psychiatric disorder is that the experience of obsessions, and the performance of rituals, reaches such an intensity or frequency that it causes significant psychological distress and interferes in a significant way with psychosocial functioning. The guideline of at least one hour spent on symptoms per day is often used as a measure of 'significant interference'. However, among patients who try to avoid situations that bring on anxiety and compulsions, the actual symptoms may not consume an hour. Yet the quantity of time lost from having to avoid objects or situations would clearly constitute interfering with functioning. Consider, for instance, a welfare mother who throws out more than $100 of groceries a week because of contamination fears. Although this behaviour has a major effect on her functioning, it might not consume one hour per day.

Patients with OCD describe their experience as having thoughts (obsessions) that they associate with some danger. The sufferer generally recognises that it is his or her own thoughts, rather than something imposed by someone else (as in some paranoid schizophrenic patients). However, the disturbing thoughts cannot be dismissed, and simply nag at the sufferer. Something must then be done to relieve the danger and mitigate the fear. This leads to actions and thoughts that are intended to neutralise the danger. These are the compulsions. Because these behaviours seem to give the otherwise 'helplessly anxious' person something to combat the danger, they are temporarily reassuring. However, since the 'danger' is typically irrational or imaginary, it simply returns, thereby triggering another cycle of the briefly reassuring compulsions. From the standpoint of classic conditioning, this pattern of painful obsession followed by temporarily reassuring compulsion eventually produces an intensely ingrained habit. It is rare to see obsessions without compulsions.

The two most common obsessions are fears of contamination and fear of harming oneself or others, while the two most common compulsions are checking and cleaning.

Reading

Questions 1 - 5

*Look at the statements (Questions 1 - 5) and the lists of disorders (**A - G**) below.*

*Match each statement with the correct disorder **A - G**.*

*Write the correct letter **A - G** next to questions 1 - 5 below.*

NB *There are more disorders than descriptions, so you will not use them all.*

1	can be positive in small doses but is generally associated with pressure	......A......
2	feeling that there is danger constantly present	......G......
3	has experiences that may or may not be part of the 'real' world	......D......
4	active to the point of losing concentration and becoming disruptive	......E......
5	good at art but not at communicating	......B......

TYPES OF DISORDERS

A   Stress

B   Autistic Spectrum Disorder

C   Attention Deficit Disorder

D   Schizophrenia

E   Attention Deficit Hyperactivity Disorder

F   Depression

G   Obsessive Compulsive Disorder

Reading Tip:

Remember that there is more than one way to read a text. It is not always necessary to read slowly and carefully. Remember that you are reading texts in order to answer questions and that should be your main focus.

Practice Test 2

Questions 6 - 9

Complete the table below.

Write **NO MORE THAN THREE WORDS** from the passage for each answer.

Disorder	Personality Trait Exhibited by Sufferer
Autism Spectrum Disorder	May excel in activities of a 6 ....*creative*........ nature.
Attention Deficit Disorder	May appear 7 .*quiet and dreamy*........ .
Schizophrenia	May respond to experiencing episodes of the disease by behaving in very 8 .*unusual ways*........ .
Depression	May experience feelings of futility that lead to thoughts of 9 ....*suicide*........ .
Obsessive Compulsive Disorder	May frequently experience feelings of doubt and anxiety.

Questions 10 - 13

Choose the correct letter, **A, B, C** or **D**.

10   Which disorder could cause visible physical changes?
  A   Autistic Spectrum Disorder
  B   Stress
  C   Schizophrenia
  D   Depression

11   Episodes of which disorder may last for a limited period of time?
  A   ADHD
  B   Autistic Spectrum Disorder
  C   schizophrenia
  D   depression

12   Which disorder can be triggered by the death of a loved one?
  A   Autistic Spectrum Disorder
  B   ADHD
  C   Stress
  D   OCD

13   What characterises sufferers of OCD?
  A   the fear of going outside
  B   the performance of rituals
  C   the desire to hurt others
  D   the feeling that they are helpless to ease their distress

Reading

READING PASSAGE 2

*You should spend about 20 minutes on **Questions 14 - 26**, which are based on Reading Passage 2 below.*

THE DEVELOPING WORLD

A

THE DEVELOPING WORLD - the economically underdeveloped countries of Asia, Africa, Oceania and Latin America - is considered as an entity with common characteristics, such as poverty, high birth rates, and economic dependence on the advanced countries. Until recently, the developing world was known as 'the third world'. The French demographer Alfred Sauvy coined the expression (in French) in 1952 by analogy with the 'third estate' - the commoners of France before and during the French Revolution - as opposed to priests and nobles, comprising the first and second estates respectively. 'Like the third estate', wrote Sauvy, 'the third world is nothing, and it wants to be something'. The term therefore implies that the third world is exploited, much as the third estate was exploited and that, like the third estate, its destiny is a revolutionary one. It conveys as well a second idea, also discussed by Sauvy – that of non-alignment, for the developing world belongs neither to the industrialised capitalist world nor to the industrialised former communist bloc. The expression 'third world' was used at the 1955 conference of Afro-Asian countries held in Bandung, Indonesia. In 1956 a group of social scientists associated with Sauvy's National Institute of Demographic Studies, in Paris, published a book called 'Le Tiers-Monde'. Three years later, the French economist Francois Perroux launched a new journal, on problems of underdevelopment, with the same title. By the end of the 1950s the term was frequently employed in the French media to refer to the underdeveloped countries of Asia, Africa, Oceania and Latin America. Present-day politicians and social commentators, however, now use the term 'developing world' in a politically correct effort to dispel the negative connotations of 'third world'.

B

Countries in the developing world have a number of common traits: distorted and highly dependent economies devoted to producing primary products for the developed world; traditional, rural social structures; high population growth and widespread poverty. Nevertheless, the developing world is sharply differentiated, for it includes countries on various levels of economic development. And despite the poverty of the countryside and the urban shanty towns, the ruling elites of most third world countries are wealthy.

C

This combination of conditions in Asia, Africa, Oceania and Latin America is linked to the absorption of the developing world into the international capitalist economy, by way of conquest or indirect domination. The main economic consequence of Western domination was the creation, for the first time in history, of a world market. By setting up sub-economies linked to the West throughout the developing world, and by introducing other modern institutions, industrial capitalism disrupted traditional economies and, indeed, societies. This disruption led to underdevelopment.

D

Because the economies of underdeveloped countries have been geared to the needs of industrialised countries, they often comprise only a few modern economic activities, such as mining or the cultivation of plantation crops. Control over these activities has often remained in the hands of large foreign firms. The prices of developing world products are usually determined by large buyers in the economically dominant countries of the West, and trade with the West provides almost all the developing world's income. Throughout the colonial period, outright exploitation severely limited the accumulation of capital within the foreign-dominated countries. Even after decolonisation (in

the 1950s, 1960s, and 1970s), the economies of the developing world grew slowly, or not at all, owing largely to the deterioration of the 'terms of trade' – the relationship between the cost of the goods a nation must import from abroad and its income from the exports it sends to foreign countries. Terms of trade are said to deteriorate when the cost of imports rises faster than income from exports. Since buyers in the industrialised countries determined the prices of most products involved in international trade, the worsening position of the developing world was scarcely surprising. Only the oil-producing countries – after 1973 – succeeded in escaping the effects of Western domination of the world economy.

E

No study of the developing world could hope to assess its future prospects without taking into account population growth. While the mortality rate from poverty-related diseases continues to cause international concern, the birth rate continues to rise at unprecedented levels. This population explosion in the developing world will surely prevent any substantial improvements in living standards, as well as threaten people in stagnant economies with worsening poverty and starvation levels.

Reading

Questions 14 - 18

Reading Passage 2 has five paragraphs, **A - E**.

Choose the most suitable heading for each paragraph from the list of headings below.

*Write the appropriate number **i - viii** in spaces 14 - 18 below.*

List of Headings

i	The great divide between rich and poor.
ii	The status and destiny of the developing world follows a European precedent.
iii	Economic progress in the developing world slowed down by political unrest.
iv	More people, less food.
v	Western countries refuse to acknowledge their history of colonisation.
vi	Open trade is the main reason these countries become impoverished.
vii	Rivalry in the developing world between capitalist and former communist bloc countries.
viii	Prices and conditions set by outsiders.

14	Paragraph **A**	....ii....
15	Paragraph **B**	....i....
16	Paragraph **C**	....vi....
17	Paragraph **D**	....viii....
18	Paragraph **E**	....iv....

Reading Tip:

If you are having a difficult time with a particular question, simply leave it and go on to the next one. If you have time you can come back and answer that question later.

Questions 19 - 22

Do the following statements agree with the information given in Reading Passage 2?

In spaces 19 - 22 below, write

YES	if the statement agrees with the information
NO	if the statement contradicts the information
NOT GIVEN	if there is no information on this

19   Agriculture still plays a role in the economy of developing countries. ....**YES**........

20   The population of the developing world increases at such a fast rate because they constantly need to renew the labour force.   ....**NOT GIVEN**........

21   Countries that spend more on imports than they earn from exports can experience problems.   ....**YES**........

22   Like the developing world, oil rich countries are also victims of dominance by Western powers.   ....**NO**........

Questions 23 - 26

Complete each sentence with the correct ending **A - F** below.

Write the correct letter **A - F** in spaces 23 - 26 below.

23   Countries in the developing world   ....**D**........
24   The term 'the third world' implies   ....**F**........
25   One factor that is prevalent in the developing world is   ....**A**........
26   One consequence of the terms of trade was   ....**E**........

A	economic dependence on developed countries.
B	that decolonisation took a long time to achieve.
C	dictate the needs of industrialised countries.
D	share common characteristics.
E	that many economies stagnated.
F	a society that wants something it does not have.

Reading

READING PASSAGE 3

*You should spend about 20 minutes on **Questions 27 - 40**, which are based on Reading Passage 3 below.*

BIOMETRICS

A

The term "biometrics" is derived from the Greek words bio (life) and metric (to measure). It refers to technologies for measuring and analysing a person's physiological or behavioural characteristics, such as fingerprints, irises, voice patterns, facial patterns and hand measurements, for identification and verification purposes. One of the earliest known examples of biometrics in practice was a form of fingerprinting used in China in the 14th century. Chinese merchants stamped children's palm prints and footprints on paper with ink to distinguish the young children from one another. This method of biometrics is still being practised today.

B

Until the late 1800s, identification largely relied upon 'photographic memory.' In the 1890s, an anthropologist and police desk clerk in Paris named Alphonse Bertillon sought to fix the problem of identifying convicted criminals and turned biometrics into a distinct field of study. He developed a method of multiple body measurements which was named after him - *Bertillonage*. Bertillon based his system on the claim that measurement of adult bones does not change after the age of 20. He also introduced a cataloguing system, which enabled the filing and checking of records quite quickly. His system was used by police authorities throughout the world, until 1903, when two identical measurements were obtained for two different persons at Fort Leavenworth prison. The prison switched to fingerprinting the following day and the rest of the world soon followed, abandoning Bertillonage forever. After the failure of Bertillonage, the police started using fingerprinting, which was developed by Richard Edward Henry of Scotland Yard, essentially reverting to the same methods used by the Chinese for years.

C

In the past three decades biometrics has moved from a single method (fingerprinting) to more than ten different methods. Hundreds of companies are involved with this development and continue to improve their methods as the technology available to them advances. As the industry grows, however, so does the public concern over privacy issues. Laws and regulations continue to be drafted and standards are beginning to be developed. While no other biometric has yet reached the wide range of use of fingerprinting, some are beginning to be used in both legal and business areas.

D

Identification and verification have long been in practice by presenting a personal document, such as a licence, ID card or a passport. It may also require personal information such as passwords or PINs. For security reasons, often two, or all three, of these systems are combined but as times progress, we are in constant need for more secure and accurate measures. Authentication by biometric verification is becoming increasingly common in corporate and public security systems, consumer electronics and point-of-sale applications. In addition to security, the driving force behind biometric verification has been convenience. Already, many European countries are introducing a biometric passport which will carry a paper-thin computer chip to store the facial image and at least one additional biometric identifier. This will help to counter fraudulent efforts to obtain duplicate passports and will verify the identity of the holder against the document.

E

Identification and verification are mainly used today in the fight against crime with the methods of fingerprint and DNA analysis. It is also used in security for granting access rights by voice pattern recognition. Additionally, it is used for personal comfort by identifying a person and changing personal settings accordingly, as in setting car seats by facial recognition. Starting in early 2000, the use of biometrics in schools has become widespread, particularly in the UK and USA. A number of justifications are given for such practices, including combatting truancy, and replacing library cards or meal cards with fingerprinting systems. Opponents of school biometrics have raised privacy concerns against the creation of databases that would progressively include the entire population.

F

Biometric devices consist of a reader or scanning device, software that converts the gathered information into digital form, and a database that stores the biometric data for comparison with previous records. When converting the biometric input, the software identifies specific points of data as match points. The match points are processed using an algorithm into a value that can be compared with biometric data in the database. There are two types of biometrics: behavioural and physical. Behavioural biometrics are generally used for verification while physical biometrics can be used for either identification or verification.

G

Iris-pattern and retina-pattern authentication methods are already employed in some bank automatic teller machines. Voice waveform recognition, a method of verification that has been used for many years with tape recordings in telephone wiretaps, is now being used for access to proprietary databanks in research facilities. Facial-recognition technology has been used by law enforcement to pick out individuals in large crowds with considerable reliability. Hand geometry is being used in industry to provide physical access to buildings. Earlobe geometry has been used to disprove the identity of individuals who claim to be someone they are not (identity theft). Signature comparison is not as reliable, all by itself, as other biometric verification methods but offers an extra layer of verification when used in conjunction with one or more other methods. No matter what biometric methodology is used, the identification verification process remains the same. A record of a person's unique characteristic is captured and kept in a database. Later on, when identification verification is required, a new record is captured and compared with the previous record in the database. If the data in the new record matches that in the database record, the person's identity is confirmed.

H

As technology advances, and time goes on, more and more private companies and public utilities will use biometrics for safe, accurate identification. However, these advances will raise many concerns throughout society, where many may not be educated on the methods. Some believe this technology can cause physical harm to an individual using it, or that instruments used are unsanitary. For example, there are concerns that retina scanners might not always be clean. There are also concerns as to whether our personal information taken through biometric methods can be misused, tampered with, or sold, eg. by criminals stealing, rearranging or copying the biometric data. Also, the data obtained using biometrics can be used in unauthorised ways without the individual's consent. Much still remains to be seen in the effectiveness of biometric verification before we can identify it as the safest system for identification.

Reading

Questions 27 - 31

Reading Passage 3 has eight paragraphs, **A - H**.

Which paragraph contains the following information?

Write the correct letter A - H in spaces 27 - 31 below.

27	possible health hazards associated with the use of biometrics	.........H.........
28	convicted criminals were not the first to be identified by the use of biometrics	.........A.........
29	the application of mathematics in assessing biometric data	.........F.........
30	despite its limitations, biometrics has become a commercial field of activity	.........C.........
31	some biometric methods are useful only in conjunction with others	.........G.........

Reading Passage 3
Justification of the Answers

27. H - 'some believe this technology may cause physical harm....'

28. A - One of the earliest known examples of biometrics in practice was a form of fingerprinting used in China in the 14th century....... to distinguish young children from one another'

29. F - 'The match points are processed using an algorithm'.

30. C - 'Hundreds of companies are involved with new methods'.

31. G - Signature comparison is not as reliable, all by itself as other biometric verification'.

32. Paragraph C - 'As the industry grows, however, so does the public concern over **privacy issues**.'

33. Paragraph E - 'Additionally, it is used for **personal comfort** by identifying a person and changing personal settings accordingly, as in setting car seats by facial recognition.'

34. Paragraph G - 'A record of a person's **unique characteristic** is captured and kept in a database.'

Questions 32 - 34

Complete the sentences below.

*Choose **NO MORE THAN TWO WORDS** from the passage for each answer.*

32 Members of the public are becoming increasingly worried about the

.............**privacy issues**........ that may accompany the use of biometrics.

33 Biometrics can be used to improve the .....**personal comfort/car seats**.....

of drivers and passengers.

34 Regardless of the technology used, it has one common purpose:

to find somebody's .....**unique characteristic**..... and store it on computer.

> ### Reading Tip:
> Always remain conscious of time limits.
> Never spend too much time on just one question.

Questions 35 - 40

*Complete the summary with the list of words **A - L** below.*

*Write the correct letter **A - L** in spaces 35 - 40 below.*

BIOMETRICS

As long ago as the 14th century, the Chinese made use of biometrics in order to tell young children apart, but it was only in the 1890s when it was first used by the authorities as a means of 35 ......identification.. in criminal cases. The system developed by the Frenchman Bertillon – that of measuring adult bones - was flawed, however, and so police adopted 36 ...fingerprinting.. as a more reliable way of identifying suspects. Governments, companies and even schools employ biometric technology to ensure, for example, that people do not enter a country illegally, gain access to certain buildings, or assume someone else's 37 ...identity...... . Apart from security, another important 38 ......factor.... behind biometric verification has been 39 ...convenience.. . The use of biometrics, however, has its critics, who say that the data collected could be used for different purposes without our 40 ....approval... .

A identification	B security	C convenience
D scanning	E fingerprinting	F identity
G violation	H measuring	I justification
J approval	K factor	L apprehension

Reading Passage 3
Justification of the Answers

35. Paragraph B - *'In the 1890s, an anthropologist and police desk clerk in Paris named Alphonse Bertillon sought to fix the problem of **identifying** convicted criminals and turned biometrics into a distinct field of study.'*
36. Paragraph B - *'After the failure of Bertillonage, the police started using **fingerprinting**, ... '*
37. Paragraph G - *'individuals who claim to be someone they are not (**identity** theft).'*
38. Paragraph D - *' ... the **driving force** behind biometric verification... "*
39. Paragraph D - *'In addition to security, the driving force behind biometric verification has been **convenience**. .....'*
40. Paragraph H - *'Also, the data obtained using biometrics can be used in unauthorised ways without the individual's **consent**.'*

Practice Test 2

Writing

WRITING TASK 1

You should spend about 20 minutes on this task.

> *The graph below shows the working hours for men and women in the developing world between the years 1998 and 2003.*
>
> *Summarise the information by selecting and reporting the main features, and make comparisons where necessary.*

Write at least 150 words.

WRITING TASK 2

You should spend about 40 minutes on this task.

Write about the following topic:

> *Most people in the world have to work to earn a living. However, many people work only for the financial gain that it involves, and not for any other rewards that a job can offer.*
>
> *What do you think the main considerations when deciding what job to take should be?*

Give reasons for your answer and include any relevant examples from your own knowledge or experience.

Write at least 250 words.

Writing Tip:
Writing Task 2 carries more marks than Writing Task 1, so leave plenty of time for it.

Speaking

Speaking Tip:
Try to give yourself time to think
before answering the questions.

PART 1   (4-5 minutes)

The examiner asks the candidate about him/herself, his/her home, work or studies and other familiar topics.

Leisure Time

- What do you like to do to relax in your free time?
- What is your idea of a perfect weekend?
- Do you prefer to watch TV or go to the cinema?
- What forms of entertainment exist in the area where you live?

PART 2   (2 minutes)

You will have to talk about the topic for one to two minutes. You have one minute to think about what you are going to say. You can make some notes to help you if you wish.

> **Describe a sport you enjoy doing or watching.**
>
> **You should say**
> - **what the sport or activity is**
> - **what its main features are**
> - **when and where you first played or saw it**
>
> **and explain why you like it.**

PART 3   (4-5 minutes)

Discussion topics:

Sports

- What personal benefits may be gained by participating in sports?
- What qualities do you think are necessary in order to work as part of a team?
- Why do you think some people enjoy extreme, or dangerous, sports?

Financial Aspect of Sports

- Many sports are cost prohibitive. Can you think of any? Why are they so expensive?
- Do you think that some professional sports people earn too much money?
- Would you pay money for a T-shirt or other gear with a team logo? Why or why not?

Test 3

Listening

Listening - Section 1
F: **(1)** The screen went blank.
M: And **(2)** it's plugged in, not running on battery?

Check the **Audioscript** in the **Self-Study Guide** for the **Justification of the Answers for ALL the Sections of the Listening Test**

SECTION 1   Questions 1 - 10

Complete the form below.

Write **NO MORE THAN THREE WORDS AND/OR A NUMBER** *for each answer.*

TOM'S COMPUTER MAINTENENCE

Customer Information Form

Date: *Sunday, 12th May*

Example: *Answer:*

Reason for call: .... *computer problem* ....
....

What happened: the screen **1** .... went blank ....

Troubleshooting checklist:

☑ restarted computer

☑ The computer is **2** .... plugged in .... - not running on battery

Activity when the problem occurred: **3** .... on the/using the internet

Possible diagnosis: **a virus**

Anti-virus programme: 4 .... not sure ....

Appointment

Location: 5 .... Morningside (area) ....

Time scheduled for visit: 6 .... 7:45 ....

Street address: *14* **7** .... Branston .... *Crescent, 2F3*

Customer name: *Sandra* **8** .... Sarrencen ....

Name on buzzer: *the same as above*

Fee: 9 .... £60 .... *for the first hour's work, then £40 per hour*

Estimated time for job: *less than* **10** .... half an hour ....

SECTION 2   *Questions 11 - 20*

Questions 11 - 17

*Choose the correct letter, **A**, **B** or **C**.*

11 The speaker's job requires
    A a great deal of walking.
    (**B**) extensive travel.
    C clean water.

12 Why is this story being told?
    (**A**) to promote Charity-Water
    B for entertainment purposes
    C to encourage Helen

13 Why do the charity workers usually surprise communities?
    A It makes people happy.
    B It is difficult to spread news.
    (**C**) It makes their work easier.

14 When villagers heard of the charity workers' arrival, they
    (**A**) had a party.
    B were suspicious.
    C took no notice.

15 Helen is feeling
    (**A**) ecstatic about her new life.
    B curious about the charity workers.
    C nostalgic about her old life.

16 What did the speaker notice about Helen?
    A that she had bathed recently
    (**B**) the care she took with her appearance
    C that she was wearing a green uniform

17 Making someone feel beautiful was
    A part of the speaker's job description.
    (**B**) an unexpected bonus for the speaker.
    C of little importance to the speaker.

Questions 18 - 20

*In what **THREE** ways did the new well improve Helen's life?*
*Choose **THREE** letters **A - G**.*

            18 ......   **19** ......   **20** ......

A Her children enjoyed better health.	(**E**) She had more choices and options.	
B It increased her household income.	**F** She made new friends in her village.	
(**C**) It gave her more free time.	**G** It allowed her to go to school.	
(**D**) She got a leadership position.		

Listening

SECTION 3   Questions 21 - 30

Questions 21 - 25

Complete the sentences below.

*Write **NO MORE THAN TWO WORDS AND/OR A NUMBER** for each answer.*

21 Jessica is interviewing Dr. Kitching for ....**an article**............... for the school newspaper.

22 Everyone Jessica knows is rather ....**puzzled**............ about how to ask for references.

23 Dr. Kitching gives Jessica permission to ....**record**............... their conversation.

24 Dr. Kitching writes more than ......**50 references**.......... a year.

25 The majority of .....**(the) requests**.................. are in the spring or early summer when students start thinking about their future.

Questions 26 - 30

Complete the flow-chart below.

*Choose **FIVE** answers from the box and write the correct letter **A - G** next to questions 26 - 30.*

A. message

B. meeting

C. information

D. exam

E. telephone call

F. course

G. email

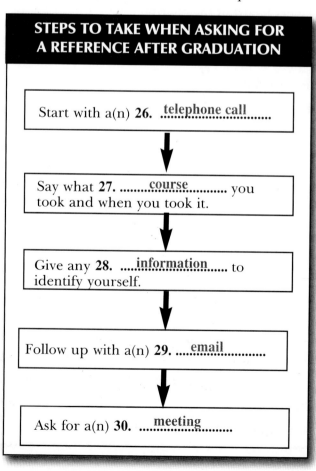

STEPS TO TAKE WHEN ASKING FOR A REFERENCE AFTER GRADUATION

Start with a(n) **26.** ...**telephone call**....

Say what **27.** ....**course**......... you took and when you took it.

Give any **28.** .....**information**..... to identify yourself.

Follow up with a(n) **29.** .....**email**.......

Ask for a(n) **30.** ......**meeting**........

SECTION 4   *Questions 31 - 40*

Questions 31 - 40
Complete the notes below.
Write **NO MORE THAN THREE WORDS** *for each answer.*

Date: *6th November*

Lecture Topic: **Primate Behaviour**

Review - Last lecture we talked about how physical features apply to:

- *living primates*
- *classification*
- *31* ....the fossil record...............

- *Human evolution is not just about how people have 32* ....changed physically...., *but also about how our behaviour evolved.*
- *The most notable thing about humans is not just that they walk on two legs but that they can 33* ....reason and/or imagine.........

Primate Cognitive Abilities

Cognition = the amount of 34......thought........ *that goes into a behaviour.*

It's difficult to come up with 35 ....experiments...... *to measure cognition.*

How sentient are the 36 ....great apes................... *?*

Sentient = there is 37 ....presence of............. *conscious thought*

Behaviours that support the presence of conscious thought in primates:

- *Various sorts of 38*.........altruism.......... *(helping others without benefit)*
- *"Machiavellian Intelligence" or deliberate 39* ....social deception......
- *Chimps can be language trained - highly intelligent*

- *Cognition and intelligence in primates has deep 40* ....moral and political....... *ramifications.*

Reading

READING PASSAGE 1

You should spend about 20 minutes on **Questions 1 - 13**, *which are based on Reading Passage 1 below*

PROJECT: Reform Of The Prison System In The UK

Penal progress:

The UK's large prison population is fuelled by a high level of recidivism - when criminals repeatedly relapse into crime. This project for a model prison tackles issues of architecture, management and funding in an enlightened attempt to achieve lasting rehabilitation.

Project:

The penal system is one of the most direct manifestations of the power of the state, but is often also a revealing reflection of the national psyche and the public's attitude to punishment and rehabilitation. Surprisingly, for a prosperous, progressive Western democracy, the UK has a lamentable penal record. Britain's prison population is currently in excess of 60,000 (up 50 per cent from a decade ago) making it the second largest in Europe. The average cost of keeping an individual prisoner incarcerated for a year is £27,000 (ten times the average expenditure on a secondary school pupil in the state sector). Despite such substantial investment, over half of British prisoners re-offend within two years of release.

Such high rates of recidivism is a serious problem. It means that the prison population is continuing to grow at an alarming rate (recently by as many as 700 a week), so overcrowding is endemic, hampering opportunities for education and rehabilitation and lowering staff and prisoner morale. To ease this pressure, the UK government is investing in the prison estate at historic levels, with 12,000 new prison places proposed within the next few years. Yet, like their nineteenth-century predecessors, Britain's 'new Victorian' prisons are designed for security and control rather than for the rehabilitation and education which is increasingly recognised as what prisoners need. Most are poorly

educated young men under 30 (at least 60 per cent of whom are functionally illiterate and innumerate), so without education and skills few will be able to build meaningful lives away from crime, no matter how often they go to prison, or how long they spend there.

Any transformation of the penal system must start with the redesign of prison buildings. Prison architecture has a clearly discernible effect on behaviour, operational efficiency, interaction and morale. Last year, architects Buschow Henley were commissioned by a think tank organisation working with the Home Office Prison Service to research and develop an alternative prison model that focuses more intensely on rehabilitation through a concentrated programme of intellectual, physical and social education. The model is not intended as a blueprint but rather a series of principles that might be adapted to support the wider concept of the 'Learning Prison' in which other aspects such as organisation, management and funding would obviously play a part. Key to this is the introduction of a system that groups together prisoners in small communities or 'houses' of between 30 and 40 inmates. This has two important consequences. First, the more compact spatial organisation of the house reduces staff time spent on supervising and escorting prisoners. Second, the system places educational and other facilities at the heart of the building, within easy reach at all times of day, reinforced by a supportive social environment. This model also enables resources to be dramatically redeployed, from a current estimated ratio of 80:20 (costs of security versus rehabilitation) to a predicted reversed figure of 20:80, freeing up much-needed funds to invest in educational programmes, thereby helping to promote rehabilitation, reduce recidivism and initiate a virtuous cycle.

In Buschow Henley's scheme, the proposed group size of 30-40 has the potential for social accountability - each prisoner being known within the community and personally accountable for his behaviour. Houses are semi-autonomous, not just dormitories, with communal, as opposed to centralised, facilities. Circulation is simplified and reduced. Buildings are arranged in a chess-board formation, as opposed to pavilions marooned in space, each with a discrete external area that can be productively used for sport, games or gardening with a minimum of supervision.

Individual cells are replanned to make them less like domestic lavatories and more conducive to learning. In an inversion of the conventional layout, the bed is placed lengthways along the external wall at high level, freeing up space below. Storage is built in and each inmate is provided with a moveable table equipped with electronic tools for study. Washing facilities are contained in a small adjoining space (included in the basic 8 sqm allowance) so reducing pressure on prison staff to manage inmate hygiene and ablution. Each cell is paired with a neighbouring 'buddy' cell linked by sliding doors controlled by individual prisoners to mitigate the risk of self-harm.

While this new type of prison appears to be somewhat liberal, the arrangement of spaces and functions both inside and out is actually tightly controlled. Paradoxically, however, this proscription enables a greater range of activities to take place, and makes general supervision easier. In this environment the prisoners are judged not by their degree of conformity, but by the scope of their activities and achievements, so laying the foundations for genuine rehabilitation. As Martin Narey, Director General of the UK Prison Services observes, 'We have got to accept that prison must be a humane and constructive place, not least because all but 23 of my population are going home some day.'

Reading

Questions 1 - 5

Complete each sentence with the correct ending, A - H, below.
*Write the correct letter **A - H** in spaces 1 - 5 below.*

1   The agenda of current British prison systems is primarily   1. .....E.........

2   The primary role of prisons should be   2. .....B.........

3   The new prison scheme will create   3. ...G...........

4   Existing prison architecture causes   4. ..C...........

5   The positive results of reducing the number of prisoners in one space include   5. ...A.........

A   improved security, supervision and education.

B   rehabilitation and education.

C   reduced efficiency, morale and interaction.

D   reduced risk of self harm.

E   security and control.

F   an alternative prison model

G   a learning environment rather than a punitive compound.

H   organisation, management and funding.

Reading Passage 1
Justification of the Answers

1 E - Paragraph 3: "Britain's 'new Victorian' prisons are designed for security and control rather than for the rehabilitation...."

2 B - Paragraph 3: "...rather than for the rehabilitation and education which is increasingly recognised as what prisoners need."

3 G - Paragraph 4: 'concept of the 'Learning prison'.'

4 C - Paragraph 4: 'Any transformation of the penal system must start with the redesign of prison buildings. Prison architecture has a clearly discernible effect on behaviour, operational efficiency, interaction and morale.'

5 A - Paragraph 4: "First, the more compact spatial organisation of the house reduces staff time spent on supervising and escorting prisoners. Second, the system places educational and other facilities at the heart of the building, ...'

6. A - 'last year, architects Buschow Henley were commissioned by a think tank organization working with the Home Office Prison Service to research and develop an alternative prison model' This is clearly a progressive attitude.

7. C - 'Such high rates of recidivism means that the prison population is continuing to grow at an alarming rate'.

8. B - The final paragraph mentions a number of ways that the new layout of prisons helps to educate and rehabilitate prisoners and to boost their self esteem through social interaction and education within the system.

9. C 'the bed is placed lengthways along the external wall at high level, freeing up space below. Storage is built in .....'

10. Paragraph 5: 'each with a **discrete external area** that can be productively used for sport'

11. Paragraph 6: 'the **bed** is placed lengthways along the external wall at high level'

12. Paragraph 6: '**Storage** is built in.'

13. Paragraph 6: 'neighbouring 'buddy' cell linked by **sliding doors**'

Questions 6 - 9

*Choose the correct letter **A**, **B**, **C** or **D**.*

6   The project to reform the penal system in the UK

    Ⓐ   is progressive.
    B   is inexpensive.
    C   will eliminate the need for supervision.
    D   is, primarily, to make prisoners more comfortable.

7   The proposal to create 12,000 new prison places, within the next few years, indicates that

    A   prison cells are too small.
    B   a lot of money is invested into educating offenders.
    Ⓒ   there is an increasing population of offenders in the UK.
    D   the government is getting tougher on offenders.

8   The proposed changes to prison architecture are designed primarily to

    A   improve the aesthetic value of the building.
    Ⓑ   boost self-esteem and social behaviour.
    C   allow prisoners more living space.
    D   increase running costs within prisons.

9   Why is the bed placed lengthways along the external wall at high level?

    A   to make room below for washing facilities
    B   for the improvement of the inmates' hygiene
    Ⓒ   to allow room below for storage and shelves
    D   to make room for sliding doors

Questions 10 - 13

Label the diagram below.

*Write **NO MORE THAN THREE WORDS** from the passage for each answer.*

Prison Plan

Semi-autonomous cell buildings

Cell Design

Cell door   Cell door

Table and electronic tools

Washing facilities

Buddy Cell

Main Cell

13 .....sliding doors.....

10 .....(discrete) external area..... for recreational activities

Built in 12 .....storage..... unit   Raised 11 .....bed.....

External Wall

Practice Test 3

Reading

READING PASSAGE 2

*You should spend about 20 minutes on **Questions 14 - 26**, which are based on Reading Passage 2 belo*

SPECIAL OLYMPICS

CONDITIONS OF PARTICIPATION

To be eligible for participation in the Special Olympics an individual with an intellectual disability must agree to observe and abide by the SOC Sports Rules. 'Mental Retardation' refers to substantial limitations in present functioning. It is characterised by significantly sub-average intellectual functioning, existing concurrently with related limitations in two or more of the following applicable adaptive skill areas: communication, self-care, home living, social skills, community use, self-direction, health and safety, functional academics, leisure and work. Mental retardation manifests itself before the age of 18. The following four assumptions are essential to the application of the definition:

1.   Valid assessment considers cultural and linguistic diversity as well as differences in communication and behavioural factors.
2.   The existence of limitations in adaptive skills occurs within the context of community environments typical of the individual's age-peers and is indexed to the person's individualised needs for support.
3.   Specific adaptive limitations often co-exist with strengths in other adaptive skills or other personal capabilities.
4.   With appropriate support over a sustained period, the life functioning of the person with mental retardation will generally improve.

The term 'mental retardation' is a diagnostic term used to describe the condition defined above. In keeping with the current language practised within the field, the term 'mental retardation' is no longer commonly used. In its place, if it is absolutely necessary to use a label, i.e. in an educational setting or in a SOC/NCCP Technical Programme, then the term that is in keeping with the current practices is *a person with an intellectual disability*. Special Olympics was created and developed to give individuals with an intellectual disability the opportunity to train and compete in sport activities. No person shall, on the grounds of gender, race, religion, colour, national origin or financial constraint be excluded from participation in, or be denied the benefits of, or otherwise be subjected to discrimination under any programme or activity of Special Olympics. Flexibility is left to the Local, Region/Zone, Chapter and National Special Olympics organisations for determining the eligibility of the participants because of the variety of situations and needs that exist in the many localities where Special Olympics programmes have been and will be instituted. Inclusion is preferred to exclusion when eligibility is in question. Individuals who have both an intellectual disability and multiple disabilities may participate in Special Olympics programmes and competitions.

A. *Participation by individuals with Down Syndrome who have Atlantoaxial Instability.*

There is evidence from medical research that up to 15 percent of individuals with Down Syndrome have a defect in the cervical vertebrae C-1 and C-2 in the neck. This condition exposes Down Syndrome individuals to the heightened possibility of a neck injury if they participate in activities that hyperextend or radically flex the neck or upper spine.

B. *SOC requires temporary restriction of individuals with Down Syndrome from participation in certain activities.*

1) Accredited Programmes may allow all individuals with Down Syndrome to continue in most Special Olympics sports training and competition activities. However, such individuals shall not be permitted to participate in sport training and competitions which, by their nature, result in hyperextension, radical flexion or direct pressure on the neck or upper spine. Such sports training and competition activities include: the butterfly stroke and diving starts in swimming, diving, pentathlon, high jump, equestrian sports, artistic gymnastics, soccer, alpine skiing and any warm-up exercise placing undue stress on the head and neck.

2) Restriction from participation in the above-listed activities shall continue until an individual with Down Syndrome has been examined (including X-ray views of full extension and flexion of the neck) by a physician who has been briefed on the nature of the Atlantoaxial Instability condition, and the results of such an examination demonstrate that the individual does not have the Atlantoaxial Instability condition.

3) For any individual diagnosed as having Atlantoaxial Instability condition, the examining physician shall notify the athlete's parents or guardians of the nature and extent of the individual's condition and such athlete shall be allowed to participate in the activities listed in 1) above only if the athlete submits written certification from two physicians combined with an acknowledgment of the

risks signed by the adult athlete or his/her parent or guardian if the athlete is a minor.

4) It is the responsibility of parents/guardians to monitor the individual and take appropriate action if neurological symptoms appear.

Terminology note: the term intellectual disability is used to replace the clinical term of Mental Retardation. Intellectual disability is not a disease, nor should it be confused with mental illness. People with mental disabilities have both a slower rate of learning and a limited capacity to learn. They may also have difficulty managing the ordinary activities of daily living, understanding the behaviour of others, and determining their own appropriate social responses (adaptive behaviour). Children with intellectual disabilities grow into adults with intellectual disabilities; they do not remain 'eternal children'.

People with intellectual disabilities constitute one of the largest groups of citizens with disabilities. There are an estimated 156 million individuals in the world who have intellectual disabilities. Intellectual disability cuts across lines of race, education, and social and economic background. It can occur in anyone. Hereditary components are known to account for only a fraction of the cases of intellectual disability. There are well over 350 causes of intellectual disability and in three-quarters of the cases the specific cause is unknown. About 87 percent of all people with intellectual disabilities are mildly afflicted and in many respects are indistinguishable from people who do not have intellectual disabilities.

Reading

Questions 14 - 20

Do the following statements agree with the information given in Reading Passage 2?

In spaces 14 - 20 below, write

TRUE	*if the statement agrees with the information*
FALSE	*if the statement contradicts the information*
NOT GIVEN	*if there is no information on this*

14   To be eligible to take part in the Special Olympics, the athlete has to be not only less than intellectually capable, but must also be lacking in a number of other functions. ....**TRUE**..........

15   People with intellectual disabilities never improve their lives. ....**FALSE**..........

16   All people with intellectual disabilities need the written permission of a parent or guardian in order to participate. ....**FALSE**..........

17   Down Syndrome participants often excel in their chosen field of athletic activity. ....**NOT GIVEN**..........

18   People with Down Syndrome cannot participate in any swimming events. ....**FALSE**..........

19   If you have Down Syndrome, your neck may be at risk of damage in certain sports. ....**TRUE**..........

20   Participation in sports helps people with intellectual disabilities to improve their communication and social skills. ....**NOT GIVEN**..........

Reading Passage 2
Justification of the Answers

14. TRUE - " 'Mental retardation' refers to substantial limitations in present functioning. It is characterised by significantly sub-level intellectual functioning existing concurrently with related limitations in two or more of the following applicable adaptive skill areas."
15. FALSE - 'With appropriate supporters over a sustained period, the life functioning of the person with mental retardation will generally improve'.

16. FALSE - Parental consent is only required 'if the athlete is a minor.'
17. NOT GIVEN - the article does not say that Down Syndrome participants often excel in their chosen sport.
18. FALSE - They cannot take part in some activities, which are listed in B.1.
19. TRUE - '15% of individuals with Down Syndrome have a defect in the cervical vertebrae C-1 and C-2 in the neck. This condition exposes Down Syndrome individuals to the heightened possibility of a neck injury if they participate in activities that hyperextend or radically flex the

neck or upper spine'.
20. NOT GIVEN - Nowhere in the article does it say that participating in sports improves the communication and social skills of those with intellectual disabilities.

Questions 21 - 23

Choose the correct letter A, B, C or D.

21   What were the objectives of the Special Olympics document?
   A   to inform the public what they are to expect from the Special Olympics
   B   to provide information for future candidates
   C   to promote awareness in the general population of the plight of disabled people
   D   to list the problems intellectually disabled people have

22   What does the passage say about intellectual disability?
   A   The majority of cases are inherited.
   B   Sufferers of the condition outnumber those with physical disabilities.
   C   In most cases, the cause of the condition cannot be determined.
   D   It may be determined by race, education, or social and economic background.

23   What word best describes the Special Olympics participation policy?
   A   inconsistent
   B   ambiguous
   C   controversial
   D   non-discriminatory

> **Reading Passage 2**
> **Justification of the Answers**
> **21. B** - The title 'Conditions of participation' indicates this.
> **22. C** - 'There are well over 350 causes of intellectual disability and in three-quarters of the cases the specific cause is unknown'.
> **23. D** - 'No person shall, on the grounds of gender, race, religion, colour, national origin or financial constraint, be excluded from participation in the Special Olympics.
>
> **24. A** '15 percent of individuals with Down Syndrome have a defect in the cervical vertebrae C-1 and C-2 in the neck.'
> **25. C** Soccer is listed as one of the high-risk sports and the article states that 'an acknowledgement of the risks signed by the adult athlete or his/her parents/guardian if the athlete is a minor' is necessary to participate in these sports.
>
> **26. F** - 'Accredited programmes may allow all individuals with Down Syndrome to continue in most Special Olympics sport training and competition activities. However, such individuals shall not be permitted to participate in sport training and competitions, which, by their nature, result in hypertension, radical flexion or direct pressure on the neck or upper spine'.

Questions 24 - 26

Which **THREE** of the following facts relating to Down Syndrome are mentioned ?

Choose three letter A - F.

24. ___   25. ___   26. ___

   A   It is thought that about one Down Syndrome person in every seven has Atlantoaxial Instability.

   B   A person with Down Syndrome cannot participate in any winter competitions.

   C   Down Syndrome sufferers with Atlantoaxial Instability who are minors need permission from a guardian to play soccer.

   D   Down Syndrome sufferers are unable to flex the upper spine.

   E   Down Syndrome athletes need to wear a neck brace to participate in the Special Olympics.

   F   Down Syndrome athletes can take part in sports that do not directly affect the neck or spine without any preconditions being fulfilled.

Reading

READING PASSAGE 3

You should spend about 20 minutes on **Questions 27 - 40**, *which are based on Reading Passage 3 belo*

Migrants and Refugees:
Racial Discrimination and Xenophobia

Today, one in every 50 human beings is a migrant worker, a refugee or asylum seeker, or an immigrant living in a foreign country. Current estimates by the United Nations and the International Organisation for Migration indicate that some 150 million people live temporarily or permanently outside their countries of origin (2.5% of the world population). Many of

these, 80-97 million, are estimated to be migrant workers with members of their families. Another 12 million are refugees outside their country of origin. These figures do not include the estimated 20 million Internally Displaced Persons forcibly displaced within their own country, nor the tens of millions more of internal migrants, mainly rural to urban, in countries around the world.

Increasing ethnic and racial diversity of societies is the inevitable consequence of migration. Increasing migration means that a growing number of states have become or are becoming more multi-ethnic, and are confronted with the challenge of accommodating peoples of different cultures, races, religions and languages. Addressing the reality of increased diversity means finding political, legal, social and economic mechanisms to ensure mutual respect and to mediate relations across differences. But xenophobia and racism have become manifest in some societies which have received substantial numbers of immigrants, as workers or as asylum-seekers. In those countries the migrants have become the targets in internal disputes about national identity. In the last few decades, the emergence of new nation states has often been accompanied by ethnic exclusion.

As governments grapple with the new realities of their multi-ethnic societies, there has been a marked increase in discrimination and violence directed against migrants, refugees and other non-nationals by extremist groups in many parts of the world. The lack of any systematic documentation or research over time makes it unclear whether there is a real increase in the level of abuse or in the level of exposure and reporting. Unfortunately, there is more than enough anecdotal evidence to show that violations of the human rights of migrants, refugees and other non-nationals are so generalised, widespread and commonplace that they are a defining feature of international migration today.

The extent of racial discrimination and xenophobia is often played down and sometimes denied by authorities. Racial discrimination is defined in international law as being: *any distinction, exclusion, restriction or preference based on race, colour, descent or national or ethnic origin which has the purpose or effect of nullifying or impairing the recognition, enjoyment or exercise, on an equal footing, of human rights and fundamental freedoms in the political, economic, social, cultural or any other field of public life.*

Racism and xenophobia are distinct phenomena, although they often overlap. While racism generally implies distinction based on difference in physical characteristics, such as skin colour, hair type, facial features, etc, xenophobia denotes behaviour specifically based on the perception that 'the other' is foreign to or originates from outside the community or nation. By the standard dictionary definition, xenophobia is the intense dislike or fear of strangers or people from other countries. As a sociologist puts it, 'xenophobia is an attitudinal orientation of hostility against non-natives in a given population.'

The definition of xenophobia, and its differentiation from racism and racial discrimination, is a still-evolving concept. One of the regional Preparatory Meetings for a recent World Conference suggested that:

- Racism is an ideological construct that assigns a certain race and/or ethnic group to a position of power over others on the basis of physical and cultural attributes, as well as economic wealth, involving hierarchical relations where the superior race exercises domination and control over others.
- Xenophobia describes attitudes, prejudices and behaviour that reject, exclude and often vilify persons, based on the perception that they are outsiders or foreigners in the community, society or with respect to national identity.

In many cases, it is difficult to distinguish between racism and xenophobia as motivations for behaviour, since differences in physical characteristics are often assumed to distinguish a person from the common identity. However, manifestations of xenophobia occur against people of identical physical characteristics, even of shared ancestry, when such people arrive, return or migrate to states or areas where occupants consider them outsiders.

Reading

Questions 27 - 30

Complete each sentence with the correct ending, A - F, below.
Write the correct letter, A - F, in the spaces below.

27 An upward trend in violence perpetrated against non-national minority groups by radical nationals

27. ...D...........

28 Where racism occurs, the dominant group promotes a hierarchical system in which it

28. ...F...........

29 Persons not considered to be culturally or physically distinct from the majority

29. ...C...........

30 Racism differs from xenophobia in that victims of the former

30. ...A...........

A are always culturally or physically distinct from the perpetrators of the acts of wrongdoing.

B tend to share a likeness with the perpetrators of the crime.

C may still find themselves the victims of xenophobic behaviour.

D has been observed in many different parts of the world.

E will eventually reach a position of total submission.

F has a controlling hand in the affairs of one or more of the other sections of society.

Questions 31 - 34

Choose the correct letter A, B, C or D.

31   Which of the following migrants are there more of?
    A   internally displaced persons
    B   refugees
    C   internal migrants
    (D)   immigrant workers

32   The author of the text believes that
    A   racism is inevitable when people emigrate.
    (B)   governments are finding it difficult to stop racism and xenophobia.
    C   the exploitation of minority groups deters others from migrating.
    D   xenophobia does not exist within minority groups.

33   There is no real way of knowing how many migrants are discriminated against because
    (A)   not all racial abuse cases are documented or looked into.
    B   the number of migrants is increasing at an alarming rate.
    C   migrants don't complain about being abused.
    D   only serious cases are documented.

34   People in authority sometimes
    A   exaggerate the seriousness of the problem.
    B   create the problem.
    (C)   deny there is a problem.
    D   are eager to solve the problem.

Questions 35 - 40

Do the following statements agree with the information given in Reading Passage 3?

In spaces 35 - 40 below, write

TRUE	*if the statement agrees with the information*
FALSE	*if the statement contradicts the information*
NOT GIVEN	*if there is no information on this*

35	Most migrants flee their country of origin because of political or social disorder.	NOT GIVEN
36	Most internal migrants leave the countryside for the cities.	TRUE
37	Governments are often reluctant to acknowledge that racial discrimination and xenophobia exist.	TRUE
38	Migrants are exploited and abused because they create a sense of insecurity for extremist groups.	NOT GIVEN
39	People who are racist or xenophobic are uneducated and hostile.	NOT GIVEN
40	People returning to their country of ancestry do not face xenophobia.	FALSE

Reading Passage 3
Justification of the Answers

27. D - Paragraph 3 - is correct because: 'there has been a marked increase [upward trend] in discrimination and violence directed against migrants, refugees and other non-nationals by extremist groups in many parts of the world.'

28. F - Paragraph 6 - is correct because: 'Racism is an ideological construct that assigns a certain race and/or ethnic group to a position of power [having a controlling hand] over others [other sections of society] on the basis of physical and cultural attributes'.

29. C - Paragraph 7 - is correct because: 'manifestations of xenophobia occur against people of identical physical characteristics [not physically distinct], even of shared ancestry [not culturally distinct]'.

30. A - Paragraph 6 - is correct because: 'Racism is an ideological construct that assigns

a certain race and/or ethnic group to a position of power over others on the basis of physical and cultural attributes"

31. 'Many of these, 80-97 million, are estimated to be migrant workers with members of their families.' (Paragraph 1)

32. B 'but xenophobia and racism have become manifest in some societies'.

33. A - 'the lack of any systematic documentation or research over time makes it unclear whether there is an increase in the level of abuse'.

34. 'xenophobia is often played down and sometimes denied by authorities.' (Paragraph 3)

35. NOT GIVEN. Although the article mentions that some immigrants are refugees, it does not say why.

36. TRUE. The article states that there are

'tens of millions more internal immigrants, mainly rural to urban'.

37. TRUE. 'The extent of racial discrimination and xenophobia is often played down and sometimes denied by authorities.'

38. NOT GIVEN. The text states that 'there has been marked discrimination and violence directed against migrants, refugees and other non-nationals by extremist groups' but it does not say that this is because they create a sense of insecurity.

39. NOT GIVEN. There are no links made between education and racism or xenophobia.

40. FALSE. The text mentions 'manifestations of xenophobia occur against people of identical physical characteristics, even of shared ancestry, when such people arrive, return or migrate to states or areas where occupants consider them outsiders.'

Writing

Writing Tip:
Remember to use the data in Writing Task 1 correctly.

WRITING TASK 1

You should spend about 20 minutes on this task.

> *The graph below shows the rate of attendance for primary and secondary schools for boys and girls across the world.*
>
> *Summarise the information by selecting and reporting the main features, and make comparisons where necessary.*

Write at least 150 words.

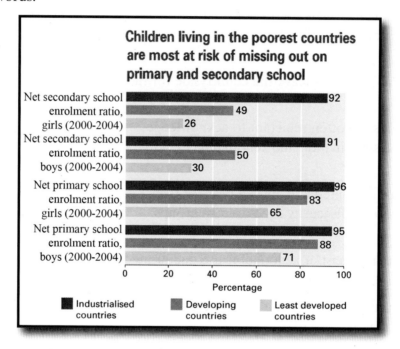

WRITING TASK 2

You should spend about 40 minutes on this task.

Write about the following topic:

> *In many places, prisons are overcrowded and expensive for governments to maintain. Yet, when offenders are released, they end up back in prison a short while later. Does prison work? Should lawbreakers be rehabilitated or punished?*

Give reasons for your answer and include any relevant examples from your own knowledge or experience.

Write at least 250 words.

Speaking

> **Speaking Tip:**
> Don't memorise answers

PART 1   (4-5 minutes)

The examiner asks the candidate about him/herself, his/her home, work or studies and other familiar topics.

Jobs

- What would the ideal job for you be, and why?
- How easy is it to get a job in your country?
- What are the typical working hours in your country?
- How do people in your country like to relax when they're not working?

PART 2   (2 minutes)

You will have to talk about the topic for one to two minutes. You have one minute to think about what you are going to say. You can make some notes to help you if you wish.

> **Describe a time when you got into trouble, either at school or at home.**
>
> **You should say:**
> - **why you got into trouble**
> - **if you were punished for what you did**
> - **how getting into trouble affected you**

PART 3   (4-5 minutes)

Discussion topics:

Crime
- What sort of crimes are common where you live?
- What do you think makes people commit serious crimes?
- Do you think that some forms of entertainment, such as video games, promote violence?

Punishing law breakers
- Do people who break the law in your country receive the correct punishment?
- Is the death penalty ever acceptable?
- Are there any alternatives to putting someone in jail?

Test 4

Listening

SECTION 1 *Questions 1 - 10*

Questions 1 - 4

Choose the correct letter A, B, C or D.

Example:
Where did Julie leave her car?
- (A) in the underground parking lot
- B in the outdoors parking lot
- C opposite the university building
- D near the Student Services office

1 What are the regulations for the underground parking area, level 1?
- A Undergraduate parking is allowed.
- (B) Postgraduate parking only is allowed.
- C Staff parking only is allowed.

2 If you don't have a parking permit, what action will be taken?
- A Your car will have a wheel clamped.
- B You will pay a fine only.
- (C) Your car will be towed away and you will pay a fine.

3 How does Julie usually travel to university?
- A by car
- (B) by rail
- C by bus

4 Where is Student Services located?
- A in the Science Department
- B next to the football field
- (C) between the cafeteria and the Science Department

Listening - Section 1
(1) <u>that area is for postgraduate students</u> and not...
J: Oh, no. It's the first time I've brought my car. I **(3)** <u>usually catch the train in.</u>
(2) <u>probably been towed away.</u>

Check the **Audioscript in the Self-Study Guide** for the **Justification of the Answers for ALL the Sections of the Listening Test**

Questions 5 - 10

Complete the release form below.
Write **NO MORE THAN THREE WORDS AND/OR A NUMBER** *for each answer.*

Application for the release of a vehicle in compound.
Name: 5 .... **Julie Karas** ....
Address: 6 .... **15 Fremont Avenue** ....
District: 7 .... **Hawkesley** ....
Faculty: 8 .... **Science** ....
Registration number: 9 .... **IKE 614T** ....
Make of car: 10 .... **Fiat Panda** ....

Listening Tip:
Remember that rephrasing what you hear is NOT necessary. Just write down the words you hear.

SECTION 2 *Questions 11 - 20*

Questions 11 - 14
What facilities are available at each campsite?
Write the correct letter A, B or C next to questions 11 - 14.

11	Biddlecombe Cascades	B
12	Crystal Falls	C
13	17 Mile Falls	C
14	Edith River Crossing	A

A a checkpoint but no toilets
B toilets but no checkpoint
C a checkpoint and toilets

Questions 15 - 20
Label the map below.
Write the correct letter, A - H, next to the questions 15 - 20.

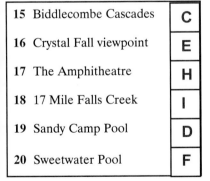

15	Biddlecombe Cascades	C
16	Crystal Fall viewpoint	E
17	The Amphitheatre	H
18	17 Mile Falls Creek	I
19	Sandy Camp Pool	D
20	Sweetwater Pool	F

Listening

SECTION 3 *Questions 21 - 30*

Questions 21 - 25

Which person has the following opinion about the incident in 2008?

Write the correct letter, A, B or C next to questions 21 - 25.

21 It was very funny.

22 Some people must have faced serious consequences.

23 It caused embarrassment.

24 It was a very immature thing to do.

25 We are being punished for it.

C
B
A
A
B

A Laura
B Jamie
C Denise

Questions 26 - 30

Complete the flow chart below.

*Choose **SIX** answers from the box and write the correct letter, **A - G**, next to questions 26 - 30.*

Experimental Design Procedure For Final Year Projects in Chemistry

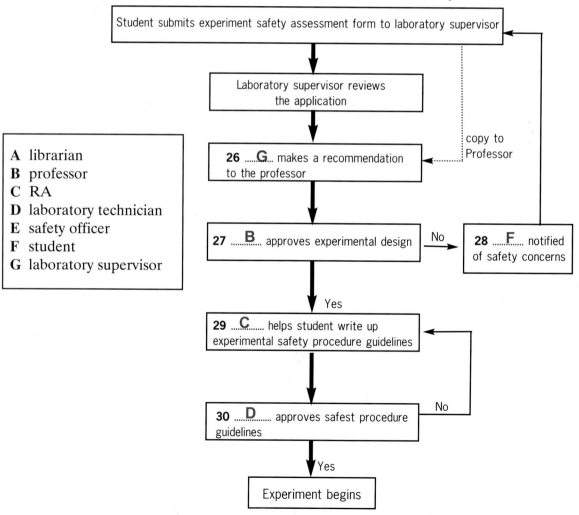

A librarian
B professor
C RA
D laboratory technician
E safety officer
F student
G laboratory supervisor

Student submits experiment safety assessment form to laboratory supervisor

Laboratory supervisor reviews the application

copy to Professor

26 ....G... makes a recommendation to the professor

27 ....B.... approves experimental design → No → 28 ....F..... notified of safety concerns

Yes

29 ..C...... helps student write up experimental safety procedure guidelines

No

30 ....D...... approves safest procedure guidelines

Yes

Experiment begins

SECTION 4 *Questions 31 - 40*

Questions 31-36
Label the map below.
Write the correct letter, A-H, next to questions 31-36.

The Biomes in Brazil

N

31 ...B....

36 ...D....

35 ...E....

34 ...G....

32 ...A...

Atlantic Ocean

33 ...H....

A　Atlantic rain forest
B　Amazonian rain forest
C　Brazilian forest
D　Caatinga
E　Cerrado
F　Grassland
G　Pantanal
H　Pampas

Questions 37 - 40
Complete the table below.
Write **NO MORE THAN ONE WORD AND/OR A NUMBER** *for each answer.*

ANIMAL PRODUCTION (in millions) in the Biomes of Brazil			
AREA	Cattle	Goats	Sheep
Cerrado	37......72.3....	none	none
Caatinga	23.9	8.8	38.....8.1.....
Pantanal	39......3........	none	none
Pampas	26	40.....none..	6

Reading

READING PASSAGE 1

*You should spend about 20 minutes on **Questions 1 - 13**, which are based on Reading Passage 1 below*

ALTERNATIVE ENERGY SOURCES

A

There are many reasons why we are looking towards alternative energy sources. With many countries signing the Kyoto Treaty, efforts to reduce pollutants and greenhouse gases are a primary focus in today's culture. Alternative, or renewable, energy sources show significant promise in helping to reduce the amount of toxins that are by-products of energy use. Not only do they protect against harmful by-products, but using alternative energy helps to preserve many of the natural resources that we currently use as sources of energy. To understand how alternative energy use can help preserve the delicate ecological balance of the planet, and help us conserve the non-renewable energy sources like fossil fuels, it is important to know what types of alternative energy are out there.

B

Alternative energy sources are resources that are constantly replaced and are usually less polluting. They are not the result of the burning of fossil fuels or splitting of atoms. The use of renewable energy is contributing to our energy supply. Some alternative energy sources are: biomass energy, geothermal energy, hydroelectric power, solar power, wind power, fuel cells, ocean thermal energy conversion, tidal energy, and wave energy.

C

Biomass is renewable energy that is produced from organic matter. Biomass fuels include wood, forest and mill residues, animal waste, grains, agricultural crops, and aquatic plants. These materials are used as fuel to heat water for steam or processed into liquids and gases, which can be burned to do the same thing. With more use of biomass at lower production costs and better technology, the United States could generate as much as four-and-a-half times more biopower by 2020. It is estimated that biomass will have the largest increase among renewable energy sources, rising by 80 percent and reaching 65.7 billion KW in 2020.

D

Geothermal energy uses heat from within the earth. Wells are drilled into geothermal reservoirs to bring the hot water or steam to the surface. The steam then drives a turbine-generator to generate electricity in geothermal plants. In some places this heat is used directly to heat homes and greenhouses, or to provide process heat for businesses or industries. Reykjavik, Iceland, is heated by geothermal energy. Most geothermal resources are concentrated in the western part of the United States. Geothermal heat pumps use shallow ground energy to heat and cool homes, and this technique can be employed almost anywhere. With technological improvements much more power could be generated from hydrothermal resources. Scientists have been experimenting by pumping water into the hot dry rock that is 3-6 miles below the earth's surface for use in geothermal power plants.

E

Hydroelectric (hydropower) energy employs the force of falling water to drive turbine-generators to produce electricity. Hydropower produces more electricity than any other alternative energy source. It has been estimated that hydroelectric power will decline from 389 billion KW in the US in 1999 to 298 billion KW in 2020. This decline is expected because most of the best sites for hydropower have already been developed and because of concerns about the adverse impact that large-scale hydroelectric facilities may have on the environment.

F

Solar energy is generated without a turbine or electromagnet. Special panels of photovoltaic cells capture light from the sun and convert it directly into electricity. The electricity is stored in a battery. Solar energy can also be used to directly heat water for domestic use (solar thermal technology). The domestic photovoltaic (PV) industry could provide up to 15% of new US peak electricity capacity that is expected to be required in 2020.

G

Wind energy can be used to produce electricity. As wind passes through the blades of a windmill, the blades spin. The shaft that is attached to the blades turns and powers a pump or turns a generator to produce electricity. Electricity is then stored in batteries. The speed of the wind and the size of the blades determine how much energy can be produced. Wind energy is more efficient in windier parts of the country. Most wind power is produced from wind farms — large groups of turbines located in consistently windy locations. Wind, used as a fuel, is free and non-polluting and produces no emissions or chemical wastes. Wind-powered electricity is gaining in popularity.

H

Fuel cells are electrochemical devices that produce electricity through a chemical reaction. Fuel cells are rechargeable, contain no moving parts, are clean, and produce no noise. Scientists are exploring ways that they could be used as a power source for nearly exhaust-free automobiles and how they can be used as electricity-generating plants. The high cost of manufacturing fuel cells has prevented the mass use of this valuable energy source.

I

Ocean sources. Oceans, which cover more than 70% of the earth, contain both thermal energy from the sun's heat and mechanical energy from the tides and waves. Ocean thermal energy conversion (OTEC) converts solar radiation to electric power. OTEC power plants use the difference in temperature between warm surface waters heated by the sun and colder waters found at ocean depths to generate electricity. The power of tides can also be harnessed to produce electricity. Tidal energy works by harnessing the power of changing tides but it needs large tidal differences. The tidal process utilises the natural motion of the tides to fill reservoirs, which are then slowly discharged through electricity-producing turbines. Wave energy conversion extracts energy from surface waves, from pressure fluctuations below the water surface, or from the full wave. Wave energy also uses the interaction of winds with the ocean surface. This technology is still in the exploratory phase in the United States.

Reading

Questions 1 - 2

The writer mentions a number of facts relating to alternative power sources.

Which **TWO** of the following facts are mentioned?

A	International co-operation has yet to result in the largescale implementation and effective use of alternative power sources.
B	One alternative energy source in particular will have a great impact in the years to come.
C	A side-effect of one of these forms of energy is the production of chemical waste.
D	Expense is the main factor that is an obstacle to developing one of these forms of energy.
E	Approximately one in five US homes will be using one of these forms of energy within twenty years.
F	One attraction of these forms of energy in general is the relatively low production costs.

Questions 3 and 4

*Choose the correct letter **A, B, C** or **D**.*

3   Geothermal energy is produced by

       A   heating the air below the surface of the ground.
       B   employing the force of falling water.
       C   extracting water or steam from beneath the earth's surface.
       D   using the earth's natural electricity.

4   Which form of alternative energy does not involve the use of turbines?

       A   wind energy
       B   geothermal energy
       C   tidal energy
       D   fuel cell energy

Questions 5 - 8

Do the following statements agree with the information given in Reading Passage 1?

In spaces 5 - 8 below, write

TRUE	*if the statement agrees with the information*
FALSE	*if the statement contradicts the information*
NOT GIVEN	*if there is no information on this*

5	Wind power is the most efficient form of alternative energy.	NOT GIVEN
6	Wave energy can be derived from a number of sources.	TRUE
7	Alternative energy sources serve several purposes.	TRUE
8	Fossil fuels are needed in at least one of these alternative energy sources.	FALSE

Reading Passage 1
Justification of the Answers

1. B 'it is estimated that Biomass will have the largest increase among renewable energy sources, rising by 80 percent and reaching 65.7 billion kW in 2020'.

2. D 'the high cost of manufacturing fuel cells has prevented the mass use of this valuable energy source'.

3. C 'wells are drilled to into geothermal reservoirs to bring the hot water or steam to the surface'.

4. D 'fuel cells are electromagnetic devices that produce electricity through a chemical reaction'.

5. NOT GIVEN the energy forms are not compared in terms of efficiency.

6. TRUE 'Wave energy conversion extracts energy from surface waves, from pressure fluctuations below the surface, or from the full wave. Wave energy also exploits the interaction of winds with the ocean surface.

7. TRUE 'not only do they protect against harmful by-products, but using alternative energy helps to preserve many of the natural resources that we currently use as energy'.

8. FALSE alternative energy sources 'are not the result of burning fossil fuels or splitting of atoms'.

9. Paragraph A 'Alternative, or renewable, energy sources show significant promise in helping to reduce the **amount of toxins** that are by-products of energy use.'

10. Paragraph B 'The use of **renewable energy** is contributing to our energy supply.'

11. Paragraph C 'Biomass is renewable energy that is produced from **organic matter**.'

12. Paragraph D '**Geothermal energy** uses heat from within the earth.'

13. Paragraph H 'The **high cost** of manufacturing fuel cells has prevented the mass use of this valuable energy source.'

Questions 9 - 13

Complete the sentences.
Choose **NO MORE THAN THREE WORDS** *from the passage for each answer.*

9   By using alternative energy sources, we can cut the ......**amount of toxins**......... that are produced by current power sources.

10   In addition to fossil fuels and atom splitting, we presently use ......**renewable energy**...... as part of our power source.

11   Renewable energy called biomass is produced from .....**organic matter**............ .

12   The renewable energy that comes from within the earth is called ...**geothermal energy**......

13   One of the reasons that fuel cells are not widely used is the ....**(high) cost**...... of manufacturing.

Reading

READING PASSAGE 2

You should spend about 20 minutes on **Questions 14 - 26**, *which are based on Reading Passage 2 below.*

Colour Blindness

Colour blindness results from an absence or malfunction of certain colour-sensitive cells in the retina. The retina is a neuro-membrane lining the inside back of the eye, behind the lens. The retina contains both rod cells (active in low light or night vision but which cannot distinguish colour) and cone cells (active in normal daylight, sensitive to colour). Cone cells, also called photoreceptors, are concentrated mostly in the central part of the retina, in an area called the macula. Cone cells provide clear, sharp colour vision. The cones contain light-sensitive pigments that are sensitive to the range of wavelengths. There are three different types of cones with one sensitive to short wavelengths, or the colour blue, one sensitive to medium wavelengths, or the colour green, and the other sensitive to higher wavelengths, or the colour red. All of these cells send information about colour to the brain via the optic nerve which connects to the retina at a point very close to the macula. Normal persons, referred to as trichromats, are able to match all colours of the spectrum by using a combination of these three fundamental colour sensitivities. Hence, the huge variety of colours we perceive stems from the cone cells' response to different compositions of wavelengths of light.

There are many types of colour blindness. When there are deficiencies in the cones, either at birth or acquired in other ways, the cones are not able to distinguish the particular wavelengths and thus, that colour range is seen differently. Those with defective colour vision have a deficiency or absence in one or more of the pigments. People with a deficiency in one of the pigments (the most common type of colour vision problem) are called anomalous trichromats. When one of the cone pigments is absent and colour is reduced to two dimensions, dichromacy occurs. These individuals normally know they have a colour vision problem and it can affect their lives on a daily basis. They see no perceptible difference between red, orange, yellow, and green. All these colours that seem so different to the normal viewer appear to them to be the same colour. Missing the cones responsible for green and red hues can also affect the sensitivity to brightness.

Most cases of colour blindness, about 99%, are inherited, resulting from partial or complete loss of function in one or more of the different cone systems and affect both eyes without worsening over time. The most common are red-green hereditary (genetic) photoreceptor disorders collectively referred to as "red-green colour blindness". It affects 8% of all males of European origin and 0.4% of all females. The gene for this is carried in the X chromosome. Since males have an X-Y pairing and females have X-X, colour blindness can occur much more easily in males and is typically passed to them by their mothers. In other words, females may be carriers of colour blindness, but males are more commonly affected. People with this disorder cannot identify red or green by itself but can if among a coloured group. Other forms of colour blindness are much more rare. They include problems in discriminating blues from yellows. Both colours are seen as white or grey. This disorder occurs with equal frequency in men and women and usually accompanies certain other physical disorders, such as liver disease or diabetes.

The rarest forms of all is total colour blindness, monochromacy, where one can only see grey or shades of black, grey and white as in a black-and-white film or photograph. Monochromacy occurs when two or all three of the cone pigments are missing and colour and lightness vision is reduced to one dimension. Another term for total colour blindness is *achromatopsia*, the inability to see colour.

Inherited colour vision problems cannot be treated or corrected. Some acquired colour vision problems can be treated with surgery, such as the removal of a cataract, depending on the cause. Certain types of tinted filters and contact lenses may also help an individual to distinguish different colours better. Additionally, computer software has been developed to assist those with visual colour difficulties and those with mild colour deficiencies to learn to associate colours with certain objects and are usually able to identify colour in the same way as everyone else. One frequent problem encountered is with traffic lights, and worst of all, warning lights: colour-blind people always know the position of the colours on the traffic light - in most situations; red on top, yellow in the centre, green on the bottom. But warning lights present an entirely different problem. In this situation there is only one light; no top or bottom, no right or left, just one light that is either red or yellow.

Colour vision problems can have a significant impact on a person's life, learning abilities and career choices. On an everyday basis, there are some annoyances and frustrations: not being able to differentiate between green or ripe tomatoes when preparing food, for example, or buying clothes that to the 'normal' eye seem positively garish. However, people with colour vision problems usually learn to compensate for their inability to see colours. Although there is little or no treatment for colour blindness, most colour deficient persons compensate well for their defect and may even discover instances in which they can discern details and images that would escape normal-sighted persons. At one time the US Army found that colour blind persons can spot camouflage colours in cases where those with normal colour vision are typically fooled.

Reading

Questions 14 - 20

*Complete each sentence with the correct ending **A - K** from the box below.*

*Write the correct letter **A - K** in spaces 14 - 20 below.*

14	Colour blindness can be caused by a birth defect, or	H
15	Surprisingly, some people who are colour blind	F
16	People with hereditary colour blindness	B
17	Because of our genetic make-up, colour blindness	C
18	Red-green genetic photoreceptor disorders mean that people	J
19	People with monochromacy	E
20	The inability to see certain lights	G

A	can see better at night than during the day.
B	cannot be treated by surgery.
C	can affect men much more easily than women.
D	can affect their sensitivity to bright lights.
E	can see no colour at all, other than shades of black, grey and white.
F	can see things that people with normal vision cannot.
G	can have very dangerous consequences for colour blind people.
H	can be acquired or inherited.
I	can mean having to wear contact lenses.
J	cannot distinguish certain colours if they stand alone.
K	can match all colours of the spectrum.

Reading Passage 2
Justification of the Answers

14. H 'Most cases of colour blindness, about 99% are hereditary'.

15. F 'colour blind persons can spot camouflage colours where those with normal colour vision are fooled by it'.

16. B 'inherited colour vision problems cannot be treated or corrected'.

17. C 'Since males have an X-Y pairing and females have X-X, colour blindness can occur much more easily in males'.

18. J 'people with this disorder cannot identify red or green by itself, but can if among a coloured group'.

19. E 'monochromacy, where one can only see grey, or shades of black, grey and white'.

20. G They may not be able to tell which colours are which in the case of warning lights.

Questions 21 - 23

*Choose the correct letter **A**, **B**, **C** or **D**.*

21   What causes colour blindness?
  A   the absence of rod cells
  B   the malfunction of rod cells
  C   the malfunction of cone cells
  D   the retina's inability to detect light

> **21. C** 'Colour blindness results from an absence or malfunction of certain colour sensitive cells in the retina.' These cells are called cone cells.
> **22 D** 'The rarest form of all is total colour blindness, monochromacy' and 'another term for total colour blindness is achromatopsia'.
> **23. D** 'buying clothes that to the 'normal' eye seem positively garish'.

22   Which group of people are the least common?
  A   people who cannot detect blues from yellows
  B   anachromous trichromats
  C   people with dichromacy
  D   people with achromatopsia

23   What would colour blind people consider an everyday nuisance?
  A   not being able to identify the colour of warning lights
  B   not being able to tell an apple from a tomato
  C   not being able to cook
  D   not being able to buy matching clothes

> **24.** 'All of these cells send information about colour to the brain via the **optic nerve** which connects to the retina at a point very close to the macula.'
> **25.** '*The* **retina** *is a neuro-membrane lining the inside back of the eye, behind the lens.*'
> **26.** 'Cone cells, also called photoreceptors, are concentrated mostly in the central part of the retina, in an area called the **macula**.'

Questions 24 - 26

Complete the diagram below.

*Choose **NO MORE THAN TWO WORDS** from the passage for each answer.*

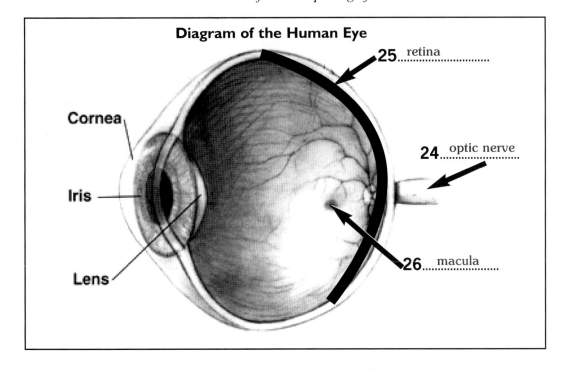

Diagram of the Human Eye

25 retina

Cornea

24 optic nerve

Iris

26 macula

Lens

Reading

READING PASSAGE 3

You should spend about 20 minutes on **Questions 27 - 40**, *which are based on Reading Passage 3 belo*

Population growth sentencing millions to hydrological poverty

A

At a time when drought in the United States, Ethiopia, and Afghanistan is in the news, it is easy to forget that far more serious water shortages are emerging as the demand for water in many countries simply outruns the supply. Water tables are now falling on every continent; literally scores of countries are facing water shortages as the tables fall and wells go dry. We live in a water-challenged world, one that is becoming more so each year as 80 million additional people stake their claims to the Earth's water resources. Unfortunately, nearly all the projected 3 billion people to be added over the next half century will be born in countries that are already experiencing water shortages. Even now many in these countries lack enough water to drink, to satisfy cleanliness needs, and to produce food.

B

By 2050, India is projected to have added 519 million people and China 211 million. Pakistan is projected to have added nearly 200 million, going from 151 million at present to 348 million. Egypt, Iran, and Mexico are slated to increase their populations by more than half by 2050. In these and other water-short countries, population growth is sentencing millions of people to hydrological poverty, a local form of poverty that is difficult to escape.

C

Even with today's 6 billion people, the world has a huge water deficit. Using data on over-pumping for China, India, Saudi Arabia, North Africa, and the United States, Sandra Postel, author of *Pillar of Sand: Can the Irrigation Miracle Last?* reports the annual depletion of aquifer to be at 160 billion cubic meters or 160 billion tons. Using the rule of thumb that it takes 1,000 tons of water to produce 1 ton of grain, this 160-billion-ton water deficit is equal to 160 million tons of grain or one-half the US grain harvest.

D

Average world grain consumption is just over 300 kilograms per person per annum - one third of a ton per person per year - and grain reserves directly or indirectly feed 480 million people globally. Stated otherwise, 480 million of the world's 6 billion people are being fed with grain produced with the unsustainable use of water.

E

Over-pumping is a new phenomenon, one largely confined to the last half century. Only since the development of powerful diesel- and electrically-driven pumps have we had the capacity to pull water out of aquifer faster than it is replaced by precipitation. Some 70 percent of the water consumed worldwide, including both that diverted from rivers and that pumped from underground, is used for irrigation, while some 20 percent is used by industry, and 10 percent for residential purposes. In the increasingly intense competition for water among sectors, agriculture almost always loses. The 1,000 tons of water used in India to produce 1 ton of wheat worth perhaps $200 can also be used to expand industrial output by easily $10,000, or 50 times as much. This ratio helps explain why, in the American West, the sale of irrigation water rights by farmers to cities is an almost daily occurrence.

F

In addition to population growth, urbanisation and industrialisation also expand the demand for water. As developing country villagers, traditionally reliant on the village well, move to urban high-rise apartment buildings with indoor plumbing, their residential water use can easily triple. Industrialisation takes even more water than urbanisation. Rising affluence in itself generates additional demand for water. As people move up the food chain, consuming more beef, pork, poultry, eggs, and dairy products, they use more grain. A US diet rich in livestock products requires 800 kilograms of grain per person a year, whereas diets in India, dominated by a starchy food staple such as rice, typically need only 200 kilograms. Using four times as much grain per person means using four times as much water.

G

Once a localised phenomenon, water scarcity is now crossing national borders via the international grain trade. The world's fastest growing grain import market is North Africa and the Middle East; an area that includes Morocco, Algeria, Tunisia, Libya, Egypt, and Iran. Virtually every country in this region is simultaneously experiencing water shortages and rapid population growth.

H

As the demand for water in the region's cities and industries increases, it is typically satisfied by diverting water from irrigation. The loss in food production capacity is then offset by importing grain from abroad. Since 1 ton of grain represents 1,000 tons of water, this becomes the most efficient way to import water.

I

Last year, Iran imported 7 million tons of wheat, eclipsing Japan to become the world's leading wheat importer. This year, Egypt is also projected to move ahead of Japan. Iran and Egypt have nearly 70 million people each. Both populations are increasing by more than a million a year and both are pressing the limits of their water supplies.

J

The water required to produce the grain and other foodstuffs imported into North Africa and the Middle East last year was roughly equal to the annual flow of the Nile River. Stated otherwise, the fast-growing water deficit of this region is equal to another Nile flowing into the region in the form of imported grain.

K

It is now often said that future wars in the region will more likely be fought over water than oil. Perhaps, but given the difficulty in winning a water war, the competition for water seems more likely to take place in world grain markets. The countries that will "win" in this competition will be those that are financially strongest, not those that are militarily strongest. The world water deficit grows larger with each year, making it potentially more difficult to manage. If we decided abruptly to stabilise water tables everywhere by simply pumping less water, the world grain harvest would fall by some 160 million tons, or 8 percent, and grain prices would go off the chart. If the deficit continues to widen, the eventual adjustment will be even greater.

L

Unless governments in water-short countries act quickly to stabilise their populations and to raise water productivity, their water shortages may soon become food shortages. The risk is that the growing number of water-short countries, including population giants China and India, with rising grain-import needs will overwhelm the exportable supply in food surplus countries, such as the United States, Canada, and Australia. This in turn could destabilise world grain markets. Another risk of delay in dealing with the deficit is that some low-income, water-short countries will not be able to afford to import needed grain, trapping millions of their people in hydrological poverty; thirsty and hungry, unable to escape.

M

Although there are still some opportunities for developing new water resources, restoring the balance between water use and developing a sustainable supply will depend primarily on demand-side initiatives, such as stabilising population and raising water productivity. Governments can no longer separate population policy from the supply of water. And just as the world turned to raising land productivity a half century ago when the frontiers of agricultural settlement disappeared, so it must now turn to raising water productivity. The first step toward this goal is to eliminate the water subsidies that foster inefficiency. The second step is to raise the price of water to reflect its cost. Shifting to more water-efficient technologies, more water-efficient crops, and more water-efficient forms of animal protein offers a huge potential for raising water productivity. These shifts will move faster if the price of water more closely reflects its real value.

Reading

> **Reading Tip:**
> Make sure you are aware of the different types of texts that may be on the test and how to approach each one.

Questions 27 - 32

Do the following statements agree with the information given in Reading Passage 3?
In spaces 27 - 32 below, write

> **TRUE**   *if the statement agrees with the writer's claims*
> **FALSE**   *if the statement contradicts the writer's claims*
> **NOT GIVEN**   *if it is impossible to say what the writer thinks about this*

27	Vegetarians drink less water than meat eaters.	**NOT GIVEN**
28	A typical Indian diet requires less grain than a typical USA diet.	**TRUE**
29	Growing grain uses more water than raising beef.	**FALSE**
30	People that move from the country to the city may increase their water consumption considerably.	**TRUE**
31	Future conflicts will be fought as much over food as they will over oil.	**FALSE**
32	Egypt and Japan also import 7 million tons of oil annually.	**NOT GIVEN**

Questions 33 - 36

Reading passage 3 has 13 paragraphs A - M.
Which paragraph contains information about the following threats to water supplies?
Write the correct letter A - M in spaces 33 - 36 below.

33 The volume of water that is needed for irrigation in grain production.	Paragraph	**C**
34 Over-pumping our underground water supplies.	Paragraph	**E**
35 Population growth will be responsible for a new type of water-related poverty.	Paragraph	**B**
36 Industrialisation demands greater water supplies.	Paragraph	**F**

Questions 37 - 40

*Choose the correct letter **A**, **B**, **C** or **D**.*

37   Our water supply is running low because

   A   grain is now exported globally.

   (B)   the world's population is increasing rapidly.

   C   more people are moving to cities.

   D   people waste water foolishly.

38   People who have a high meat diet cause more water to be used because

   (A)   it takes more grain to feed livestock than it does a human.

   B   the industrial processes to produce meat require a lot of water.

   C   livestock drink a lot of water.

   D   packaging of meat products goes through an intensive washing process.

39   What would reduce the use of water without adversely affecting the food supply?

   A   growing fewer crops

   B   increasing water subsidies

   C   diverting water from irrigation

   (D)   falling population levels

40   If there is a water war, who will win?

   A   the driest countries

   (B)   the richest countries

   C   the countries that are more forceful

   D   the countries that have the biggest population

Reading Passage 3
Justification of the Answers

27. NOT GIVEN - Paragraph F - although less water is used in the production of rice than of grain to feed cattle, it does not state that vegetarians actually drink less water than meat eaters; it would vary from person to person depending on their diet.

28. TRUE - Paragraph F - 'A US diet rich in livestock products requires 800 kilograms of grain per person a year, whereas diets in India, dominated by a starchy food staple such as rice, typically need only 200 kilograms.'

29. FALSE - Paragraph F- 'As people move up the food chain, consuming more beef, pork, poultry, eggs, and dairy products, they use more grain.' and 'Using four times as much grain per person means using four times as much water.'

30. TRUE - Paragraph F -'in addition to population growth, urbanization and industrialization also expand the demand for water. As developing country villagers, traditionally reliant on the village well, move to urban high-rise apartment buildings with indoor plumbing, their residential water use can easily triple.'

31. FALSE - Paragraph K - 'It is now often said that future wars in the region will more likely be fought over water than oil'. - not food

32. NOT GIVEN - Paragraph I - Both countries are mentioned but the text discusses importing grain not oil.

33. C - 'it takes 1,000 tons of water to pro-duce 1 ton of grain.'

34. E there are many references to over-pumping throughout the whole of the paragraph.

35. B this 'population growth is sentencing millions of people to hydrological poverty'.

36. F 'urbanisation and industrialisation also expand the demand for water'.

37. B 'We live in a water-challenged world, one that is becoming more so each year as 80 million additional people make their claims to the Earth's water resources'.

38. A - 'A US diet rich in livestock products requires 800 kilograms of grain per person a year, whereas diets in India, dominated by a starchy food staple such as rice, typically need only 200 kilograms'.

39. D - 'Unless governments in water-short countries act quickly to stabilise their popula-tions and to raise water productivity, their water shortages may soon become food shortages.'

40. B - 'those that are financially strongest'

Writing

WRITING TASK 1

You should spend about 20 minutes on this task.

> *The graph below shows the daily water consumption for Americans in their homes.*
>
> *Summarise the information by selecting and reporting the main features, and make comparisons where necessary.*

Write at least 150 words.

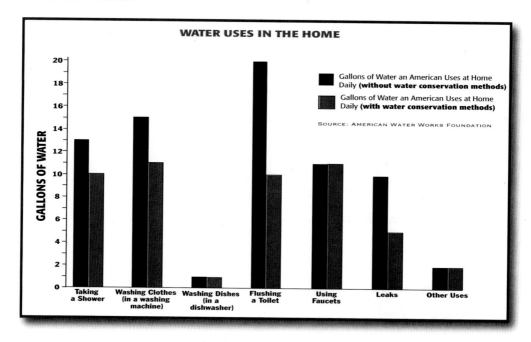

WRITING TASK 2

You should spend about 40 minutes on this task.

Write about the following topic:

> *If racism and xenophobia are attitudes that we are taught, not born with, then the problems that come from them can be resolved.*
>
> *Discuss this view and give your own opinion.*

Give reasons for your answer and include any relevant examples from your own knowledge or experience.

Write at least 250 words.

Speaking

> **Speaking Tip:**
> Don't worry if, in Part 2, the examiner stops you.
> This means you have said enough.

PART 1   (4-5 minutes)

The examiner asks the candidate about him/herself, his/her home, work or studies and other familiar topics.

Studies

- What do you think is the most useful subject you have studied?
- What are you currently studying / planning to study at university?
- Why have you chosen this field?
- What do you hope to do after you graduate?

PART 2   (2 minutes)

You will have to talk about the topic for one to two minutes. You have one minute to think about what you are going to say. You can make some notes to help you if you wish.

> **Describe someone you know who comes from a different country or who has a different origin from you.**
>
> **You should say:**
> - **what you like about this person**
> - **what you have learned about their culture from the friendship you have formed**
> - **if knowing this person has encouraged you to experience other cultures**

PART 3   (4-5 minutes)

Discussion topics:

Other cultures
- How important is it to learn about other people's cultures?
- What difficulties can people living in a foreign country experience?
- What benefits can there be for people living in a foreign country?

A global culture
- Do you believe in stereotypes about different nationalities?
- Are you in favour of adopting a universal language?
- What negative effects might come from a country losing its traditional culture?

Test 5

Listening

Listening - Section 1
E: (1) For an alumnus, that's two hundred and forty pounds annually, or one hundred pounds for a month.

E: Well, we do offer a really excellent facility. For the cost, members have access to the **(2)** Emily Pankhurst Fitness Centre, which is a ....
Check the **Audioscript** in the **Self-Study Guide** for the **Justification of the Answers for ALL the Sections of the Listening Test**

SECTION 1   Questions 1 - 10

Questions 1 - 5

Complete the notes below.

Write **NO MORE THAN THREE WORDS AND/OR A NUMBER** *for each answer.*

Ratner Athletics Centre

Example: Current students get membership for .... **no charge / free** ....

- a yearly membership costs 1 .... **£240** .... for alumni

- Features offered include:
  - the Emily Pankhurst 2 .... **fitness centre** ....
  - the Dalton 3 .... **swimming pool** ....
  - personal 4 .... **trainers** .... at an extra charge

- Hours: 6 a.m. to 5 **midnight/24.00** .... on weekdays and 6 a.m. to 9 p.m. on weekends

---

Questions 6 - 10

Complete the form below.

Write **NO MORE THAN THREE WORDS AND/OR A NUMBER** *for each answer.*

NEW CUSTOMER MEMBERSHIP FORM

- **Customer name:** Shannon 6 .... **Fleet** ....
- **Street Address:** 7 .. **24 Whitehall Close** ....
- **City:** Newcastle
- **Postcode:** 8 .. **NE0 1EN** ....
- **Telephone number:** 9 .. **9765 484 493** ......
- **Payment method:** cash
- **Proof of address:** 10 .. **electricity bill** ....

SECTION 2   *Questions 11 - 20*

> **Listening Tip:**
> Make sure your answers make sense within the context of what you're listening to.

Complete the notes below.

Write **NO MORE THAN TWO WORDS** *for each answer.*

Orientation Meeting for students studying abroad in South America

Remember to sign the attendance lists on the way out!

To get a student visa you must make a folder of health information including:

- vaccination **11** .... records ....

- proof you don't have a serious **12** ..... contagious disease ....

Have a consultation with a doctor specialised in **13** .... travel medicine .... to get

information on:

- what vaccines you will need to get

- **14** .... medication .... for malaria

- what to expect if you have any existing **15** .... health issues ....

Health issues in South America

Malaria is a concern for most people going to South America.

- In each country, it is **16** .... present .... in some areas but not others.

- You must **17** .... keep informed .... and not travel to high risk areas if you

  are not protected.

To prevent insect bites:

- wear long-sleeved shirts and **18** ..... long trousers ....

- use insect repellent on **19** ..... bare skin .... and flying-insect spray in rooms

- stay indoors in the peak biting periods of **20** .... dusk .... and ... dawn ....

Listening

SECTION 3   *Questions 21 - 30*

Questions 21 - 23

Which opinion does each person express about filling out the evaluation forms?
*Choose your answer from the box and write the letters **A - F** next to questions 21 - 23.*

A They encourage students to work hard.	
B Important changes have been made because of the forms.	Joshua **21** ....D.......
C We could be judged because of what we write.	
D It is alright to say that you don't have an opinion.	Ethan **22** ....E.......
E Probably no one reads them anyway.	
F They are required; if we don't do them we will get bad marks.	Lily **23** ....B.......

Questions 24 - 30

Complete the table below.

Write **NO MORE THAN THREE WORDS AND/OR A NUMBER** *for each answer.*

Opinions about project:	Lily	Joshua	Ethan
Initial Suggested Rating	24 ....4......	25 ....5......	26 ...4.5......
Good Points	nothing specific	27 well thought out	choice between 28 two topics
Bad Points	no practical point / choices were both 29 boring	should have given us 30 more time	no opinion

SECTION 4 *Questions 31 - 40*

Questions 31 - 40

Complete the flow-chart below.

Write **NO MORE THAN THREE WORDS** *for each answer.*

Product Life Cycle
Marketing Aims by Stage

Stage 1: Market Introduction

Features:

- Costs **31** ...... *very high* ....
- Sales volumes **32** ...... *low* ....

Marketing Strategy:

<u>Step 1</u>

Get the brand noticed by the

33 ...... *target market* ....

<u>Step 2</u>

Encourage potential customers to

34 ...... *try the product* ....

Stage 2: Growth

Features:

- Economies **35** ...... *of scale* ....

  lead to reduced costs and rise in sales.

Marketing Strategy:

<u>Step 1</u>

Find a way to **36** ...... *reward* ....

return customers.

<u>Step 2</u>

Differentiate the **37** ...... *brand* ....

from rival products.

Stage 3: Maturity

Features:

- Sales will **38** ...... *peak* ....
- Competition will be **39** ...... *intense* ....

Marketing Strategy:

<u>Step 1</u>

Continue to point out the differences
between your product and rival brands.

<u>Step 2</u>

Find new **40** ...... *applications* .... for
the product.

Reading

READING PASSAGE 1

*You should spend about 20 minutes on **Questions 1 - 13**, which are based on Reading Passage 1 below*

CONTROLLING DEATHWATCH BEETLES

All of the organisms that damage timber in buildings are part of the natural process that takes dead wood to the forest floor, decomposes it into humus and recycles the nutrients released back into trees. Each stage in this process requires the correct environment and if we replicate this in our buildings then the organisms belonging to that part of the cycle will invade. A poorly maintained roof is, after all, just an extension of the forest floor to a fungus.

The first fact to remember about deathwatch beetles in your building is that they have probably been there for centuries and will continue long after you have gone. Beetle damage in oak timbers is a slow process and if we make it slower by good maintenance then the beetle population may eventually decline to extinction. The second fact is that natural predation will help you. Spiders are a significant predator and will help to keep the beetle population under control. They will speed up the decline of a beetle population in a well-maintained building.

The beetles fly to light and some form of light trap may help to deplete a population. The place in which it is used must be dark, so that there is no competing light source, and the air temperature must rise above about 17°C during the emergence season (April to June) so that the beetles will fly. Beetle holes do not disappear when the beetles have gone so it is sometimes necessary to confirm active infestation if remedial works are planned. This is generally easy with beetle damage in sapwood because the holes will look clean and have sharp edges, usually with bore dust trickling from them. Infestation deep within modified heartwood is more difficult to detect, particularly because the beetles will not necessarily bite their own emergence holes if plenty of other holes are available. This problem may be overcome by clogging the suspected holes with furniture polish or by covering a group of holes tightly with paper or card. Any emerging beetles will make a hole that should be visible, so that the extent and magnitude of the problem can be assessed. Unnecessary pesticide treatments must be avoided.

Sometimes a building cannot be dried enough to eradicate the beetles or a localised population will have built up unnoticed. A few scattered beetles in a building need not cause much concern, but dozens of beetles below a beam-end might indicate the need for some form of treatment if the infested timber is accessible. Insecticides formulated as a paste can be effective – either applied to the surface or caulked into pre-drilled holes – but the formulations may only be obtainable by a remedial company.

Surface spray treatments are generally ineffective because they barely penetrate the surface of the timber and the beetles' natural behaviour does not bring it into much contact with the insecticide. Contact insecticides might also kill the natural predators.

Heat treatments for entire buildings are available and the continental experience is that they are effective. They are also likely to be expensive but they may be the only way to eradicate a heavy and widespread infestation without causing considerable structural degradation of the building.

Two other beetles are worth a mention.

The first is the House Longhorn Beetle (*Hylotrupes bajulus*). This is a large insect that produces oval emergence holes that are packed with little cylindrical pellets. The beetles restrict their activities to the sapwood of 20th century softwood, although there is now some evidence that they will attack older softwood. The beetle larvae can cause considerable damage but infestation has generally been restricted to the south-west of London, possibly because they need a high temperature before the beetles will fly. Old damage is, however, frequently found elsewhere, thus indicating a wider distribution in the past, and infested timber is sometimes imported. This is an insect that might become more widespread because of climate change.

The second is the Lyctus or powderpost beetle. There are several species that are rather difficult to tell apart. These beetles live in the sapwood of oak. The beetles breed rapidly so that many cylindrical beetles may be present and the round emergence holes resemble those of the furniture beetle. This is, and has always been, a pest of newly installed oak. Timbers with an exploded sapwood surface are frequently found in old buildings and the damage will have occurred during a few decades after the timbers were installed. Our main interest with these beetles is that they seem to have become more common of late. Beetle infestation within a few months of a new oak construction will be Lyctus beetles in the sapwood and not furniture beetles. The problem can be avoided by using oak with minimal sapwood content. The beetle infestation will cease after a few years but spray treatment may be necessary if an infestation is heavy.

Reading

Reading Tip:
Make sure you answer as many questions as you can in the time allotted.

Questions 1 - 4

Complete each sentence with the correct ending A - H below.

Write the correct ending A - H in spaces 1 - 4 below.

1 One species of the beetle population may spread ....F..........

2 You can detect the presence of beetles ....B..........

3 You may kill household spiders ....D..........

4 Beetles will disappear at a faster rate ....A..........

A if the building is kept in good condition.

B if you clog the suspected holes with furniture polish, paper or card.

C if the temperature rises to above about 17°C during the emergence season.

D if you use a contact insecticide.

E if it was installed a few decades earlier.

F if changes in weather patterns continue.

G if the use of surface treatments is avoided.

H if the wood has a low sapwood concentration.

Reading Passage 1
Justification of the Answers

1. F 'This is an insect that might become more widespread because of climate change' (The House Longhorn Beetle).
2. B 'This problem may be overcome by clogging the suspected holes ....'.
3. D 'Contact insecticides might also kill the natural predators' - spiders.
4. A 'Beetle damage in oak timbers is a slow process and if we make it slower by good maintenance then the beetle population may eventually decline to extinction'.

5. FALSE 'Infestation deep within modified heartwood is more difficult to detect, particularly because the beetles will not necessarily bite their own emergence holes if plenty of other holes are available'.
6. FALSE 'clogging the suspected holes with furniture polish or by covering a group of holes tightly with paper or card. Any emerging beetles will make a hole that should be visible, so that the extent and magnitude of a problem can be assessed'. - so they aren't trapped
7. FALSE they are effective
8. NOT GIVEN - 'Surface spray treatments are generally ineffective' however no mention is made whether the House Longhorn Beetle is an exception.
9. TRUE 'Heat treatments may be the only way to eradicate a heavy and widespread infestation without causing considerable structural degradation of the building'.
10. C 'good maintenance then the beetle population may eventually decline to extinction.'.
11. D 'The beetles fly to light and some form of light trap may help to deplete a population. The place in which it is used must be dark, so that there is no competing light source'.
12. B 'Surface spray treatments are generally ineffective because they barely penetrate the surface of the timber and the beetles' natural behaviour does not bring it into much contact with the insecticide'.
13. B 'Old damage is, however, frequently found elsewhere, thus indicating a wider distribution in the past, and infested timber is sometimes imported'.

Questions 5 - 9

Do the following statements agree with the information given in Reading Passage 1?

In spaces 5 - 9 below, write

TRUE	*if the statement agrees with the writer's claims*
FALSE	*if the statement contradicts the writer's claims*
NOT GIVEN	*if it is impossible to say what the writer thinks about this*

5 Infestation by beetles deep within modified heartwood can be identified
   by the type of hole visible.   **FALSE**

6 Clogging a hole with furniture polish or paper will trap the beetle inside permanently.   **FALSE**

7 Paste insecticides are less effective than any other kind.   **FALSE**

8 Surface spray treatments are sometimes effective for the House Longhorn Beetle   **NOT GIVEN**

9 Heat treatments tend to cause less damage than other treatments.   **TRUE**

Questions 10 - 13

Choose the correct letter A, B, C or D.

10 The point the writer makes about deathwatch beetles is that

   A   they must be eliminated quickly.
   B   only natural predation will keep them under control.
   C   with good maintenance it may be possible to eliminate them.
   D   they are there to stay and do great damage.

11 One way to trap deathwatch beetles is to attract them to

   A   daylight.
   B   a totally dark environment.
   C   a constantly warm environment.
   D   a light trap in a dark place.

12 Surface spray treatments are not effective because

   A   the beetles are immune to them.
   B   they do not reach the beetles.
   C   they react poorly to wooden surfaces.
   D   they attract other harmful creatures.

13 Damage by the House Longhorn Beetle is sometimes found further afield than London because

   A   temperatures have increased.
   B   the timber was not local timber.
   C   there was no effective treatment previously.
   D   the type of timber has changed.

Reading

READING PASSAGE 2

You should spend about 20 minutes on **Questions 14 - 26**, *which are based on Reading Passage 2 below.*

Therapeutic Jurisprudence:

An Overview

Therapeutic jurisprudence is the study of the role of the law as a therapeutic agent. It examines the law's impact on emotional life and on psychological well-being, and the therapeutic and antitherapeutic consequences of the law. It is most applicable to the fields of mental health law, criminal law, juvenile law and family law.

The general aim of therapeutic jurisprudence is the humanising of the law and addressing the human, emotional and psychological side of the legal process. It promotes the perspective that the law is a social force that produces behaviours and consequences. Therapeutic jurisprudence strives to have laws made or applied in a more therapeutic way so long as other values, such as justice and due process, can be fully respected. It is important to recognise that therapeutic jurisprudence does not itself suggest that therapeutic goals should trump other goals. It does not support paternalism or coercion by any means. It is simply a way of looking at the law in a richer way, and then bringing to the table some areas and issues that previously have gone unnoticed. Therapeutic jurisprudence simply suggests that we think about the therapeutic consequences of law and see if they can be factored into the processes of law-making, lawyering, and judging.

The law can be divided into the following categories: (1) legal rules, (2) legal procedures, such as hearings and trials and (3) the roles of legal actors -the behaviour of judges, lawyers, and of therapists acting in a legal context. Much of what legal actors do has an impact on the psychological well-being or emotional life of persons affected by the law, for example, in the dialogues that judges have with defendants or that lawyers have with clients. Therefore, therapeutic jurisprudence is especially applicable to this third category.

Therapeutic jurisprudence is a relatively new phenomenon. In the early days of law, attitudes were very different and efforts were focused primarily on what was wrong with various sorts of testimony. While there were good reasons for that early emphasis, an exclusive focus on what is wrong, rather than also looking at what is right and how these aspects could be further developed, is seriously short-sighted. Therapeutic jurisprudence focuses attention on this previously under-appreciated aspect, encouraging us to look very hard for promising developments, and to borrow from the behavioural science literature, even when this literature has nothing obviously to do with the law. It encourages people to think creatively about how promising developments from other fields might be brought into the legal system.

Recently, as a result of this multidisciplinary approach, certain kinds of rehabilitative programmes have begun to emerge that look rather promising. One type of cognitive behavioural treatment encourages offenders to prepare relapse prevention plans which require them to think through the chain of events that lead to criminality. These reasoning and rehabilitation type programmes teach offenders cognitive self-change, to stop and think and figure out consequences, to anticipate high-risk situations, and to learn to avoid or cope with them. These programmes, so far, seem to be reasonably successful.

From a therapeutic jurisprudence standpoint, the question is how these programmes might be brought into the law. In one obvious sense, these problem-solving, reasoning and rehabilitation-type programmes can be made widely available in correctional and community settings. A way of linking them even more to the law, of course, would be to make them part of the legal process itself. The suggestion here is that if a judge or parole board becomes familiar with these techniques and is about to consider someone for probation, the judge might say, 'I'm going to consider you but I want you to come up with a preliminary relapse prevention plan that we will use as a basis for dis-cussion. I want you to figure out why I should grant you probation and why I should be comfortable that you're going to succeed. In order for me to feel comfortable, I need to know what you regard to be high-risk situations and how you're going to avoid them or cope with them.'

If that approach is followed, courts will be promoting cognitive self-change as part and parcel of the sentencing process itself. The process may operate this way; an offender would make a state-ment like 'I realise I mess up on Friday nights; therefore, I propose that I will stay at home on Friday nights.' Suddenly, it is not a judge imposing something on the offender. It's something that the offender has come up with him or herself, so he or she should think it is fair. If a person has a voice in his rehabilitation, then he is more likely to feel a commitment to it, and with that commit-ment, presumably, compliance will increase dramatically.

Reading

Questions 14 - 20

Complete the notes below.

*Choose **NO MORE THAN ONE WORD** from the passage for each answer.*

NOTES: Therapeutic Jurisprudence

Therapeutic Jurisprudence: study of the law as a therapeutic 14 ....**agent**..........

and the therapeutic and 15 ....**antitherapeutic**.......... consequences

of the law.

Goal:

the 16 ....**humanising**.......... of the law,

but NOT at the expense of 17 ....**justice**.......... and due process

Applicable to:

especially applicable to the role of legal 18 ....**actors**.......... such as judges and lawyers

Therapeutic jurisprudence = new attitude

1.   It asks people to seek out 19 ....**promising**.......... developments, not problems.

2.   It urges people to think 20 ....**creatively**.......... and borrow from other fields.

Reading Passage 2 Justification of the Answers	
14. Paragraph 1: 'Therapeutic jurisprudence is the study of the role of the law as a therapeutic **agent**'.	**17.** Paragraph 2: ' ...so long as other values, such as **justice** and due process, can be fully respected... '
15. Paragraph 1: ' ...and the therapeutic and **antitherapeutic** consequences of the law'.	**18.** Paragraph 3: 'therapeutic jurisprudence is especially applicable to this third category' i.e. '(3) the roles of legal **actors**'.
16. Paragraph 2: 'The general aim of therapeutic jurisprudence is the **humanising** of the law'	**19.** Paragraph 4: ' encouraging us to look very hard for **promising** developments... '
	20. Paragraph 4: 'It encourages people to think **creatively**.... "

Questions 21 - 23

Complete the sentences.

Choose **NO MORE THAN THREE WORDS** *from the passage for each answer.*

---

21   One aspect of cognitive behavioural treatment includes the preparation of
........**relapse prevention plans**.... by offenders.

22   The treatment requires offenders to consider the ....**chain of events**.........
that lead to a crime being committed.

23   Treatment programmes encourage offenders to recognise ....**high-risk situations**.........
before they happen, and know what to do in case they do happen.

Reading Passage 2 Justification of the Answers	
21. Paragraph 5.: 'One type of cognitive behavioural treatment encourages offenders to prepare *relapse prevention plans* which require ...'.	**24. NOT GIVEN** - Paragraph 5: Although rehabilitation programs are said to 'look rather promising' no concrete information is given or claim made about how greatly they reduce the chances of criminals re-offending.
22. Paragraph 5: ' ....which require them to think through the *chain of events* that lead to criminality.'	**25. TRUE** - Paragraph 6: 'From a therapeutic jurisprudence standpoint, the question is how these programmes might be brought into the law .... to make them part of the legal process itself'.
23. Paragraph 5: 'to anticipate *high-risk situations*, and to learn to avoid or cope with them.'	**26. FALSE** - Paragraph 7: A prisoner does not decide on punishment, but has a 'voice in his rehabilitation'.

Questions 24 - 26

Do the following statements agree with the information given in Reading Passage 2?
In spaces 24 - 26 below, write

TRUE	*if the statement agrees with the information*
FALSE	*if the statement contradicts the information*
NOT GIVEN	*if there is no information on this*

---

24   The use of rehabilitative programs has been proved to greatly
reduce the chance of a criminal re-offending.   **NOT GIVEN**
....

25   Therapeutic jurisprudence aims to make cognitive behavioural
treatment a part of the legal process itself.   **TRUE**
....

26   Offenders might be encouraged by judges to take part in deciding
what their punishment should be.   **FALSE**
....

Reading

READING PASSAGE 3

*You should spend about 20 minutes on **Questions 27 - 40**, which are based on Reading Passage 3 belo*

S L E E P

WHY WE SLEEP

As the field of sleep research is still relatively new, scientists have yet to determine exactly why people sleep. However, they do know that humans must sleep and, in fact, people can survive longer without food than without sleep. And people are not alone in this need. All mammals, reptiles and birds sleep.

Scientists have proposed the following theories on why humans require sleep:

- Sleep may be a way of recharging the brain. The brain has a chance to shut down and repair neurons and to exercise important neuronal connections that might otherwise deteriorate due to lack of activity.

- Sleep gives the brain an opportunity to reorganise data to help find a solution to problems, process newly-learned information and organise and archive memories.

- Sleep lowers a person's metabolic rate and energy consumption.

- The cardiovascular system also gets a break during sleep. Researchers have found that people with normal or high blood pressure experience a 20 to 30% reduction in blood pressure and 10 to 20% reduction in heart rate.

- During sleep, the body has a chance to replace chemicals and repair muscles, other tissues and aging or dead cells.

- In children and teenagers, growth hormones are released during deep sleep.

When a person falls asleep and wakes up is largely determined by his or her circadian rhythm, a day-night cycle of about 24 hours. Circadian rhythms greatly influence the timing, amount and quality of sleep.

For many small mammals such as rodents, sleep has other particular benefits, as it provides the only real opportunity for physical rest, and confines the animal to the thermal insulation of a nest. In these respects, sleep conserves much energy in such mammals, particularly as sleep can also develop into a torpor, whereby the metabolic rate drops significantly for a few hours during the sleep period. On the other hand, humans can usually rest and relax quite adequately during wakefulness, and there is only a modest further energy saving to be gained by sleeping. We do not enter torpor, and the fall in metabolic rate for a human adult sleeping compared to lying resting but awake is only about 5-10%.

A sizeable portion of the workforce are shift workers who work and sleep against their bodies' natural sleep-wake cycle. While a person's circadian rhythm cannot be ignored or reprogrammed, the cycle can be altered by the timing of things such as naps, exercise, bedtime, travel to a different time zone and exposure to light. The more stable and consistent the cycle is, the better the person sleeps. Disruption of circadian rhythms has even been found to cause mania in people with bipolar disorder.

The 'seven deadly sins' formulated by the medieval monks included Sloth. The Bible in Proverbs 6:9 includes the line: 'How long will you sleep, O sluggard? When will you arise out of your sleep?' But a more nuanced understanding of sloth sees it as a disinclination to labour or work. This isn't the same as the desire for healthy sleep. On the contrary, a person can't do work without rest periods and no one can operate at top performance without adequate sleep. The puritan work ethic can be adhered to and respect still paid to the sleep needs of healthy humans. It is wrong to see sleep as a shameful activity.

Usually sleepers pass through five stages: 1, 2, 3, 4 and REM (rapid eye movement) sleep. These stages progress cyclically from 1 through REM then begin again. A complete sleep cycle takes an average of 90 to 110 minutes. The first sleep cycles each night have relatively short REM sleeps and long periods of deep sleep but later in the night, REM periods lengthen and deep sleep time decreases. Stage 1 is light sleep where you drift in and out of sleep and can be awakened easily. In this stage, the eyes move slowly and muscle activity slows. During this stage, many people experience sudden muscle contractions preceded by a sensation of falling. In stage 2, eye movement stops and brain waves become slower with only an occasional burst of rapid brain waves. When a person enters stage 3, extremely slow brain waves called delta waves are interspersed with smaller, faster waves. In stage 4, the brain produces delta waves almost exclusively. Stages 3 and 4 are referred to as deep sleep, and it is very difficult to wake someone from them. In deep sleep, there is no eye movement or muscle activity. This is when some children experience bedwetting, sleepwalking or night terrors.

In the REM period, breathing becomes more rapid, irregular and shallow, eyes jerk rapidly and limb muscles are temporarily paralysed. Brain waves during this stage increase to levels experienced when a person is awake. Also, heart rate increases, blood pressure rises and the body loses some of the ability to regulate its temperature. This is the time when most dreams occur, and, if awoken during REM sleep, a person can remember the dreams. Most people experience three to five intervals of REM sleep each night. Infants spend almost 50% of their time in REM sleep. Adults spend nearly half of sleep time in stage 2, about 20% in REM and the other 30% is divided between the other three stages. Older adults spend progressively less time in REM sleep.

As sleep research is still a relatively young field, scientists did not discover REM sleep until 1953, when new machines were developed to monitor brain activity. Before this discovery it was believed that most brain activity ceased during sleep. Since then, scientists have also disproved the idea that deprivation of REM sleep can lead to insanity and have found that lack of REM sleep can alleviate clinical depression although they do not know why. Recent theories link REM sleep to learning and memory.

Reading

Reading Tip:
Often it is helpful to skim the questions before reading the text.

Questions 27 - 30

*Choose the correct letter, **A, B, C** or **D**.*

27   Among other functions, sleep serves to

   A   help the adult body develop physically.

   B   push daily problems from our minds.

   C   accelerate the learning process significantly.

   (**D**)   re-energise parts of the brain.

28   'Torpor' can be described as

   (**A**)   a very deep sleep.

   B   a long state of hibernation.

   C   the sleep all non-human mammals experience.

   D   a light sleep.

29   Unlike small mammals, humans

   A   don't sleep to conserve energy.

   B   don't sleep properly.

   (**C**)   save only a small amount of energy by sleeping.

   D   show no decrease in their metabolic rate when they sleep.

30   In stage 3 deep sleep

   A   the eyes move slowly and there's little muscle activity.

   (**B**)   there is an alternation of delta waves and small fast waves.

   C   there is an occasional burst of rapid brain waves.

   D   there are no small fast waves.

**Reading Passage 3
Justification of the Answers**

27. D - 'Sleep may be a way of recharging the brain.'

28. A - 'Whereby metabolic rate drops significantly for a few hours.'

29. C - 'there is only a modest further energy saving to be gained by sleeping.'

30. B - 'When a person enters stage 3, extremely slow brain waves called delta waves are interspersed with smaller, faster waves.'

31. p. 135 Paragraph 3 - '*Stage 1 is **light sleep** where you drift in and out of sleep and can be awakened easily.*'

32. p. 135 Paragraph 3 - '*In stage 2, eye movement stops and **brain** waves become slower....*'

33. p. 135 Paragraph 3 - '*When a person enters stage 3, extreme-*

ly slow brain waves called delta waves are interspersed with **smaller, faster waves.**'

34. p. 135 Paragraph 3 - '*Stages 3 and 4 are referred to as **deep sleep**, ...*'

35. p. 135 Paragraph 4 - '*In the REM period, **breathing** becomes more rapid, irregular and shallow..*'

36. p. 134 Paragraph 2 - '*..... to exercise important neuronal connections that might otherwise **deteriorate** due to lack of activity.*'

37. p. 134 Paragraph 2 - '*Sleep lowers a person's **metabolic rate.**.*'

38. p. 134 Paragraph 3 - '*We do not enter **torpor**, ...*'

39 - 40. p. 134 Paragraph 4 - '*When a person falls asleep and wakes up is largely determined by his or her **circadian rhythm**, a **day-night cycle** of about 24 hours.*'

Questions 31 - 35

Complete the flow-chart below.

Write **NO MORE THAN THREE WORDS** for each answer.

The Stages of Sleep

The individual drifts in and out of consciousness and can be woken up easily as they are only in a
31 ......**light sleep**...... . Eye movement is slow and there is reduced muscle activity.

↓

The speed of **32** ......**brain**...... activity slows and all movement of the eyes tends to stop.

↓

Brain activity is dominated by delta waves, with a scattering of **33** ...**smaller, faster waves**... also in evidence.

↓

In a state of **34** ......**deep sleep**......, the brain emits delta waves almost exclusively. It is hard to wake the individual.

↓

A period of rapid eye movement follows, during which **35** ......**breathing**...... patterns are not consistent and limb muscles enter a temporary state of paralysis.

Questions 36 - 40

Complete the summary.

Choose **NO MORE THAN TWO WORDS** from the passage for each answer.

Sleep is so essential to a person that he can actually go longer without food than without sleep. During sleep, the brain has the chance to close down and do some repair work on neuronal connections which could otherwise **36** ......**deteriorate**...... in a state of inactivity. Sleep also gives the brain the opportunity to organise data, especially newly-learned information.

During this rest period, the **37** ......**metabolic rate**...... drops and energy consumption goes down. At the same time, the cardiovascular system has a much-needed rest. While they go into a deep sleep, humans don't fall into **38**......**torpor**...... , unlike some small animals such as rodents. A **39** ......**day-night cycle**...... of 24 hours is described as a person's **40** ...**circadian rhythm**...... , and this greatly influences a person's amount of sleep, and the type of sleep he gets.

Writing

WRITING TASK 1

You should spend about 20 minutes on this task.

> *The charts below show the average annual spending for Canadian households in the year 1972 and the year 2002.*
>
> *Summarise the information by selecting and reporting the main features, and make comparisons where necessary.*

Write at least 150 words.

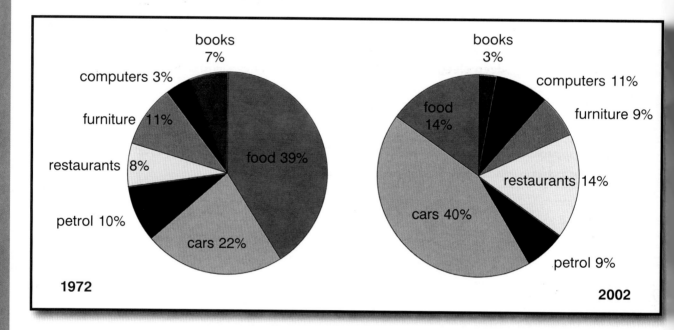

> **Writing Tip:**
> Be sure to write clearly and concisely.
> Focus on organization as much as content.

WRITING TASK 2

You should spend about 40 minutes on this task.

Write about the following topic:

> *The state of the environment is now a cause for concern in all countries across the world. Apart from government measures and policies, what can individuals do on a personal level to combat the negative effects that our lifestyles have on the environment?*

Give reasons for your answer and include any relevant examples from your own knowledge or experience.

Write at least 250 words.

Speaking

> **Speaking Tip:**
> Remember that you are allowed to correct
> yourself if you realise you've made a mistake.

PART 1 (4-5 minutes)

The examiner asks the candidate about him/herself, his/her home, work or studies and other familiar topics.

Pets

• Is it common in your country for families to have pets?
• Which pets are most popular?
• Did you have a pet when you were a child?
• What is the attraction of having a pet, in your opinion?

PART 2 (2 minutes)

You will have to talk about the topic for one to two minutes. You have one minute to think about what you are going to say. You can make some notes to help you if you wish.

> **Describe the types of things you have in your house. You should say:**
>
> • **if your home is big or small**
> • **what type of furniture you have**
> • **if you have modern appliances like a DVD player, computer, mobile phone, etc.**
> • **what else you would like to have in your home that you do not have already.**

PART 3 (4-5 minutes)

Discussion topics:

Lifestyle

• How important is it for you to have all the latest modern gadgets?
• Is having a luxurious home important to you?
• If you have extra money, do you prefer to spend it on a physical thing, or on an experience?

Technology and Lifestyle

• What advances in technology do you consider to be the most important, and why?
• How have mobile phones affected the way we communicate on an everyday basis?
• Computers have had a great effect on the way we live and work. What do you think will influence the way we lead our lives in the future?

Test 6

Listening

SECTION 1   Questions 1 - 10

Questions 1 - 8

Complete the notes below.

Write **NO MORE THAN TWO WORDS AND/OR A NUMBER** *for each answer.*

Fairview Lake Camping Centre

The three functions of the centre are:
- conference centre
- *Example:* <u>educational institution</u>
- place for fun-filled weekends

The customer wants to bring children who have **1** .... <u>**failed exams**</u> .....
SPORTS: Sailing, windsurfing, volleyball, rowing, and a sport most children have never tried which is **2** <u>**archery**</u> ....

Accommodation Facilities

- The Birch Units - sleeps **3** ... <u>**8 people**</u> ....
- Greenback Row - sleeps the same number of people
- Cabins 1 - 3: sleep 10 people
- Cabins **4** ... <u>**5, 6 /(5 and 6)**</u> : sleep 12 people each

◄--►

Mr Bryson's booking arrangements

- The customer would bring **5** .... <u>**22**</u> .... students for the course.
- He would like to book the course starting Sunday **6** .... <u>**June 24th**</u> ....
- The cost for one week would be **7** .... <u>**£425**</u> .... per child.
- The school's telephone number is **8** .... <u>**1304 647864**</u> ....

Questions 9 and 10

Choose the correct letter A, B or C.

9 The receptionist suggests Mr Bryson's group eat with the other groups because

   A it works out cheaper that way.

   B it's more sociable.

   C you can do your own cooking.

10 Before he decides whether to accept the course or not, Mike Bryson will

   A check with a higher authority.

   B ask for lower prices.

   C see what the children have to say.

SECTION 2   Questions 11 - 20

Questions 11 - 15

Label the map below. Write the correct letter, A – G, next to questions 11 – 15.

11	Petting Zoo	.........C......
12	Toddler's Play Pool	......B......
13	Bouncy Castle and Fairy Palace	......A......
14	Winter Wonderland	.........G......
15	Craft Zone	......D......

Questions 16 - 20

*Label the diagram below. Write **NO MORE THAN TWO WORDS** for each answer.*

Practice Test 6

Listening

SECTION 3   *Questions 21 - 30*

Questions 21 - 22

*Choose **TWO** letters A - E.*

Which **TWO** courses does the summer school offer?

(A) preparation courses for graduate studies	(D) graduate studies
B teacher training	E management training course
C future employment	

Questions 23 - 27

Choose the correct letter A, B or C.

23 Paddy is interested in the sports programme because
   A he needs a qualification to teach PE.
   (B) he wants to improve his general teaching skills.
   C he has been told to follow it.

24 The swimming course concentrates on
   A competitive swimming.
   B teaching beginners.
   (C) technical aspects of swimming.

25 Paddy is interested in the equestrian course because
   A he thinks it will help him get better employment.
   (B) there is great interest in this sport in his present school.
   C he has always been interested in riding.

26 The beginners on the equestrian course will be taught
   (A) basic horsemanship.
   B only dressage and show jumping.
   C only flat work and show jumping.

27 When is the deadline for enrolment?
   A mid-April
   B late April
   (C) early May

Questions 28 - 30

Complete the summary below.

*Write **NO MORE THAN TWO WORDS** for each answer.*

Paddy is also interested in a course on 28 ....**rhythmic gymnastics**...., but he knows nothing about it. Conveniently, it is a 29 ......**weekend course**...... so it doesn't matter that he is back at school. Apart from that, he is advised to take a 30 ......**dance course/class**......, which will teach him body awareness, and an appreciation of music.

SECTION 4   Questions 31 - 40

Questions 31 - 40

Complete the nots below.

Write **NO MORE THAN TWO WORDS AND/OR A NUMBER** *for each answer.*

Sending your child to University

- Someone with a higher education earns **31** ....**50%**........ more than someone without.

- In 1997 maintenance grants abolished and **32** ....**tuition fees**........... introduced.

- University fees increasing, up to **33** ....**£6,000**............... a year.

- Average undergraduate needs **34** ....**£25,000**.................. for 3 years.

- Almost 80% of students' cost are **35** ....**living expenses**........... .

PAYING FOR YOUR CHILD'S EDUCATION

- Students' tuition can be paid for, in part, if they join the **36** ....**armed forces**........... .

- The RAF will sponsor, but students must do at least **37** ....**4 years**........... service commitment.

- Students good at sport might secure a **38** ....**(sports) scholarship**........ .

- The University of Kent gives a **39** ....**£1,500**........... cricket bursary to promising players.

Student Loans:

- Maximum **40** ....**yearly loan**............ is 5,000 pounds.

- Needn't be paid back until after graduation.

Reading

READING PASSAGE 1

*You should spend about 20 minutes on **Questions 1 - 13**, which are based on Reading Passage 1 below.*

GRAFFITI

A

The word 'graffiti' derives from the Greek word *graphein,* meaning *to write*. This evolved into the Latin word *graffito*. Graffiti is the plural form of *graffito*. Simply put, graffiti is a drawing, scribbling or writing on a flat surface. Today, we equate graffiti with the 'New York' or 'Hip Hop' style which emerged from New York City in the 1970s. Hip Hop was originally an inner city concept. It evolved from the rap music made in Brooklyn and Harlem in the late 1960s and early 1970s. Donald Clarke, a music historian, has written that rap music was a reaction to the disco music of the period. Disco was centred in the rich, elitist clubs of Manhattan and rap emerged on street corners as an alternative. Using lyrical rhythms and 'beat boxing' the music was a way to express feelings about inner-city life. Hip Hop emerged as turntables began to be used to form part of the rhythm by 'scratching' (the sound created by running the stylus over the grooves of an LP). As Hip Hop music emerged so did a new outlet for artistic visibility. Keith Haring began using posters to place his uniquely drawn figures and characters in public places. Soon he began to draw directly on subway walls and transit posters. The uniqueness of his drawings eventually led to their being shown in galleries and published in books and his art became 'legitimate'.

B

At about the same time as Keith Haring, a delivery messenger began writing 'Taki 183' whenever he delivered documents. Soon his name was all over the city. Newspapers and magazines wrote articles about him and Keith Haring, and soon both became celebrities. This claim to fame attracted many young people, especially those involved with rapping, and they began to imitate 'Taki 183', as a

means to indicate the writer's presence, i.e. the age old statement of *I was here*. Graffiti was soon incorporated into the Hip Hop culture and became a sort of triad with rapping and breakdancing. Breakdancing has since lost much of its initial popularity, while rapping has emerged as a major style in American music. New York City was inundated with graffiti during the late seventies and early eighties, but as media coverage faded so did the graffiti. Then, in the mid-eighties a national TV programme did a graffiti story and set off a graffiti wildfire which has since gone global.

C

In the past, graffiti artists usually worked alone, but the size and complexity of pieces as well as safety concerns motivated artists to work together in crews, which are groups of graffitists that vary in membership from 3 to 10 or more persons. A member of a crew can be down with (affiliated with) more than one crew. To join a crew, one must have produced stylish pieces and show potential for developing one's own, unique style. A crew is headed by a king or queen who is usually that person recognised as having the best artistic ability among the members of the crew. One early crew wrote TAG as their crew name, an acronym for Tuff Artists Group. Tag has since come to mean both graffiti writing, 'tagging' and graffiti, a 'tag'. Crews often tag together, writing both the crew tag and their own personal tags. Graffiti has its own language with terms such as: piece, toy, wild-style, and racking.

D

At first pens and markers were used, but these were limited as to what types of surfaces they worked on, so very quickly everyone started using spray paint. Spray paint could mark all types of surfaces and was quick and easy to use. However, the spray nozzles on the spray cans proved inadequate to create the more colourful pieces. Caps from deodorant, insecticide, and other aerosol cans were substituted to allow for a finer or thicker stream of paint. As municipalities began passing graffiti ordinances outlawing graffiti implements, clever ways of disguising paint implements were devised. Shoe polish, deodorant roll-ons and other seemingly innocent containers were emptied and filled with paint. Markers, art pens and grease pens obtained from art supply stores were also used. In fact, nearly any object which can leave a mark on most surfaces is used by taggers, though the spray can is the medium of choice for most taggers.

E

As graffiti has grown, so too has its character. What began as an urban lower-income protest, graffiti now spans all racial and economic groups. While many inner-city kids are still heavily involved in the graffiti culture, taggers range from the ultra-rich to the ultra-poor. There is no general classification of graffitists. They range in age from 12-30 years old, and there are male and female artists. One tagger recently caught in Philadelphia was a 27-year-old stockbroker who drove to tagging sites in his BMW. Styles have dramatically evolved from the simple cursory style, which is still the most prevalent, to intricate interlocking letter graphic designs with multiple colours called 'pieces' (from masterpieces). Gang markings of territory also fit the definition of graffiti, and they mainly consist of tags and messages that provide 'news' of happenings in the neighbourhood.

F

Graffiti shops, both retail and on-line, sell a wide variety of items to taggers. Caps, markers, magazines, T-shirts, backpacks, shorts with hidden pockets, even drawing books with templates of different railroad cars can be purchased. Over 25,000 graffiti sites exist on the world wide web; the majority of these are pro-graffiti. Graffiti vandalism is a problem in nearly every urban area in the world. Pro-graffiti web sites post photos of graffiti from Europe, South America, the Philippines, Australia, South Africa, China and Japan. Billions of dollars worldwide are spent each year in an effort to curb graffiti.

G

While most taggers are simply interested in seeing their name in as many places as possible and as visibly as possible, some taggers are more content to find secluded warehouse walls where they can practise their pieces. Some of these taggers are able to sell twelve-foot canvases of their work for upwards of $10 - $12,000. As graffiti was introduced to the art world, two trends happened. One, the art world of collectors, dealers, curators, artists and the like helped graffitists evolve in style, presumably by sharing their artistic knowledge with the newcomers. Two, the exposure helped to expand graffiti into all parts of the world. Furthermore, more progressive cities have recognised the talent of graffitists by providing a means for them to do legal graffiti art which has helped to foster the art form and lessen the amount of graffiti art that appears in the city as vandalism. Likewise, organisations who support graffiti artists seek out places to do legal graffiti such as abandoned buildings, businesses, or community walls in parks. What this shows is that some graffiti, particularly in the form of spraycan art, is recognised as art by the conventional art world.

Reading

Questions 1 - 7

Reading Passage 1 has seven paragraphs, **A - G.**

Choose the correct heading for each paragraph from the list of headings below.

*Write the correct number **i - x** in spaces 1 - 7 below.*

i	Becoming mainstream art		
ii	The Culture Of Graffiti	**1** Paragraph A	x
iii	Tools Of The Trade	**2** Paragraph B	viii
iv	Internet Art Styles	**3** Paragraph C	ii
v	Crossing Boundaries	**4** Paragraph D	iii
vi	Cashing In On The Craze	**5** Paragraph E	v
vii	Trends In Street Music	**6** Paragraph F	vi
viii	Gradually gaining popularity	**7** Paragraph G	i
ix	A Solitary Existence		
x	From Ancient To Modern		

Reading Passage 1
Justification of the Answers

1. A is **x** as the paragraph describes the ancient origins of the term graffiti and then moves on to discuss the modern use of the term.

2. B is **viii** because the paragraph discusses another graffiti artist who is considered to have revolutionised the art form.

3. C is **ii** as the paragraph details the lifestyle, values and traditions of the graffiti artists.

4. D is **iii** because it discusses the equipment that is used by graffiti artists; the tools of their trade.

5. E is **v** because it describes how graffiti is no longer restricted to the lower classes, but has transcended class and race boundaries.

6. F is **vi** because it highlights how many shops have exploited the graffiti industry for commercial gain.

7. G is **i** because this paragraph discusses how graffiti is now acknowledged as a valid art form.

8. NOT GIVEN as the article mentions the laws, but not how effective they were.

9. TRUE - Paragraph **A** states 'as hip hop music emerged so did a new outlet for artistic visibility'

10. FALSE - not hostility, it just wasn't recognised as high art at first.

11. F as 'what began as an urban, lower-income protest, graffiti now spans all racial and economic groups'.

12. C - this is stated in paragraph **E.**

13. E 'shoe polish, deodorant roll-ons and other seemingly innocent containers were emptied and filled with paint.'

Questions 8 - 10

Do the following statements agree with the information given in Reading Passage 1?

In spaces 8 - 10 below, write

TRUE	*if the statement agrees with the writer's claims*
FALSE	*if the statement contradicts the writer's claims*
NOT GIVEN	*if it is impossible to say what the writer thinks about this*

8   The introduction of anti-graffiti laws managed to curb its spread in some cities.   .....**NOT GIVEN**.....

9   Along with Hip Hop music came a new way of visual expression.   .....**TRUE**.....

10   There was hostility towards graffiti artists among the established art community.   .....**FALSE**.....

Questions 11 - 13

Complete each sentence with the correct ending **A - F** below.

Write the correct letter **A - F** in spaces 11 - 13 below.

11   Graffiti is flourishing in the 21st century as
     people from all backgrounds have begun to   .....**F**.....

12   As graffiti has developed, it has come to   .....**C**.....

13   Graffiti artists used many ingenious methods to   .....**E**.....

A	use it as a means of expression of rebellion against law enforcement.
B	become increasingly more difficult to succeed in the art world.
C	transcend race, status and gender.
D	realise that inner-urban areas where poverty is the norm are decreasing.
E	conceal their intentions from law enforcement officers.
F	embrace it as a means of expression.

Reading

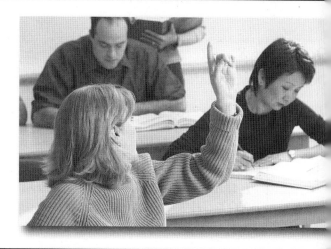

READING PASSAGE 2

You should spend about 20 minutes on
Questions 14 - 26, which are based on
Reading Passage 2 below.

DISTANCE LEARNING

A   Distance learning is not a recent innovation in education, correspondence courses having been used for over 150 years, but new interactive technologies are providing new opportunities and strategies for teaching at a distance. Several studies have compared face-to-face classrooms to distance classrooms in order to evaluate differences in student performance and quality of instruction. A meta-analysis of these studies showed that distance-learning students performed equally well and some distance courses outperformed their classroom counterparts.

This result has been consistent over many studies across many disciplines; advances in communication technology and innovative methods of delivery of instruction at a distance have challenged the idea that laboratory courses can only be delivered in a face-to-face laboratory setting. In engineering, for example, virtual laboratories have been used to teach thermodynamics, electronic circuits, and other experimental courses as well. Programmes in nursing, engineering, technology and other sciences are beginning to use different technologies and innovative methods to deliver courses via distance-learning methodology in order to reach students in different locations and boost enrolment. A survey of online distance-learning programmes revealed a large increase in student enrolment. The availability of distance courses has made it possible for some people to attend college because courses are accessible within their locality or the time of course delivery is convenient for them.

This opportunity for learning has not been without its critics who keep a close eye on the quality of instruction, and rightly so as with any form of instructional delivery. Quality issues are a major concern for those who intend to pursue degree programmes via distance learning, especially with the proliferation of distance learning programmes. Although it is difficult for academics to agree on specific standards that constitute quality in distance learning, nonetheless, attributes such as accreditation standards for programmes, evaluating students' experiences, teacher-student interaction, student-to-student interaction, learning resources for the learner, learner assessment and performance, instructional resources for faculty, faculty training, and learner satisfaction are valid criteria. These and many other factors can determine the quality of delivery of instruction in both distance and face-to-face classrooms.

B   ***Distance Learning Technologies and Innovation in Laboratory Course Delivery***
In a selected UK university, five departments that offered laboratory courses in Technology and Engineering via distance learning used combinations of a variety of instructional technologies. The technologies most used were Interactive Microwave TV, (two-way audio and video), compressed video, Internet, CDs, computer software (virtual software), and video tapes. At the selected university in the UK, interviews were conducted on-site with faculty and staff. A wide range of teaching materials, student portfolios, and a secure website were observed. In addition to the Internet, CDs, and video, the university used the following innovative ways to deliver laboratory courses.

Residential and Summer Schools

Residential and summer schools serve a similar purpose; the difference is the duration.

The summer school is one week long and combines labs, lectures, and problem sessions.

In general, these schools provide four key features, providing the opportunity for students to:

1. undertake experimental work considered too hazardous for a student working at home.
2. undertake lab work using more sophisticated equipment, or equipment too expensive to provide at home.
3. undertake assessed lab-work.
4. work together with fellow students.

Some courses even arranged to take students on a study trip, perhaps to a company with special processes, or to a geographic site of interest.

C   Demonstration Laboratory

The demonstration laboratory introduces students to the work they are going to undertake, illustrating how to proceed, how to make particular types of measurements, etc. It also covers topics considered too dangerous for students or situations in which the equipment is not available at the residential school. Many of these demonstrations are recorded on video to control both the process taught and the quality of the teaching across numerous groups of students at different levels.

D   Support Services Provided to Faculty and Students Engaged in Distance Learning

All the departments that offer distance learning courses offer support services to students and faculty. The support services include e-mail systems, graduate assistants, course websites, proctors, telephone conferencing, electronic library materials, and instructional designers to work with faculty to design and develop courses. At the selected university in the UK, interviews with instructional designers and faculty revealed the significant role played by instructional designers. Although they are not the content experts, they advise faculty, for example, on how information is presented on a website or the format in which the

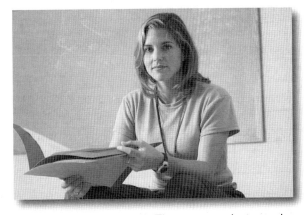

information is presented. The purpose is to maintain a standard format and quality in print materials, including electronic resources. The selected university in the UK also provides a support service to faculty that is unique from other institutions in this study: staff tutors who are regionally based to provide the link between the university faculty and students within the regions. The staff tutors have a key role in quality assurance, especially in facilitating effective teaching of the university faculty's courses, and are responsible for the selection, monitoring, and development of part-time Associate Lecturers. They contribute to faculty research and the development and presentation of courses. The staff tutors are highly qualified in their fields, and as such, bridge the distance gap between the university faculty and students at different locations.

E
The UK university, by using innovative strategies such as the Residential and Summer Schools, Field Trips and Demonstration Laboratories in combination with other technologies, is able to teach all its laboratory courses via distance learning to its nearly 200,000 students within and outside the UK. Distance learning is not meant to replace a face-to-face classroom, but it is one major way to make education more accessible to society. As advances in communication and digital technology continue, residential or demonstration labs may someday be replaced with comparable experiences provided through distance education.

Reading

Reading Tip:
Practise distinguishing supporting
details from the main idea.

Questions 14 - 18

Reading Passage 2 has five sections **A - E**.

Which section contains the following information?

*Write the correct letter **A - E** in spaces 14 - 18 below.*
NB Some sections may be used more than once.

14   One aspect of the course is that students can gain first-hand experience
     in a working environment and on educational excursions.   ....**B**........

15   Where the instruction takes place is not
     a critical factor in students' achievements.   ....**A**........

16   This method of instruction is not designed to
     replace traditional teaching techniques.   ....**E**........

17   In the future, the use of technology may mean students
     will not have to attend practical instruction sessions.   ....**E**........

18   Attending laboratory courses allows students to benefit from the
     use of expensive equipment not otherwise available to them.   ....**B**........

Reading Passage 2
Justification of the Answers

14. B the paragraph details many different teaching methods and locations including study trips.

15. A the paragraph details how distance learning courses are just as successful as those courses taught on-site.

16. E 'distance learning is not meant to replace a face-to-face classroom, but is one major way to make education more accessible to society'.

17. E 'as advantages in communication and digital technology continue, residential or demonstration labs may someday be replaced with comparable experiences provided through distance education'.

18. B as students can 'undertake lab work using more sophisticated equipment, or equipment too expensive to provide at home.

19. B as students 'undertake assessed lab work' at residential or summer schools.

20. D 'they advise the faculty, for example, on how information is presented on a website or the format in which the information is presented'.

21. C as 'staff tutors are responsible for the selection, monitoring and development of part-time Associate Lecturers.'

22. C because the paragraph mentions 'Quality issues are a major concern for those who intend to pursue degree programmes via distance learning, especially with the proliferation of distance learning programmes. '

23. NOT GIVEN as the text makes no reference to this although paragraph A does say that Universities try to overcome this lack of interaction.

24. YES - 'residential and summer schools serve a similar purpose; the difference is the duration'.

25. NO. The article devotes a whole paragraph (C) to describing demonstration lessons.

26. NOT GIVEN - paragraph D states that instructional designers play a 'significant role' , however salaries are not mentioned.

Questions 19 - 22

Choose the correct letter A, B, C or D.

19 One purpose of the summer school is to

    A encourage students to work individually.
    B enable students to be assessed directly.
    C allow students to undertake simple experiments.
    D familiarise students with laboratory equipment.

20 Instructional designers advise faculty on the

    A course content.
    B support services for students.
    C suitability of library material.
    D visual display of coursework.

21 Staff tutors are responsible for the

    A monitoring of students' progress.
    B suitability of courses for students' needs.
    C appointment of certain teaching staff.
    D training of all teaching staff.

22 With the increasing number of distance-learning courses,

    A it has been difficult to find suitable tutors.
    B problems arise with the timing of course delivery.
    C the standard of teaching has become an issue.
    D student-to-teacher interaction is no longer relevant.

Questions 23 - 26

Do the following statements agree with the information given in Reading Passage 2?

In spaces 23 - 26 below, write

YES	*if the statement agrees with the writer's claims*
NO	*if the statement contradicts the writer's claims*
NOT GIVEN	*if it is impossible to say what the writer thinks about this*

23	Many students may find the lack of student-to-student interaction a disadvantage to this method of study.	NOT GIVEN
24	The main difference between residential and summer courses is the length of the courses they offer.	YES
25	At the UK university, difficulties exist where the teaching of science subjects involves laboratory experiments.	NO
26	Instructional designers receive very high salaries.	NOT GIVEN

Reading

READING PASSAGE 3

*You should spend about 20 minutes on **Questions 27 - 40**, which are based on Reading Passage 3 below.*

LATCHKEY CHILDREN

Latchkey child was a term coined to describe children who wore or carried house keys to school so that they could let themselves into their home when they returned from school. The term came into use during the Second World War, when fathers had gone off to war, and mothers had gone into industry, making the tanks, planes, uniforms and bullets the soldiers needed. The children went home with keys on chains, ribbons or a piece of string tied around their necks. Some mothers chose to work the night shift, called the "swing shift", and tucked their children into bed, locked the door and went to the factory. The country's response was prompt and comprehensive. Programmes were set up in factories, in schools and community centres, to gather in all the children whose parents were busy with the war effort. These programmes closed promptly when the war ended, and women resumed their roles as housewives. More than sixty years on, there are large numbers of working mothers, but unlike in wartime, the country isn't organised to care for their children.

Sadly, finding young children at home without adult supervision has become much too commonplace. Latchkey children were once found only among the lower classes, but the situation has gradually spread to the middle and upper classes. The same is true of adolescent violence. In the past, shootings and stabbings were associated primarily with inner city, or poverty stricken areas permeated with abusive families and neglectful schools. However, in recent times, the "teen violence" epidemic has penetrated society at every economic level. An increase in the number of working mothers, as well as single-parent families, combined with a decrease in extended families that once helped with childcare, has contributed to the growing ranks of latchkey kids.

According to one census, one third of all school-age children in the United States are, for some part of the week, latchkey kids, that is, they go home to an empty house or apartment. The total number may be between five and seven million children between five and thirteen years old. Marian Wright Edelman, the director of the Children's Defense Fund, thinks it's close to 16 million children. The Census Bureau found that 15% were home alone before school, 76% after school and 9% at night. Presumably, the 9% have parents who work night shifts.

One-half of all children in the country aged 12 to 14 are home alone for an average of seven hours a week. The very poor in America are less likely to leave their children alone at home, or allow them to go home alone, than families who earn twice their level of income. This is probably because the very poor live in less safe neighbourhoods, and have fewer friends or family who can step in, in case of emergency. In spite of the hours spent on the job, working mothers spend an average of five-and-a-half hours a day with their children.

When latchkey children are functioning well, we don't hear about them. But we do hear about the one-third of all complaints to child welfare agencies which involve latchkey children. We know about the 51% who are doing poorly in school. Most teachers believe that being alone at home is the number one cause of school failure. The afternoon hours are the peak time for juvenile crime. In the last 11 years, juvenile crime has increased 48%. The Carnegie Council on Adolescent Development found that 8th graders who are alone 11 hours a week are twice as likely to abuse drugs as adolescents who are busy after school.

Unsupervised children are more likely to become depressed, smoke cigarettes and marijuana and drink alcohol. They are also more likely to be the victims of crimes. When home alone, latchkey children generally watch television, eat snacks, play with pets and fight with siblings.

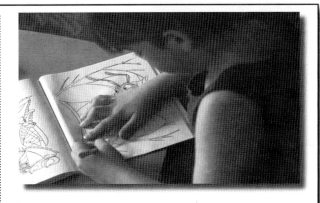

Adolescents who fall under the classification of latchkey children are more likely than others of the same age group to experience feelings of rage and isolation and to express those emotions in a physically aggressive manner. While there are certainly genetic and biological factors involved in the development of an adolescent's propensity towards acting out their feelings of rage and isolation, environment also plays a key role in this arena. Sociologists have found that many latchkey children, because they are frequently raised in dysfunctional families, are taught by example to be manipulative, secretive and unpredictable. They often instinctively develop a sense of timing and management of their emotions. These are skills that can be easily and directly used to portray a false picture of themselves and their living situation.

Making the decision: When is a child ready to be home alone? Personality characteristics, skills, and maturity are useful criteria for determining a child's readiness to be home alone. Personality doesn't generally change much with age, although children can learn to modify some of their reactions as they learn what is expected of them. There are some children who find it very difficult to be alone, some who need time and gradual exposure to become accustomed to being by themselves, and some who adapt easily.

The personality characteristics of the child who is ready to be home alone is a child who
– is not fearful, feels at ease in the world and is self-confident
– is calm, and is not excitable when something unexpected happens
– is outgoing and talks about his or her feelings and thoughts readily with parents and others
– admits wrongdoing, even when expecting disapproval
– has courage enough to resist pressure from friends and others.

In many communities there are activities for school-age children whose parents work and cannot be at home in the afternoon. The importance of looking into these is stressed by child development professionals. According to James Comer of Yale University, "the period between 10 and 15 years is a time when young people re-examine their attitudes and values. They are being pressured by peers. They need to be protected by responsible adults who will help them examine and counter some of these attitudes."

The activities available vary as does the cost. Some are more popular with children than others, and some are more rewarding, but all are preferable to sitting at home in front of the television. These programmes can vary in cost or are free, depending upon the particular activity and the age of the child. All of them offer the opportunity to acquire skills and knowledge that are useful throughout life. Children who are not learning anything for hours every week are at a distinct disadvantage compared to children who are engaged in enriching activities. In the words of T. Berry Brazelton, of Harvard University: "During these all important bridge years between childhood and adulthood, kids really do need something constructive to do, and they also still need to have their activities supervised. Most of all, they need to know that their parents care about them, are involved in their lives, and have their best interests at heart."

Practice Test 6

Reading

Questions 27 - 29

Choose **THREE** letters **A - H**.

NB Your answers may be given in any order.

Which **THREE** of the following statements are mentioned in the text?

Ⓐ   Youth crime is no longer attributable to economic background.

B   The greatest cause for concern is the children whose parents work the night shift.

C   Latchkey children whose parents have alcohol-abuse problems are more likely to drink alcohol when unsupervised at home.

D   The safer the neighbourhood, the lower the crime rate amongst adolescents.

E   Because of financial considerations, children from middle-class or upper-class backgrounds have more access to community activities.

Ⓕ   Latchkey children are not only drawn to crime; they are victims of crime, too.

G   Expense should not be a factor in allowing children to get involved in out-of-school activities.

Ⓗ   Knowing how to say no to one's peers is a sign of an adolescent's maturity.

Questions 30 - 31

Choose the correct letter **A, B, C** or **D**.

30   The writer says that during the war,

    Ⓐ   children whose parents were absent from the home were better looked after than present-day children in the same situation are.

    B   the country was slow to react to the problem of latchkey children.

    C   the role of the housewife changed forever.

    D   all wives whose husbands had gone off to fight were expected to work in industry.

31   According to the Census Bureau, most children were left alone

    A   at night.

    B   in the morning.

    Ⓒ   in the afternoon.

    D   all day.

Questions 32 - 35

Do the following statements agree with the information given in Reading Passage 3?

In spaces 32 - 35 below, write

TRUE	*if the statement agrees with the information*
FALSE	*if the statement contradicts the information*
NOT GIVEN	*if there is no information on this*

32	Latchkey children can be experts at hiding the truth about their situation.	TRUE
33	Latchkey children leave home at a very early age.	NOT GIVEN
34	Latchkey children's aggressive emotional responses are due principally to their biological make-up.	FALSE
35	Good communication skills are a measure of a child's ability to be left unsupervised.	TRUE

Reading Passage 3
Justification of the Answers

36. Paragraph 1 - '... when fathers had gone off to war, and mothers had gone into **industry**'
37. Paragraph 1 - 'The country's **response** was prompt and comprehensive.'
38. Paragraph 2 - 'Sadly, finding young children at home without **adult supervision** has become much too commonplace.'
39. Paragraph 7 - 'Adolescents who fall under the classification of latchkey children are more likely than others of the same age group to experience feelings of rage and isolation and to express those emotions in a **physically aggressive** manner.'
40. Paragraph 8 - '**Personality** characteristics, skills, and maturity are useful criteria for determining a child's readiness to be home alone.'

Questions 36 - 40

Complete the summary.

*Choose **NO MORE THAN TWO WORDS** from the passage for each answer.*

The Second World War gave rise to the phenomenon of the latchkey child, as mothers had to abandon their traditional duties and fill the places of men in 36 ....**industry**.... . Fortunately, there was a quick 37 ....**response**.......... to this by the authorities to help mothers so that their children would not be left at home unsupervised. However, now, so many years after the war, this type of support has disappeared and the problem of having children alone at home without 38 ......**adult supervision**.......... is very common . These children generally perform poorly at school, display 39 ......**(physically) aggressive**...... behaviour and may take up smoking and drinking alcohol. While 40 ....**personality**.......... and level of maturity plays a part in how a child copes with being a latchkey child, experts say that the remedy for this situation is more parental involvement and interest in their children's lives.

Writing

Writing Tip:
Do **NOT** write either Writing Task in note form or using bullet points.

WRITING TASK 1

You should spend about 20 minutes on this task.

The chart below shows the payment methods used most often by US consumers over a four-year period.

Summarise the information by selecting and reporting the main features, and make comparisons where relevant.

Write at least 150 words.

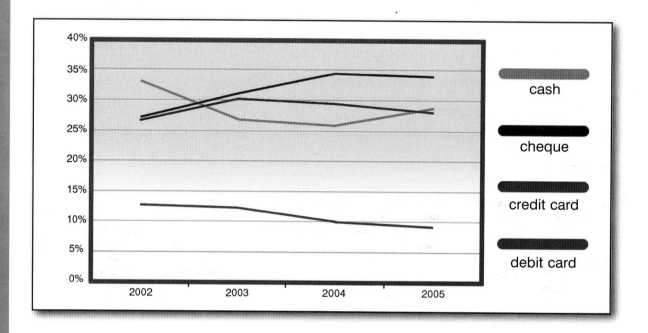

WRITING TASK 2

You should spend about 40 minutes on this task.

Write about the following topic:

We live in a world in which we are constantly exposed to advertising. To what extent does advertising influence our choices as consumers, and what effect does it have on our lifestyles?

Discuss this issue and give your opinion.

Give reasons for your answers and include any relevant examples from your own knowledge or experience.

Write at least 250 words.

Speaking

> **Speaking Tip:**
> Avoid asking the examiner if you are correct.

PART 1   (4-5 minutes)

The examiner asks the candidate about him/herself, his/her home, work or studies and other familiar topics.

Holidays
- What is your definition of the perfect holiday?
- What do you do to prepare for a holiday?
- Which areas of your country do you find the most appealing?
- What do tourists like to do when they come to visit your country?

PART 2   (2 minutes)

You will have to talk about the topic for one to two minutes. You have one minute to think about what you are going to say. You can make some notes to help you if you wish.

> **Describe a country that you would enjoy visiting.**
>
> **You should say:**
> - **where the country is**
> - **what the country is known for**
> - **which famous landmarks or tourist sites are associated with it**
> - **why you would enjoy visiting it**

PART 3   (4-5 minutes)

Discussion topics:

Tourism
- What do young people in your country like to do when they go on holiday?
- What do you think are the benefits of young people visiting foreign countries?
- Has tourism had a significant effect on your country?

Environmental impact of tourism
- How can tourism affect the environment?
- Do you think ecotourism is something we should take more seriously?
- What is your opinion of space tourism?

Test 7

Listening

Listening - Section 1
James: .... **(1)** <u>makes your total tour discount</u>, hmmmmm, fifty plus fifteen, sixty-five percent.
Jonathon: I see, and **(2)** <u>would Madrid be on that list by any</u> chance?
Check the **Audioscript** in the **Self-Study Guide** for the **Justification of the Answers for ALL the Sections of the Listening Test**

SECTION 1   Questions 1 - 10

Questions 1 - 3

Choose the correct letter A, B or C.

Example: When does the special offer finish?
  A   late March
  B   early April
  (C)   at the end of May

1   What total discount is Jonathon's school being offered?
  A   25%
  B   50%
  (C)   65%

2   Where did Jonathon first want to take his students?
  (A)   Madrid
  B   Barcelona
  C   Sainsbury

3   What is the normal price of this tour?
  A   £679
  B   £1261
  (C)   £1940

Questions 4 - 10

Complete the notes below.

*Write **NO MORE THAN THREE WORDS** for each answer.*

Mcfadden's Travel

Two main things the all-inclusive price covers:

4 ....**flights**...

5 ....**(hotel) accommodation**...

Extras also covered by the all-inclusive offer:

airport taxis, **6** ..**breakfast (every morning)**...

a city tour, **7** ..**theatre tickets**..

CLIENT DETAILS:

E-mail address of contact person: **8** ....**jonathon.presley**....... @ ....**sainsbury**...........com

Number of travellers: **49**

Date of travel: **7th of April**

Departure time: **7:00 a.m.**

Arrival time: **10:30 a.m. (local time)**

Credit Card Number: **9**   **6676 6654 9743 1251**

Expiry Date: **01-Jan-2015**

Total cost of booking: **10** £..**31,234**...........................

SECTION 2   *Questions 11 - 20*

Questions 11 - 12

Choose the correct letter A, B or C.

11 What does the word 'formula' stand for?
   (A) the rules drivers must respect
   B the type of roads used for the races
   C the way they drive

12 When did the first championship race take place?
   A in 1920
   B in 1955
   (C) in 1950

Questions 13 - 20

Complete the table below.

Write **NO MORE THAN TWO WORDS AND/OR A NUMBER** *for each answer.*

Driver	First Title	Last Title	Notable Record/s	Interesting Fact
Juan Manuel Fangio	1951	13 __1957__	won 5 world championships, a record which remained for 14 __46__ years	was the first 15 __multiple championship__ winner
Ayrton Senna	1988	1991	won the most races ever at the 16 __Monaco__ Grand Prix	is regarded as the most 17 __naturally__ __gifted__ driver ever
Alain Prost	1985	1993	won the third 18 __highest__ number of championships	was a 19 __great__ __rival__ of Senna
Michael Schumacher	1994	2004	holds many records including most drivers' championships, pole positions, race victories and fastest laps	is the 20 __greatest__ __driver__ on paper

Listening

SECTION 3   Questions 21 - 30

Questions 21 - 27

Complete the table below.

*Write **NO MORE THAN THREE WORDS AND/OR A NUMBER** for each answer.*

Bizz-Educators Inc.	
Upsides	**Downsides**
has a proven track record	wants to remain an independent entity, so this would be a hostile 25 ...takeover (bid)...
is an industry 21 ...leader...	is a production-based company
is well-respected and has a great name	is a 26 ...high risk... venture
has generated a lot of goodwill	is in a different market so there will be no synergy, and no cost savings
consistently has an annual gross profit of 22 ...£500,000...	
has a clear and ambitious 23 ...strategy...	
has very high 24 ...projected profits... for 2012 and 2013	
The official decision on whether to buy Bizz-Educators will be taken at tomorrow's 27 ...board meeting...	

Questions 28 - 30

*Choose **THREE** letters, A - G.*

What **THREE** requirements are there for the takeover of Bizz-Educators to go ahead?

(A)	Assurances that the management of Bizz-Educators won't oppose the deal.
(B)	An independent mediator be used to broker the deal.
C	An audit of the company's books.
D	That a study of the company's projected profit margin be conducted.
(E)	That the deal be kept secret until it is finalised.
F	That an analysis of the company's goodwill assets be carried out.
G	That the asking price be lowered.

SECTION 4   *Questions 31 - 40*

Complete the notes below.

*Write **NO MORE THAN TWO WORDS** for each answer.*

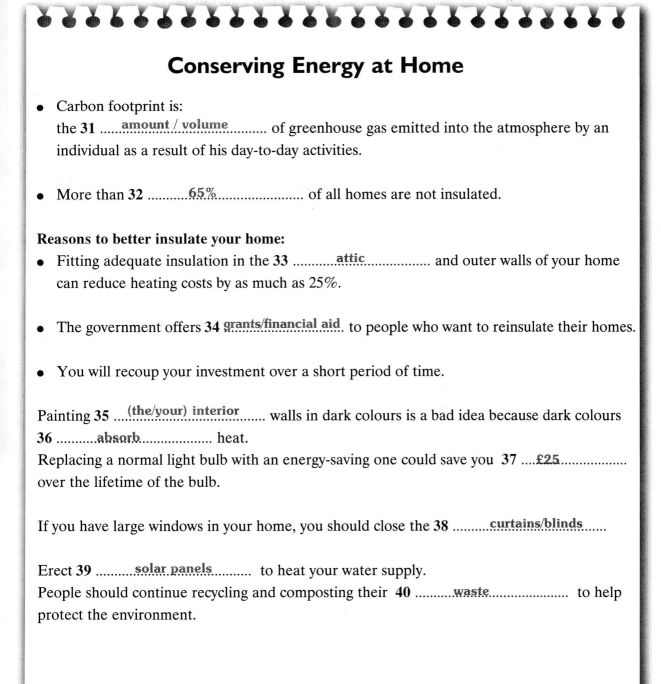

Conserving Energy at Home

- Carbon footprint is:
  the **31** ....amount / volume.......... of greenhouse gas emitted into the atmosphere by an
  individual as a result of his day-to-day activities.

- More than **32** ....65.%.................. of all homes are not insulated.

Reasons to better insulate your home:
- Fitting adequate insulation in the **33** ....attic.................. and outer walls of your home
  can reduce heating costs by as much as 25%.

- The government offers **34** grants/financial aid. to people who want to reinsulate their homes.

- You will recoup your investment over a short period of time.

Painting **35** ....(the/your) interior.......... walls in dark colours is a bad idea because dark colours
36 ....absorb.................. heat.
Replacing a normal light bulb with an energy-saving one could save you **37** ....£25..................
over the lifetime of the bulb.

If you have large windows in your home, you should close the **38** ....curtains/blinds.......

Erect **39** ....solar panels.......... to heat your water supply.
People should continue recycling and composting their **40** ....waste.................. to help
protect the environment.

Reading

READING PASSAGE 1

*You should spend about 20 minutes on **Questions 1 - 13**, which are based on Reading Passage 1 below.*

The Final Frontier for Tourism

A

For some reason humankind has always looked towards the stars and dreamt of one day making the voyage into the unknown and exploring outer space. Perhaps it is our innate curiosity, perhaps the challenge presented by the seemingly impossible; whatever the lure, the quest to venture into space has become an obsession for many.

B

On a memorable July day in 1969 one man made a giant leap for his kind. Neil Armstrong touched down on the moon as the world watched with bated breath. Was this a beginning or the culmination of years of endeavour that pushed science to its very limits? Well, it has been a long time indeed since the last moon landing, more than 40 years, but science has not stood still in the interim, nor have our dreams become any less ambitious. According to NASA, plans are afoot for a manned mission to Mars at some point after 2020. A return to the moon has been scheduled sooner - perhaps 2018 if NASA's new Crew Exploration Vehicle (CEV) is rolled out on time. It may not be Hollywood razzle-dazzle-style progress; it may even be painstakingly slow, but rest assured that plans are afoot for something very ambitious and special indeed, and NASA may be back in the headlines making waves and history again, just as it did on that faithful day in 1969, in the not-too-distant future.

C

That said, it is the prospect of space tourism for the masses that has captured the headlines recently, and this may not be such a distant dream as people would expect. In 2001, an American multimillionaire, Denis Tito, became the first space tourist, spending ten days on the International Space Station along with his crew of Russian cosmonauts, and fulfilling a lifelong ambition in the process. He described the experience rather paradoxically as 'indescribable'; everything that he thought it would be and more. A year later, South African millionaire Mark Shuttleworth followed in his footsteps. On his return to Earth he said, 'every second will be with me for the rest of my life'. Clearly these men had a once-in-a-lifetime experience, but this came at a hefty price, both paying $20 million for the pleasure of their space adventures.

D

At present, space tourism is undoubtedly reserved for an elite and wealthy few, but what of the future? If Eric Anderson, president of Space Adventures, the company that organised Tito and Shuttleworth's trips, is to be believed, it will be the next big thing. 'Everyone's looking for a new experience', he says. Indeed, Space Adventures is planning to offer rocket trips to the public for $100,000 within the next few years, so perhaps space tourism is closer than we think. Another company, The Space Island Group, is planning to build a space hotel inspired by the spaceship in the film *2001: A Space Odyssey*. Gene Meyers, the company's president, predicts that in 2020 a five-day holiday at the hotel will cost less than $25,000. Imagine, he says, a five-star hotel with all the usual luxuries, except that each morning you'll be greeted by mind-blowing views of outer space. This is certainly food for thought for adventure-seeking holiday planners. That said, unless there is a serious spike in inflation between now and 2020, $25,000 will still remain a considerable sum of money to have to part with for a recreational activity, once-in-a-lifetime or not. But that is perhaps missing the point – the prospect of affordable space travel is getting closer and closer and it is only a matter of time before it becomes a reality.

E

Other companies have even more ambitious plans. Bigelow Aerospace is spending close to $500 million on a project to build a 700-metre spaceship to fly tourists to the moon. The spaceship will be able to hold 100 guests, each with a private room offering truly unique views of the Earth's sunset. Even the Hilton Hotel Group wants to get in on the act with talk of plans to build a Hilton on the moon. For the present, only millionaires can enjoy the privilege of a space journey, but in the words of one Bob Dylan, 'The times they are a changing.' And sooner than you'd think.

Questions 1 - 5

Reading passage 1 has five paragraphs A - E.
Choose the correct heading for each paragraph A - E from the list of headings below.
Write the correct number i - viii in the spaces 1 - 5 below.

List of Headings

i   Not worth the cost

ii   Space travel; past, present and future

iii   Russian innovations

iv   A profitable investment

v   The future of tourism

vi   Insatiable desire for adventure

vii   The first space tourists

viii   Moon hotels

1	vi
2	ii
3	vii
4	v
5	viii

1 Paragraph **A**
2 Paragraph **B**
3 Paragraph **C**
4 Paragraph **D**
5 Paragraph **E**

Questions 6 - 9

Look at the following people (Questions 6 - 9) and the list of statements below.
Match each person with the correct statement, A - D.
Write the correct letter, A - D, in spaces 6 - 9.

6 Denis Tito — **C**

7 Mark Shuttleworth — **D**

8 Eric Anderson — **B**

9 Gene Meyers — **E**

A touched down on the moon in 1969

B believes space tourism will be popular in the near future

C spent ten days on the International Space Station

D was the second tourist to travel into space

E predicts space holidays will be more affordable by 2020

F will build a hotel inspired by a film

Questions 10 - 13

Do the following statements agree with the information given in Reading Passage 1?

In spaces 10 - 13 below, write:

TRUE	*if the statement agrees with the information*
FALSE	*if the statement contradicts the information*
NOT GIVEN	*if there is no information on this*

10 Bigelow Aerospace's spaceship will offer unique views of the Moon's sunset. ....**FALSE**............

11 The Hilton Hotel Group has ambitious plans to organise cheap space journeys. ....**NOT GIVEN**............

12 NASA plans to launch a mission to Mars, but first it is hoping to return to the moon. ....**TRUE**............

13 At the moment, space tourism is too expensive for ordinary people, only the very rich can travel to space. ....**TRUE**............

JUSTIFICATIONS OF THE ANSWERS

Reading Passage 1

1. vi. "humankind has always looked towards the stars and dreamt of one day making the voyage into the unknown and exploring outer space".

2. ii. "it has been a long time since the last moon landing, almost 40 years ..... According to NASA, plans are afoot for a manned mission to Mars at some point after 2020".

3. vii. "Denis Tito, became the first space tourist ... A year later, South African millionaire Mark Shuttleworth followed in his footsteps".

4. v. "At present, space tourism is undoubtedly reserved for an elite and wealthy few, but what of the future".

5. viii. "Even the Hilton group wants to get in on the act with talk of plans to build a Hilton on the moon".

6. C. Paragraph C. "Denis Tito, became the first space tourist, spending ten days on the International Space Station".

7. D. Paragraph C. "Mark Shuttleworth followed in his (Denis Tito's) footsteps".

8. B. Paragraph D. "If Eric Anderson, president of Space Adventures, the company that organised Tito and Shuttleworth's trips, is to be believed, it will be the next big thing".

9. E. Paragraph D. "Gene Meyers, the company's president, predicts that in 2020 a five-day holiday at the hotel will cost less than $25,000".

10. F Paragraph E. "The spaceship will be able to hold 100 guests, each with a private room offering 'truly unique views' of the **Earth's** sunset".

11. NG Paragraph E. "plans to build a Hilton 'on the moon'.

12. T Paragraph B. "According to NASA, plans are afoot for a planned mission to Mars at some point after 2020. A return to the moon has been scheduled sooner"

13. T Paragraph D. "At present, space tourism is undoubtedly reserved for an elite and wealthy few".

Reading

READING PASSAGE 2

You should spend about 20 minutes on Questions 14 - 26, which are based on Reading Passage 2 below.

Arctic Survivors

The Arctic is an area located at the northern-most part of the Earth and includes the Arctic Ocean, Canada, Russia, Greenland, the United States, Norway, Sweden, Finland and Iceland. It consists of an ice-covered ocean, surrounded by treeless permafrost. The area can be defined as north of the Arctic Circle, the approximate limit of the midnight sun and the polar night. The average temperature in July, which is the warmest month, is below 10 °C. Colder summer temperatures cause the size, abundance, productivity and variety of plants to decrease. Trees cannot grow in the Arctic, but in its warmest parts, shrubs are common and can reach 2 metres in height.

A thick blanket of snow lies several feet deep all over the ground. The sun appears for only a few brief hours each day before sinking below the horizon as blackness cloaks the land. As it vanishes, a bitter chill tightens its grip. The Arctic is not a place to be in the throes of winter, it is hostile to almost all animal life. Amphibians would freeze solid here. Nor can reptiles withstand the extreme cold. And yet there are animals here, animals that exhibit a remarkable tolerance of the most inhospitable conditions on the planet. Less than half a metre beneath the surface of the snow, a furry white creature, no bigger than a hamster, scurries along a tunnel. It is a collared lemming. It and other members of its family have excavated a complex home within the snow field, but it costs the lemmings a great deal to survive here. They pay by using some of their precious and scarce food supply to generate heat within their bodies so that their biochemical processes can continue to function efficiently. But in order to keep fuel costs to a minimum, they must conserve as much energy as they can. A thick insulating coat of fine fur covering all but the lemmings' eyes achieves this. Fur is the life preserver of the Arctic.

Only one class of animals has fur - the mammals. Fur is comprised of dense layers of hair follicles. Hair is composed of a substance called keratin. It grows constantly, its roots embedded in the skin and surrounded by nerve fibres so that its owner can sense any movement of the hair. It is this precious fur that gives land mammals the edge necessary to survive the harsh Arctic winter. Without it, wolves, lemmings and arctic foxes alike would surely perish.

The insulation provided by fur comes not from the fur itself, but largely from the layer of air trapped within the fur. Air is an extremely effective insulator, which is the same as saying it is a poor conductor, i.e. it has a very limited ability to conduct heat away from a warm surface. Studies reveal that if a layer of air of about five centimetres could be held in place close to the skin, it would provide the same insulation as would the impressively dense winter coat of the arctic fox. If an arctic fox or wolf is exposed to an air temperature of about minus ten degrees, the temperature near the tips of the fur will match the air temperature, but at the surface of the skin it will be closer to thirty degrees. This represents a temperature difference of around forty degrees. Such effective insulation is only made possible by the layer of trapped air contained within the long, fine and densely packed fur.

But Arctic mammals have more in their arsenal than just fur to protect them from the elements. Unlike amphibians, reptiles and other classes of animals, they are endotherms, meaning they can generate their own body heat. This is another of the defining characteristics of mammals. It is the mammalian ability to generate heat

internally that enables the arctic fox or the lemming to remain warm and active in very cold conditions. Generating heat internally, arctic mammals can regulate their body temperature independent of external conditions; this is known as thermoregulation. When arctic mammals are cold, they raise their metabolic rate and produce more heat. When they are warm, the reverse happens. Together, thermoregulation and fur make arctic mammals perfectly equipped to face the toughest conditions the arctic can throw at them.

Reading

Questions 14 - 20

Choose the correct answer A, B, C or D.

14 Animals that live in the Arctic

    (A) can withstand extremely difficult living conditions.

    B often freeze solid during winter.

    C are mainly reptilian.

    D are mostly frogs or toads

15 Where do lemmings live?

    A on the surface of the snow

    B in tunnels built under the frozen ocean

    C in wide tunnels deep underground

    (D) about 50 cm below the surface of the snow

16 Fur is

    (A) thick layers of hair.

    B common to all animal classes.

    C unhelpful to Arctic animals.

    D the life preserver only for small Arctic mammals

17 Why is trapped air a good insulator?

    A It is a good conductor of heat.

    B Air helps us to breathe.

    (C) It is a bad conductor of heat.

    D It absorbs heat and cold very well

18 If the temperature at the tip of the fur of an arctic fox is minus ten degrees, the temperature at the surface of the skin will be closer to

    A forty degrees.

    B ten degrees.

    (C) thirty degrees.

    D thirty five degrees.

19 What is an endotherm?

    (A) an animal that can generate heat inside its body

    B an animal that cannot generate heat inside its body

    C an animal that never gets cold

    D an animal that has special insulation

20 Thermoregulation and fur help arctic mammals

    A cope with hot temperatures.

    (B) protect themselves from the elements.

    C regulate the temperature of their surroundings.

    D create a layer of trapped air within their fur

JUSTIFICATIONS OF THE ANSWERS
Reading Passage 2

14. A. Paragraph 2. "And yet there are animals here, animals that exhibit a remarkable tolerance of the most inhospitable conditions on the planet".

15. D. Paragraph 2. "Less than half a metre beneath the surface of the snow, a furry white creature scurries... along a tunnel. It is a collared lemming. It and other members of its family have excavated a complex home".

16. A. Paragraph 3. "Fur is comprised of dense layers of hair follicles"

17. C. Paragraph 4. "Air is an extremely effective insulator ...... i.e. it has very limited ability to conduct heat away from a warm surface".

18. C. Paragraph 4. "If an arctic fox or wolf is exposed to an air temperature of about minus ten degrees, the temperature near the 'tips of the fur' will match the air temperature, but at the surface of the skin it will be closer to thirty degrees".

19. A. Paragraph 5. "they are endotherms, meaning they can generate their own body heat".

20. B. Paragraph 5. "Together, thermoregulation and fur make arctic mammals perfectly equipped to face the toughest conditions the arctic can throw at them".

Questions 21 - 26

Complete the summary below.

*Choose **ONE WORD ONLY** from the passage for each answer.*

The Arctic winter is something few animals can survive, but there are a select few that show an amazing **21** ......**tolerance**...... of the severe winter conditions. These animals have to use their food resources to keep their body temperature high so that the biochemical **22** ...**processes**...... inside them continue to run. One thing that helps them keep their bodies warm is their **23** ....**fur**............ which consists of thick layers of hair that provide insulation to their bodies; it is their life **24** ....**preserver**........ . The layer of trapped air that they also have provides very effective insulation from cold because it is not a good **25** ...**conductor**...... of heat. In the case of an arctic mammal getting cold, it deals with it by increasing its **26** ....**metabolic**......... rate to generate more heat.

JUSTIFICATIONS OF THE ANSWERS

Reading Passage 2

21. Paragraph 2 - 'Nor can reptiles withstand the extreme cold. And yet there are animals here, animals that exhibit a remarkable **tolerance** of the most inhospitable conditions on the planet.'

22. Paragraph 3 - 'They pay by using some of their precious and scarce food supply to generate heat within their bodies so that their **biochemical processes** can continue to function efficiently.'

23. Paragraph 3 - 'A thick insulating coat of fine **fur** covering all but the lemmings' eyes achieves this.'

24. 'Paragraph 3 - Fur is the **life preserver** of the Arctic.'

25. Paragraph 5 - 'Air is an extremely effective insulator, which is the same as saying it is a **poor conductor**, i.e. it has a very limited ability to conduct heat away from a warm surface.'

26. Paragraph 6 - 'When arctic mammals are cold, they raise their **metabolic rate** and produce more heat. When they are warm, the reverse happens.'

Reading

READING PASSAGE 3

*You should spend about 20 minutes on **Questions 27 - 40**, which are based on Reading Passage 3 below.*

Bismarck: A Master of Political and Diplomatic Juggling?

A

Otto Von Bismarck's rise up the political ladder was swift and relentless. Having entered parliament in 1847, he always harboured lofty ambitions, chief among them perhaps being the reunification of Germany into one strong, centrally controlled state, though his own personal thirst for power was arguably even stronger. On becoming Prussian Chancellor, he set about fulfilling his ambitions and in doing so proved himself to be a diplomat of some considerable skill. Victory in the Austro-Prussian war effectively ended Austria as a factor in German affairs. His political and military juggling was taken a step further when he orchestrated a situation where France declared war on Germany in 1870, making the French seem responsible for a conflict he had always intended to create. And following another swift military triumph, this time over the French, the German empire was proclaimed in January 1871.

B

In little more than nine years, Bismarck realised his lifelong ambition, steering Germany to reunification. And by defeating Austria and France in quick succession, he also created a power vacuum on mainland Europe which he was determined to fill himself. This was another opportunity for Bismarck to demonstrate his political and diplomatic cunning. He set about creating a dictatorial

Germany in which he, as head of the Prussian parliament, would automatically become chancellor of the German empire. He drafted a new German constitution to suit his own purposes and, despite maintaining a veneer of democracy, the German parliament was effectively powerless to oppose him. Provinces that were slow to support him were enticed with bribes and before long the German empire was his to command.

C

It is testament to his political skill that Bismarck achieved so much so quickly. At this point in his colourful political career he did appear, for all intents and purposes, a master of political and diplomatic juggling. But challenges lay ahead and Bismarck's next target was the Catholic church, which he deemed too powerful and a threat to his political dominance. He proceeded to enact a series of laws which seriously eroded the power of the church. However his plans backfired and Bismarck was forced to make a political U-turn. Though here again, he somehow managed to save face. The damage to his reputation was limited and indeed by the late 1870s he had even managed to win over the church whose support he now needed.

JUSTIFICATIONS OF THE ANSWERS
Reading Passage 3
27. **A.** Paragraph 2. "steering Germany to reunification. And by defeating Austria and France in quick succession...".
28. **A.** Paragraph 3. "Bismark was forced to make a political U-turn" but "even managed to win over the church whose support he now needed".
29. **C.** Paragraph 4. "despite his attempts to destroy the socialist movement, its popularity had trebled by 1890".
30. **B.** Paragraph 5. "Bismark now believed that his ambitions were best served by peace. His plan to isolate a hostile France...".
31. **D.** Paragraph 6. 'His political and diplomatic juggling, therefore, simply cannot be considered a total success.'
32. **True.** Paragraph 5. "Congress of Berlin which he hosted was an outstanding success".

33. **False.** Paragraph 5. "He built up strategic alliances with the big powers, Russia, Italy and Austria-Hungary".
34. **Not Given.** Bismark's opinion about his reign is not expressed in the passage.
35. **ii.** The paragraph describes his rise up the 'political ladder' until he became Prussian Chancellor.
36. **viii.** "despite maintaining a veneer of democracy, the German parliament was effectively powerless to oppose him".
37. **ix.** "Bismark was forced to make a political U-turn".
38. **vi.** "Bismark viewed the growing popularity of the Socialist Democratic Party as a serious threat".
39. **iii.** "after 1871, Bismark devoted a lot of his time to foreign policy".
40. **i.** The paragraph comments on his reign as chancellor and analyses his legacy in terms of his successes and failures.

D
Bismarck viewed the growing popularity of the Socialist Democratic Party as a serious threat. He bided his time and used the attempted assassination of the Kaiser as an excuse to attack the socialists in 1878, blaming them for the attempt on the Kaiser's life. He immediately arrested the leaders, banned party meetings and suppressed socialist newspapers. But despite his efforts to destroy the socialist movement, its popularity had trebled by 1890. Just as his interventions with the church had not gone as planned, Bismarck once again failed to achieve his objective; though, to his credit, he held on to power.

E
His domestic position was relatively secure after 1871 and Bismarck devoted a lot of his time to foreign policy. Having used war to unite Germany and make her great, Bismarck now believed that his ambitions were best served by peace. His plan to isolate a hostile France would require all his considerable diplomatic skills. The Dreikaiserbund agreement of 1873 between Germany, Austria-Hungary and Russia was a first step towards doing just that. The Balkan crisis, a conflict involving Russia and Austria-Hungary, severely tested his diplomatic credentials, but his answer was to offer himself as an 'honest broker' to help resolve the dispute. The subsequent Congress of Berlin which he hosted was an outstanding success and only served to

reinforce Bismarck's reputation as a shrewd diplomat. Bismarck's foreign policy would continue in this vein throughout his reign as Chancellor. He built up strategic alliances with the big powers, Russia, Italy and Austria-Hungary, in the hope that he could keep his main threats, France and Britain, isolated.

F
In truth, Bismarck's reign as chancellor of the German empire does seem to confirm him as a shrewd and wily diplomat and politician, one whose objectives were broadly achieved. Does this mean his so-called juggling was a success? Perhaps, but Bismarck left a less than perfect legacy. He created a Germany in which the Kaiser had the ultimate say in domestic affairs and enjoyed far too much power should he choose to yield it. This meant that the future of the empire largely depended on the strength and character of just one man, the Kaiser. A weak Kaiser would be disastrous for the country's welfare, and so it would soon prove. In the final analysis, Bismarck put Germany back on the map again as a great power during his reign, but we should not forget that he created the political situation that would be the downfall of his country in the end. His political and diplomatic juggling, therefore, simply cannot be considered a total success.

Reading

Practice Test 7

Questions 27 - 31

Choose the correct answer A, B, C or D.

Write the correct letter in the boxes 14-20 on your answer sheet.

27   In little more than nine years as Prussian Chancellor Bismarck had

    (A) succeeded in reuniting Germany and defeating Austria and France.

    B divided his country and lost two wars.

    C succeeded in suppressing the Socialist party.

    D abolished the parliament

28   What happened after Bismarck enacted laws to weaken the Catholic church?

    (A) He changed his policy and made the church an ally.

    B The church's influence weakened.

    C France declared war on Germany.

    D He didn't succeed and his influence was severely weakened.

29   What had happened to the Socialist party by 1890?

    A It had taken power from Bismarck.

    B It had lost its influence.

    (C) Its popularity had risen three-fold.

    D It became very powerful in the parliament.

30   After reuniting Germany what was Bismarck's belief on foreign policy?

    A He needed to wage war with all countries that posed a military threat.

    (B) Preserving the peace and isolating France would benefit him.

    C Germany needed to befriend France to form a powerful alliance.

    D He wanted to form an alliance with Britain and France.

31   The article concludes that Bismark

    A   made few mistakes and left a positive legacy.

    B   was not at all successful.

    C   was always tolerant of those who had different opinions.

    (D) was not actually a master of political juggling.

Questions 32 - 34

Do the following statements agree with the information given in Reading Passage 3?

In spaces 32 - 34 below, write

TRUE	*if the statement agrees with the information*
FALSE	*if the statement contradicts the information*
NOT GIVEN	*if there is no information on this*

32 The Congress of Berlin was a great personal success for Bismarck.   .....TRUE.....

33 Bismarck refused to build alliances with Russia or Austria.   .....FALSE.....

34 Bismarck considered his reign as German chancellor a failure.   .....NOT GIVEN.....

Questions 35 - 40

Reading passage 3 has six paragraphs, **A - F**.

Choose the correct heading, A - F, from the list of headings below.

Write the correct number, i - ix, in spaces 35 - 40 below.

35	Paragraph **A**	ii
36	Paragraph **B**	viii
37	Paragraph **C**	ix
38	Paragraph **D**	vi
39	Paragraph **E**	iii
40	Paragraph **F**	i

List of Headings

i	A critical analysis
ii	Early career and rise to power
iii	Foreign policy
iv	Powerful friends
v	Separating church and state
vi	Socialist threat
vii	Political decline
viii	Creating a virtual dictatorship
ix	A change of mind

Writing

WRITING TASK 1

You should spend about 20 minutes on this task.

The chart shows the end of year value for four major international money market indices in 2005, 2006, 2007 and 2008. [FTSE 100 = UK Market Index,   Dow Jones = US Market Index, KOSPI = Korean Market Index,   CAC 40 = French Market Index]

Summarise the information by selecting and reporting the main features, and make comparisons where relevant.

Write at least 150 words.

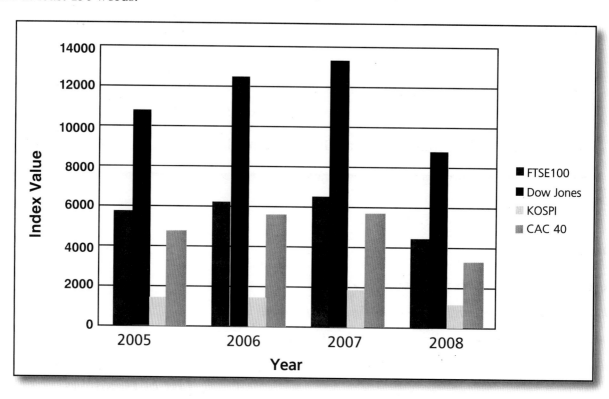

WRITING TASK 2

You should spend about 40 minutes on this task.

Write about the following topic:

Society is becoming obsessed with material goods like fast cars, designer clothes and flashy jewellery. We have stopped caring about the important things and that is why divorce rates are so high and family bonds are not as strong anymore; our value system is disintegrating.
To what extent do you agree or disagree?

Give reasons for your answer and include any relevant examples from your own knowledge or experience.

Write at least 250 words.

Speaking

PART 1   (4-5 minutes)

The examiner asks the candidate about him/herself, his/her home, work or studies and other familiar topics.

Living Arrangements
- Would you prefer to live in a traditional house or in a modern apartment building? Why?
- Can you tell me something about the area you live in?
- If you could make changes to your area or home town, what would you change?
- Would you prefer to live in a big city or in the countryside? Why?

PART 2   (2 minutes)

You will have to talk about the topic for one to two minutes. You have one minute to think about what you are going to say. You can make some notes to help you if you wish.

Describe an individual who you regard as a role model.
You should say:
- why you look up to him/her
- which of his/her characteristics you admire
and explain what, in your opinion, makes a good role model,
especially for young people today.

PART 3   (4-5 minutes)

Discussion topics:

Role Models
- Are parents ever role models? Why/Why not?
- Do you think today's celebrities are good role models?
- Should famous people think about how their actions might influence young people?

Celebrities
- Many people say there is one rule for celebrities and another for ordinary people.
  Do you believe this?
- Do celebrities have a right to their privacy or should they accept that their lives will always
  be played out in the public eye?
- Many people believe that celebrities and public figures like politicians make the worst role models.
  Do you agree?

Listening

SECTION 1   **Questions 1 - 10**

Questions 1 - 3

Choose the correct letter A, B or C.

> **Listening - Section 1**
> 1: The answer is B; three. 'for every three bottles of house red or white..... you will get a bottle free'
> 2: The answer is B; Italian. 'I think most of my friends will want to drink Italian wine.'
> Check the **Audioscript** in the **Self-Study Guide** for the **Justification of the Answers for ALL the Sections of the Listening Test**

Example: When is there a 50% discount on Lasagna?

    A On the weekends and on weekdays

    B On weekdays only

    (C) On weekends only

1   How many bottles of wine do you have to buy to get one free?

    A one

    (B) three

    C four

2   Which type of wine do David's friends prefer?

    A French

    (B) Italian

    C Spanish

3   What is the price of the champagne?

    (A) £20

    B £35

    C £25

Questions 4 - 10

Answer the questions below.

Write **NO MORE THAN THREE WORDS AND/OR A NUMBER** *for each answer.*

Belluci's Restaurant

Sam's suggestions
Would go best with the Lasagna:

4   **Mixed Salad**

5   **Greek Salad**

Other side dishes that Sam mentions:

6   **bread with herbs**

7   **cheese with peppers**

CUSTOMER DETAILS

Booking made on: *5th August*   Date when customers will be at the restaurant: **8** **27th August**

Time: *7:00 pm*   Number of people: **9** **15**

Email address: **10** **david.hamill** @ **worthing** .com

Customer phone number: *01445 333 6451*   Customer willing to have emails sent to them: *Yes*

SECTION 2   *Questions 11 - 20*

Questions 11 - 12

Choose the correct letter A, B or C.

11 How did the players hit the ball when the game first launched in the 12th century?

   A with a bat

   B with a racquet

   (C) with their bare hand

12 In the 16th century what kind of people found tennis most appealing?

   (A) royal families

   B wealthy merchants

   C everyday people

Questions 13 - 20

Complete the table below.

Write **NO MORE THAN THREE WORDS AND/OR A NUMBER** *for each answer.*

Tennis Player	Year Born	Nationality	Number of Major Titles Won	Interesting Fact
Bjorn Borg	**13** 1956	Swedish	**14** Eleven	won both Wimbledon and the French open in **15** the same year more than once
Boris Becker	1967	German	**16** Six	the youngest ever male Grand Slam singles champion at **17** 17 years 7 months.
Pete Sampras	1971	American	**18** Fourteen	He started hitting tennis balls at the age of 3
Andre Agassi	**19** 1970	American	Eight	His first **20** tournament was in La Quinta

Listening

SECTION 3   Questions 21 - 30

Questions 21 - 27

Complete the table below.

*Write **NO MORE THREE WORDS** for each answer.*

College Conference 2009	
Speakers	**Administration and Organisation**
Professor Harman - good at running 21 ...workshops... .	Invitations to all speakers have to be typed on the school's headed paper.
Mr Steve Bishop - 22 ...well-respected... among many Universities in England.	The photographer will take pictures for the school 25 ...newsletter... .
Sandra Bolton will give some Drama 23 ...seminars... .	The caterers are called 26 ...Flying Fish...
Mr Max Wallington will give a lecture about Shakespeare.	The conference will be in the main college hall and rooms 10, 11, 12 and 13.
Sean O'Brien has done a lot of work in the field of 24 ...genetics... .	The date of the next meeting will be on 27 ...Wednesday 6th June...
Geoff O'Hara has a lot of knowledge about Albert Einstein.	

Questions 28 - 30

*Choose **THREE** letters, A - G.*

What **THREE** rules, given to them by the headmaster, do the students have to follow during the conference?

28 ....   29 ....   30 ....

A   Make sure they tidy up the hall and rooms after the conference.
B   Provide cleaners for the conference.
C   Provide lunch for the speakers.
D   Make a record of what each student at the conference wants to study at University.
E   Make a record of what each student at the conference is studying now.
F   Make a record of all students who attend the conference.
G   Help organise the travel arrangements for the speakers.

SECTION 4   *Questions 31 - 40*

Questions 31 - 40

Complete the notes below.

Write **NO MORE THAN TWO WORDS** *for each answer.*

To calculate your Body Mass Index you should first take **31** ....your weight....... in kilograms and divide it by your height in metres.

Healthy Diets

- It is important to eat starchy foods with fruit and vegetables.

- There are people who **32** ...(wrongly) think....... that starchy foods are 'fattening'.
- Eat a minimum of **33** ......five portions....... of fruit and vegetables a day.
- People tend to eat too much **34** ....protein...... and you only need a certain amount to keep healthy.
- People say that **35** ....oily fish.............. can help protect against heart disease.

Exercise is good for us because:

1) it strengthens the heart

2) it tones our **36** ....muscles........................

3) it is good for the mind

- We do less exercise because we have domestic **37** ....appliances................ to do things for us.
- Adults should do at least **38** ....30 minutes................ moderate-intensity physical activity, five days a week.

A physical activity can be:

a) a lifestyle activity

b) a **39** ....structured........ activity

c) sports

Activities that produce **40** ......high physical stresses.... on the bones are necessary.

Reading

READING PASSAGE 1

*You should spend about 20 minutes on **Questions 1 - 14**, which are based on Reading Passage 1 below.*

A

The climate of the Earth is always changing. In the past it has altered as a result of natural causes. Nowadays, however, the term 'climate change' is generally used when referring to changes in our climate which have been identified since the early part of the twentieth century. The changes we've seen over recent years and those which are predicted to occur over the next 100 years are thought by many to be largely a result of human behaviour rather than due to natural changes in the atmosphere. And this is what is so significant about current climactic trends; never before has man played such a significant role in determining long-term weather patterns – we are entering the unknown and there is no precedent for what might happen next.

B

The greenhouse effect is very important when we talk about climate change as it relates to the gases which keep the Earth warm. Although the greenhouse effect is a naturally occurring phenomenon, it is believed that the effect could be intensified by human activity and the emission of gases into the atmosphere. It is the extra greenhouse gases which humans have released which are thought to pose the strongest threat. Certain researchers, such as Dr Michael Crawley, argue: 'even though this natural phenomenon does exist it is without a doubt human activity that has worsened its effect; this is evident when comparing data regarding the earth's temperature in the last one hundred years with the one hundred years prior to that.' Some scientists, however, dispute this as Dr Ray Ellis suggests: 'human activity may be contributing a small amount to climate change but this increase in temperature is an unavoidable fact based on the research data we have compiled.'

C

Scientists around the globe are looking at all the evidence surrounding
climate change and using advanced
technology have come up with predictions for our future environment
and weather. The next stage of that
work, which is just as important, is
looking at the knock-on effects of
potential changes. For example, are
we likely to see an increase in precipitation and sea levels? Does this

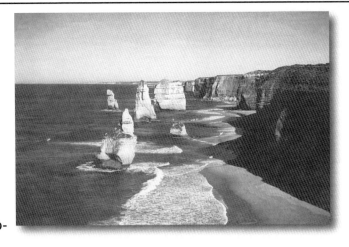

mean there will be an increase in flooding and what can we do to protect ourselves from
that? How will our health be affected by climate change, how will agricultural practices
change and how will wildlife cope? What will the effects on coral be? Professor Max
Leonard has suggested, 'while it may be controversial some would argue that climate
change could bring with it positive effects as well as negative ones'.

D

There are many institutions around the world whose sole priority is to take action against
these environmental problems. Green Peace is the organisation that is probably the most
well-known. It is an international organisation that campaigns in favour of researching
and promoting solutions to climate change, exposes the companies and governments
that are blocking action, lobbies to change national and international policy, and bears
witness to the impacts of unnecessary destruction and detrimental human activity.

E

The problem of climate change is without a doubt something that this generation and the
generations to come need to deal with. Fortunately, the use of renewable energy is
becoming increasingly popular, which means that less energy is consumed as renewable
energy is generated from natural resources—such as sunlight, wind, rain, tides, and geothermal heat—which can be naturally replenished. Another way to help the environment,
in terms of climate change, is by travelling light. Walking or riding a bike instead of driving a car uses less fossil fuels which release carbon dioxide into the atmosphere. In addition, using products that are made from recycled paper, glass, metal and plastic reduces
carbon emissions because they use less energy to manufacture than products made from
completely new materials. Recycling paper also saves trees and lets them continue to
limit climate change naturally as they remain in the forest, where they remove carbon
from the atmosphere. Professor Mark Halton, who has completed various studies in this
field, has stated: 'with all this information and the possible action that we can take, it
isn't too late to save our planet from over-heating and the even worse side-effects of our
own activity'.

Practice Test 8

Reading

Questions 1 - 5

Reading Passage 1 has 5 paragraphs, A - E. Which paragraph contains the following information?
Write the correct letter A - E in the boxes below.
NB *You may use any letter more than once.*

1   A natural phenomenon that could also affect climate change.   **B**

2   Steps we can take to help reverse the situation.   **E**

3   An explanation of what climate change is.   **A**

4   Organisations that want to help.   **D**

5   Possible effects of climate change.   **C**

JUSTIFICATIONS OF THE ANSWERS
Reading Passage 1
1. B. "The greenhouse effect is very important when we talk about climate change... the greenhouse effect is a naturally occurring phenomenon".
2. E. The paragraph discusses use of renewable energy, using less fossil fuels and recycling as actions that can be taken.
3. A. The paragraph defines climate change as "changes in our climate which have been identified since the early part of the twentieth century".
4. D. "There are many institutions around the world whose sole priority is to take action against these environmental problems".
5. C. "looking at the knock-on effects of potential changes. For example are we likely to see an increase in precipitation and sea levels?".

6. D. Paragraph C. "Professor Max Leonard has suggested, 'while it may be controversial some would argue that climate change could bring with it positive effects as well as negative ones'".
7. C. Paragraph B. "such as Dr Michael Crawley, argue: 'even though this natural phenomenon does exist it is without a doubt human activity that has worsened its effect ....'".
8. A. Paragraph E. "with all this information and the possible action we can take, it isn't too late to save our planet".
9. B. Paragraph B. "Dr Ray Ellis suggests: 'human activity may be contributing a small amount to climate change but this increase in temperature is an unavoidable fact'".

10. Yes. Paragraph B. "Although the greenhouse effect is a naturally occurring phenomenon, it is believed that the effect could be intensified by human activity and the emission of gases into the atmosphere

11. Not Given. There is no mention about nuclear energy.

12. Yes. Paragraph D. "Greenpeace is an organisation that.......exposes the companies and governments that are blocking action".

13. No. Paragraph E. "Fortunately, the regular use of renewable energy is becoming increasingly popular".

Questions 6 - 9

Look at the following people (Questions 6 - 9) and the list of statements below.
Match each person with the correct statement, A - D.
Write the correct letter, A - D, in spaces 6 - 9.

6	Professor Max Leonard	**D**
7	Dr Michael Crawley	**C**
8	Professor Mark Halton	**A**
9	Dr Ray Ellis	**B**

A We have the ability to change the situation.

B Climate change is inevitable.

C Humans have made the situation much worse.

D Climate change might not be all bad.

E Human activity and natural weather phenomena have combined with equal influence to shape climate change

F While we may not be too late to save our planet, there are bound to be some extreme side-effects of past human activity, one way or the other.

Questions 10 - 13

Do the following statements agree with the information given in Reading Passage 1?

In spaces 10 - 13 below, write

YES	*if the statement agrees with the information*
NO	*if the statement contradicts the information*
NOT GIVEN	*if there is no information on this*

10	Man is not entirely responsible for global warming.	YES
11	Scientists have come up with new evidence about the negative effects of carbon free sources of energy such as nuclear power	NOT GIVEN
12	One of the purposes of Green Peace is to find out which companies and governments are doing things which don't help the actions of environmentalists.	YES
13	Most people aren't willing to start using renewable energy.	NO

Reading

READING PASSAGE 2

You should spend about 20 minutes on Questions 14 - 26, which are based on Reading Passage 2 below.

PRIVATE SCHOOLS

Most countries' education systems have had what you might call educational disasters, but, sadly, in many areas of certain countries these 'disasters' are still evident today. The English education system is unique due to the fact that there are still dozens of schools which are known as private schools and they perpetuate privilege and social division. Most countries have some private schools for the children of the wealthy; England is able to more than triple the average number globally. England has around 3,000 private schools and just under half a million children are educated at them whilst some nine million children are educated at state schools. The overwhelming majority of students at private schools also come from middle-class families.

The result of this system is evident and it has much English history embedded within it. The facts seem to speak for themselves. In the private system almost half the students go on to University, whilst in the state system only about eight per cent make it to further education. However, statistics such as these can be deceptive due to the fact that middle class children do better at examinations than working class ones, and most of them stay on at school after 16. Private schools therefore have the advantage over state schools as they are entirely 'middle class', and this creates an environment of success where students work harder and apply themselves more diligently to their school work.

Private schools are extortionately expensive, being as much as £18,000 a year at somewhere such as Harrow or Eton, where Princes William and Harry attended, and at least £8,000 a year almost everywhere else. There are many parents who are not wealthy or even comfortably off but are willing to sacrifice a great deal in the cause of their children's schooling. It baffles many people as to why they need to spend such vast amounts when there are perfectly acceptable state schools that don't cost a penny. One father gave his reasoning for sending his son to a private school; 'If my son gets a five-percent-better chance of going to University then that may be the difference between success and failure." It would seem to the average person that a £50,000 minimum total cost of second level education is a lot to pay for a five-percent-better chance. Most children, given the choice, would take the money and spend it on more enjoyable things rather than shelling it out on a school that is too posh for its own good!

However, some say that the real reason that parents fork out the cash is prejudice: they don't want their little kids mixing with the "workers", or picking up an undesirable accent. In addition to this, it wouldn't do if at the next dinner party all the guests were boasting about sending their kids to the same place where the son of the third cousin of Prince Charles is going, and you say your kid is going to the state school down the road, even if you could pocket the money for yourself instead, and, as a result, be able to serve the best Champagne with the smoked salmon and duck.

It is a fact, however, that at many of the best private schools, your money buys you something. One school, with 500 pupils, has 11 science laboratories; another school with 800 pupils, has 30 music practice rooms; another has 16 squash courts, and yet another has its own beach.

Private schools spend £300 per pupil a year on investment in buildings and facilities; the state system spends less than £50. On books, the ratio is 3 to 1.

One of the things that your money buys which is difficult to quantify is the appearance of the school, the way it looks. Most private schools that you will find are set in beautiful, well-kept country houses, with extensive grounds and gardens. In comparison with the state schools they tend to look like castles, with the worst of the state schools looking like public lavatories, perhaps even tiled or covered in graffiti. Many may even have an architectural design that is just about on the level of an industrial shed.

Questions 14 - 20

*Choose the correct letter **A, B, C** or **D**.*

14 The English educational system differs from
    other ones because
    A it tries to make state and private education
       equal.
    B more students are educated at private schools
       than state schools.
    C it contributes to creating a class system
       within society.
    D it is more expensive to run.

15 There are more private school children who
    go to university because
    A the lessons and teachers at the private
       schools are much better.
    B their parents are very rich and can help them.
    C they have more teaching hours.
    D the schools create a successful environment.

16 A lot of parents often send their children
    to private schools
    A because they are not well-informed.
    B to show how much money they have
       to their friends.
    C to increase their chances of succeeding in the
       university exams.
    D because of the better sports facilities.

17 It is suggested that some parents of children
    at private schools are
    A prejudiced and superficial.
    B more intelligent that those with
       children at state schools.
    C well-brought up and cultivated.
    D overly protective.

18 Private schools
    A always have their own beaches.
    B teach sport that state schools do not.
    C spend more money per student than state
       schools.
    D spend more money on hiring good teachers.

19 The writer thinks that private schools buildings
    A are very attractive and luxurious.
    B generally do not look very nice.
    C are too big for the amount of students
       who attend the school.
    D are not built to suit student's needs

20 In general, what do you think the writer's
    opinion of private schools is?
    A It isn't fair that those without money can't
       attend them.
    B They divide social classes but they offer better
       facilities and a more creative environment.
    C There is little difference between private
       and state schools.
    D They have the best teachers.

JUSTIFICATIONS OF THE ANSWERS
21. Paragraph 1: *'The English education system is **unique** due to the fact .....
as private schools'*
22. Paragraph 1: *'The overwhelming majority of students .... come from
middle-class families.'*
23. Paragraph 2: *'However, statistics such as these can be **deceptive**...'*
24. Paragraph 2: *'**apply** themselves more diligently to their school work.'*
25. Paragraph 3: *'There are many parents ..... children's **schooling**.'*
26. Paragraph 6: *'Many may ... is just about on the level of an industrial **shed**.'*

Questions 21 - 26

Complete the sentences below.

*Choose **ONE WORD ONLY** from the passage for each answer.*

The fact that there are so many private schools in England, in comparison to other countries, makes
the English educational system **21** ....**unique**.... .

Most students in these schools are from **22** ..**middle-class**.. families. These students seem to do
better at exams although statistics can be **23** ..**deceptive**. .

One of the advantages of private schools is that they seem to provide students with a better, more
positive environment that encourages them to **24** ....**apply**...... themselves to their school work with
more enthusiasm.

A lot of not very well-off parents make huge sacrifices for their children's **25** ...**schooling** to help
them go to respectable universities. Unfortunately, many state school buildings some times have
the appearance of an industrial **26** ....**shed**...... .

Reading

READING PASSAGE 3

*You should spend about 20 minutes on **Questions 27 - 40**, which are based on Reading Passage 3 below*

Martin Luther King

A

Martin Luther King was born on January 15, 1929, in Atlanta, Georgia. He was the son of the Reverend Martin Luther King, Sr. and Alberta Williams King. He had an older sister, Willie Christine King, and a younger brother Alfred Daniel Williams King. Growing up in Atlanta, King attended Booker T. Washington High School. He skipped ninth and twelfth grade, and entered Morehouse College at age fifteen without formally graduating from high school. From the time that Martin was born, he knew that black people and white people had different rights in certain parts of America. If a black family wanted to eat at a restaurant, they had to sit in a separate section of the restaurant. They had to sit at the back of the cinema, and even use separate toilets. Worse, and perhaps even more humiliating still, in many southern states, if a black man was on a bus and all the seats were taken, he would have to endure the indignity of relinquishing his own seat to a white man. King could never understand the terrible injustice of this.
In 1948, he graduated with a Bachelor of Arts degree in sociology. Later, King began doctoral studies in systematic theology at Boston University and received his Doctor of Philosophy on June 5, 1955. King married Coretta Scott, on June 18, 1953 and they had four children.

B

Returning to the South to become pastor of a Baptist Church in Montgomery, Alabama, King first achieved national renown when he helped mobilise the black boycott of the Montgomery bus system in 1955. This was organised after Rosa Parks, a black woman, refused to give up her seat on the bus to a white man - in the segregated south, black people could only sit at the back of the bus. The 382-day boycott led the bus company to change its regulations, and the Supreme Court declared such segregation unconstitutional.

C

In 1957 King was active in the organisation of the Southern Leadership Christian Conference (SCLC), formed to co-ordinate protests against discrimination. He advocated non-violent direct action based on the methods of Gandhi, who led protests against British rule in India culminating in India's independence in 1947. In 1963, King led mass protests against discriminatory practices in Birmingham, Alabama, where the white population were violently resisting desegregation. The city was dubbed 'Bombingham' as attacks against civil rights protesters increased, and King was arrested and jailed for his part in the protests.

D

After his release, King participated in the enormous civil rights march, in Washington, in August 1963, and delivered his famous 'I have a dream' speech, predicting a day when the promise of freedom and equality for all would become a reality in America. In 1964 he was awarded the Nobel Peace Prize. In 1965, he led a campaign to register blacks to vote. The same year the US Congress passed the Voting Rights Act outlawing the discriminatory practices that had barred blacks from voting in the south.

E

As the civil rights movement became increasingly radicalised, King found that his message of peaceful protest was not shared by many in the younger generation. King began to protest against the Vietnam War and poverty levels in the US. On March 29, 1968, King went to Memphis, Tennessee, in support of the black sanitary public works employees who had been on strike since March 12 for higher wages and better treatment. In one incident, black street repairmen had received pay for two hours when they were sent home because of bad weather, but white employees had been paid for the full day. King could not bear to stand by and let such patent acts of racism go unnoticed. He moved to unite his people, and all the peoples of America on the receiving end of discriminatory practices, to protest for their rights, peacefully but steadfastly.

F

On his trip to Memphis, King was booked into room 306 at the Lorraine Motel, owned by Walter Bailey. King was shot at 6:01 p.m. April 4, 1968 while he was standing on the motel's second-floor balcony. King was rushed to St. Joseph's Hospital, where doctors opened his chest and performed manual heart massage. He was pronounced dead at 7:05 p.m. King's autopsy revealed that although he was only 39 years old, he had the heart of a 60 year old man.

JUSTIFICATIONS OF THE ANSWERS
Reading Passage 3
27. B. Paragraph 1. "If a black family wanted to eat at a restaurant, they had to sit in a separate section of the restaurant... He could never understand this".
28. A. Paragraph 2. "King first achieved national renown when he helped mobilise the black boycott of the Montgomery bus system".
29. D. Paragraph 3. "He advocated non-violent direct action based on the methods of Gandhi".
30. A. Paragraph 4. "In 1965, he led a campaign to register blacks to vote".
31. D. Paragraph 5. "King found that his message of peaceful protest was not shared by many in the younger generation".
32. Yes. Paragraph 2. "The 382-day boycott led the bus company to change its regulations, and the Supreme Court declared such segregation unconstitutional".

33. No. Paragraph 3. '....in Birmingham, Alabama, where the white population were violently resisting desegregation.'
34. Not Given. Paragraph 5. We only know he began to protest about the Vietnam war but there is no information about the outcome of the protest.

35. v. Paragraph A. describes his birthplace, family and education, comprising his background.
36. iv. Paragraph B. gives details about the protest and boycott of the Montgomery bus system.
37. ii. Paragraph C. "He advocated non-violent direct action".
38. i. Paragraph D. "in August 1963, and delivered his famous 'I have a dream' speech".
39. vi. Paragraph E. "King began to protest against the Vietnam war".
40. iii. Paragraph F. "in room 306 at the Lorraine motel.....King was shot at 6:01p.m.".

Reading

Question 27-31

Choose the correct letter A, B, C or D.

27   From a young age Martin Luther King

    A   wanted to protest for the rights of black people.

    B   could not understand why black people were treated differently.

    C   was not allowed to go to the cinema or to restaurants.

    D   was aware that black people were being humiliated in many northern states.

28   What initially made Martin Luther King famous?

    A   the black boycott of the Montgomery bus system

    B   becoming a pastor at a Baptist Church

    C   when Rosa Parks refused to give up her seat on a bus

    D   when he persuaded Rosa Parks not to give up her bus seat to a white man

29   What influenced Martin Luther King regarding non-violence?

    A   India's independence in 1947

    B   Christianity

    C   the Southern Leadership Christian Conference

    D   the methods of Gandhi

30   What did Martin Luther King fight for in 1965?

    A   the right of black people to vote

    B   the actions of US Congress

    C   the right to win the Nobel Peace Prize

    D   the right of black people to travel abroad

31   How did Martin Luther King feel about the civil rights movement?

    A   It was helping the war in Vietnam.

    B   It brought the younger generation together.

    C   It had been exploited by politicians who wanted to get more votes.

    D   The protesters sometimes behaved too violently.

Questions 32 - 34

Do the following statements agree with the information given in Reading Passage 3?

In spaces 32 - 34 below, write

YES	*if the statement agrees with the information*
NO	*if the statement contradicts the information*
NOT GIVEN	*if there is no information on this*

32 The black boycott of the Montgomery bus system was a success. ....**YES**.......

33 In 1963 the white people in Alabama wanted desegregation. ....**NO**.......

34 Martin Luther King achieved a lot in his protest against the Vietnam War. **NOT GIVEN**

Questions 35 - 40

Reading Passage 2 has 6 paragraphs.
Choose the correct heading for each paragraph A - F, from the list of headings.
*Write the correct number, **i - viii**, in spaces **35 - 40** below.*

35 Paragraph **A** ......**v**......

36 Paragraph **B** ......**iv**......

37 Paragraph **C** ......**ii**......

38 Paragraph **D** ......**i**......

39 Paragraph **E** ......**vi**......

40 Paragraph **F** ......**iii**......

i The memorable speech
ii Unhappy about violence
iii A tragic incident
iv Protests and action
v The background of an iconic man
vi Making his mark internationally
vii Difficult childhood
viii Black street repairmen

Writing

WRITING TASK 1

You should spend about 20 minutes on this task.

The graphs below provide information about the sales in England of three different kinds of music. The graphs together cover five decades and the sales are measured in pounds sterling. Summarise the information by selecting and reporting the main features, and make comparisons where relevant.

Write at least 150 words.

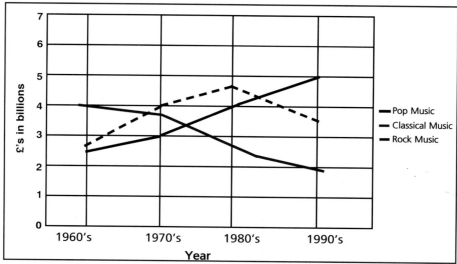

WRITING TASK 2

You should spend about 40 minutes on this task.
Write about the following topic:

It has become very common for people to borrow money. Most people have a credit card, a mortgage and often they will buy a car on credit as well. Is this a good idea or is it too risky? Discuss both views and give your own opinion.

Give reasons for your answer and include any relevant examples from your own knowledge or experience.

Write at least 250 words.

Speaking

PART 1   (4-5 minutes)

The examiner asks the candidate about him/herself, his/her home, work or studies and other familiar topics.

Sports

- What sort of sports do you like to take part in?
- Why do you enjoy playing these sports?
- Do you think it's important for people to play sports? Why?/Why not?
- Do people of all ages in your culture enjoy sports? Why?/Why not?

PART 2   (2 minutes)

You will have to talk about the topic for one to two minutes. You have one minute to think about what you are going to say. You can make some notes to help you if you wish.

> Describe some environmental voluntary work that you have done, or that you would like to.
>
> You should say:
> - What it was
> - How difficult or tiring it was
> - Whether it was effective or not
>
> and explain why you decided to take part.

PART 3   (4-5 minutes)

Discussion topics:

Economic growth and environmental protection

- Businesses should be seen as partners in cleaning up the environment and not be treated as suspects by the government. What's your opinion on that?
- Can we afford to have both continued economic growth and environmental protection?
- Can we find the solution to our energy problems using renewable energy sources?

Technology and pollution

- Do you think that technology can play a key role in solving the pollution problem?
- We may lose some jobs as we move towards environmentally friendly technologies and lifestyles, but we'll create new ones in "green" industries. Do you agree with this statement?
- Do you agree with the opinion that preventing environmental damage can be more effective and less costly in the long run?

Test 9

Listening

SECTION 1   *Questions 1 - 10*

Questions 1 - 8

Complete the form below.
Write **NO MORE THAN THREE** *words for each answer.*

DENHAM'S SHIPPING AGENCY
customer quotation form

Example:
Country of destination: *Ireland*
Name: Tim **1** .... *Lafferty* ....
Address to be collected from: **2** ...... *Abbeyfield* .. University
Town: Brighton
Postcode: **3** .. *BR8 9P3* ....

Size of container:

Length:
2.5 m

Depth: 5 .... **1.20m** ....

Width: 4 .... **1.25m** ....

Contents: books
        6 .... **Music albums** ....
        7 .... **Stationery** ......

Total estimated value: **8** ... **£3000** ....

Questions 9 - 10

Choose the correct letter, A, B, or C.

9 What is the minimum recommended cover by the agency?
   A premium
   B standard
   C economy

10 Where does the customer want the goods delivered?
    A port
    B home
    C business

SECTION 2   *Questions 11 - 20*

Questions 11 - 15

Label the plan below.
*Write **NO MORE THAN THREE WORDS** for each answer.*

14 3D Theatre

15 Modern Art Studio

13 Main Exhibition Centre

12 Art Gallery

Ticket Centre and
11 Gift Shop

Entrance

Questions 16 - 20

What does the tour guide tell her tour group about each of the following places on the day's itinerary?
Write the correct letter, A, B, or C next to questions 16 - 20 below.
NB *You may choose any letter more than once.*

16	The Aquarium	B
17	Solheim Country Club	A
18	Milltown Winery	C
19	The Zoological Gardens	A
20	The Stout Brewery	B

A They'll definitely go there.
B They might go there if time allows.
C They certainly won't go there.

Listening

SECTION 3   *Questions 21 - 30*

Questions 21 - 25

Complete the sentences below.

Write **NO MORE THAN TWO WORDS** *for each answer.*

Gyroscopes are used in laser devices and are found in many consumer **21** ...appliances... .

The purpose of the project is to design a functional, **22** ...practical... and beneficial consumer product.

The gyroscopic exercise ball can be set in motion by movements of the **23** ...lower arm... and wrist together in synch.

The gyroscopic ball could help people in **24** rehabilitation... who have lower-arm injuries.

The product could also be aimed at **25** high-performance athletes for whom lower-arm strength is very important.

Questions 26 - 30

Complete the table below.
Write **NO MORE THAN THREE WORDS AND/OR A NUMBER** *for each answer.*

	PROTOTYPE DESIGN	TESTING
Estimated Cost:	£3,000	26 ...£1,500...
Numbers of Weeks:	27 ...2...	6
	Numbers of test subjects:	28 ...15...
	Breakdown of test subjects:	5 professional athletes
		29 5 recovery patients
		5 30 ..gym members..

SECTION 4   *Questions 31 - 40*

Questions 31 - 35

Choose the correct letter, A, B or C.

31   Speakers have to know
   (A)   their material.
   B   their audience.
   C   their limitations.

32   Experienced speakers
   A   always try to wing it.
   (B)   never arrive unprepared.
   C   give the best presentations.

33   You should always rehearse
   A   with friends who can advise you.
   (B)   with all the equipment you plan on using.
   C   more than once.

34   It is a good idea to
   A   be discreet with your audience.
   B   meet your fans.
   (C)   meet and welcome your audience.

35   Taking a few deep breaths before you begin
   A   will stop you having a panic attack.
   B   will guarantee that you feel more relaxed.
   (C)   will help turn your tension into enthusiasm.

Questions 36 - 40

Complete the sentences below.

*Write **NO MORE THAN TWO WORDS** for each answer.*

Useful Tips for a Successful Presentation

- Try to **36** .....visualise......... yourself making a speech and imagine your voice loud and confident.
- Even if you make mistakes avoid making **37** ...apologies...... .
- Pay attention to your **38** body language - your words carry less meaning than your delivery.
- People usually remember less than **39** ....25%.......... of what they hear.
- Be **40** ...realistic.......... about yourself; You don't become a perfect speaker overnight.

Reading

READING PASSAGE 1

You should spend about 20 minutes on **Questions 1 - 13**, *which are based on Reading Passage 1 below.*

Taking us back to the Paradise City

Formed in 1985 by Axl Rose and then lead guitarist, Tracii Guns, and taking its name from its two founding members, the hard rock band *Guns and Roses* reached heights of success that few could or would have ever predicted. Having sold more than 100 million albums worldwide, 46 million in the States alone, to date, the band that came to symbolise the hedonistic rebelliousness of the 1980s and 90s punk-rock period has, after much speculation, resurrected itself for one more assault on the music charts. GNR, as the band has come to be known, has just begun a new world tour. And as it embarks on another chapter of its journey, we take a look back at the colourful and often controversial history of the band.

1985 – 1986

The band line-up underwent many changes in the early days. Founding member Tracii Guns' failure to attend rehearsals led to him being replaced as lead guitarist by Slash. And once Rob Gardner, the band's original drummer quit for personal reasons, Slash brought his close friend Steven Adler into the fold. With the band members now settled and the line-up complete, Axl Rose (vocals), Izzy Stradlin (rhythm guitar), Duff McKagan (bass), Slash (lead guitar) and Steven Adler (drums) embarked on their first tour, nicknamed 'Hell Tour'. It was here on the road that the band established its chemistry and though it only managed to release one four-track EP, *Like a Suicide*, during this period, the seeds of success were being sown as the band quickly earned a reputation for its impressive live performances.

1987 – 1989

On July the 21st, 1987, the band released its first album, *Appetite for Destruction*. But success wasn't by any means instant; the album lingered low in the charts for almost a year before the band's agent managed to convince MTV executives to play *Welcome to the Jungle*, the first single off the album, during their afternoon rotations. Rock and punk fans soon took notice and began requesting the video en masse. *Sweet Child of Mine* was the album's second US single and, thanks largely to growing grassroots support, the song and its accompanying music video received regular airplay and shot to the top of the US charts. A world tour and invitations to appear at major international rock festivals followed. The band was now well on its way to achieving fame and fortune.

1990 – 1993

Band members lived life on the edge and, unfortunately, drummer Adler's lifestyle got the better of him. The extent of his dependence on drugs was so bad that he could no longer perform with the band and was fired in July, 1990, to be replaced by Matt Sorum. A sixth member of the group was also added as Dizzy Reed became the band's keyboardist. And, having gotten rid of its old management team as well, the band now launched its most ambitious project to date, releasing two albums, *Use Your Illusion 1* and *Use Your Illusion 2*, at the same time. The gamble paid off spectacularly with the albums shooting to numbers one and two in the charts respectively - GNR was the first band ever to achieve such a feat. But though they were riding the crest of a wave, controversy was never far from the band members, especially vocalist Rose who was, among other things, charged with assault and accused of inciting a riot that led to several fatalities. That said, the *Use Your Illusion* Tour ended on a high, registering record attendances and lasting an incredible 28 months.

1994 – 2008

But just when it seemed that the band could do no wrong, things slowly began to unravel. Rose and Slash had personal issues and the band went on a hiatus, not recording or touring together for the best part of two years, before Slash officially quit in 1996. Most of the other band members followed Slash out and, though Rose replaced them, it was a full nine years before a much-touted comeback gig was played in Las Vegas. The band's promised new album, *Chinese Democracy*, never materialised and tour schedules were interrupted and often cancelled altogether. It wasn't until 2008, with Rose now the only remaining member of the original band, that *Chinese Democracy* was finally released.

2009 – Present

A new world tour followed the release of *Chinese Democracy* and, although it received largely positive reviews, the band has continued to be plagued by controversy; Rose is notorious for arriving late for performances and his onstage behaviour has led to much criticism. But when all's said and done, there's no denying the enduring appeal of GNR. Loyal fans still line up in their thousands to get tickets for every new tour date, just as they did all those years ago at the height of the band's success. The only difference is that today they are more hoping for than expecting a great performance, but then that's rock and roll baby!

Reading

Questions 1 - 3

Questions 1 – 3 relate to the first paragraph only. Complete each sentence with the correct ending, A – G, from the box below. You may use each letter once only.

1 Guns and Roses	B
2 The band has enjoyed	E
3 The band became	G

A takes its name from two former members.
B was named after its founding members.
C success in the States alone.
D was never a predictable band musically.
E considerable success in America.
F a symbol of success in the 1980s.
G representative of a certain attitude in music in the 80s and 90s.

Questions 4 - 7

Complete the sentences below.

*Write **NO MORE THAN ONE WORD** for each answer.*

Between 1985 and 1986 one of the original members wasn't capable of going to 4 ......rehearsals...... which forced the band to replace him.

During their first tour they managed to have good 5 ......chemistry...... and play well together.

The album *Sweet Child of Mine* got regular 6 ......airplay...... and reached the top of the charts.

Nobody can argue that they have enjoyed long-lasting 7 ......appeal...... .

Questions 8 - 13

Look at the following statements (Questions 8 - 13) and the lists of periods of time below.

Match each statement to the correct period A - D.

*Write the correct letter, **A - D**, in the spaces 8 - 13 below.*

NB You may use any letter more than once.

A	from 1985 to 1986
B	from 1987 to 1989
C	from 1990 to 1993
D	from 1994 to 2008

8	The band took a long break, during which many members decided to leave.	D
9	There was an extremely long delay before the release of the band's next album.	D
10	The relationship between band members developed in a positive way while on tour.	A
11	A damaging addiction prevented one band member from performing well and led to him being sacked.	C
12	A new member joined the band playing an instrument that hadn't been played by previous band members.	C
13	The band registered its first number-one hit single.	B

Practice Test 9

JUSTIFICATIONS OF THE ANSWERS

Reading Passage 1

8. The correct answer is **D**: "... the band went on a hiatus, not recording or touring together for the best part of two years, before Slash officially quit in 1996. Most of the other band members followed Slash out ..."

9. The correct answer is **D**: "The band's promised new album, *Chinese Democracy*, never materialised... It wasn't until 2008, with Rose now the only remaining member of the original band, that *Chinese Democracy* was finally released."

10. The correct answer is **A**: "It was here on the road that the band established its chemistry...". Chemistry between people is a positive way of interacting.

11. The correct answer is **C**: "unfortunately, drummer Adler's lifestyle got the better of him. The extent of his dependence on drugs was so bad that he could no longer perform with the band and was fired in July, 1990"

12. The correct answer is **C**: "A sixth member of the group was also added as Dizzy Reed became the band's keyboardist"

13. The correct answer is **B**: "...the song and its accompanying music video received regular airplay and shot to the top of the US charts..."

Reading

READING PASSAGE 2

You should spend about 20 minutes on Questions 14 - 26, which are based on Reading Passage 2 below.

Surf's Up

There are two major subdivisions of surfing: longboarding and shortboarding. Their respective names represent differences in the type of surfboard used. Longboards are, as the name suggests, much longer and require a different riding style to shortboards.

Surfboards were originally made of solid wood, and were large and cumbersome, often weighing in excess of 100 pounds. Nowadays, they are more commonly constructed out of polyurethane foam making them much lighter, which means better manoeuvrability for the boarder. This is especially beneficial for longboarders, whose boards can measure up to 3 metres in length. Successful longboarders must learn to carry out difficult walking manoeuvres up and down the board so as to set themselves in the optimal position for catching and riding the wave. The lighter the board, the easier it becomes to execute such manoeuvres. Shortboarders, whose boards are usually between 1.8 and 2 metres long, also benefit from greater manoeuvrability though, and are able to turn and adjust more quickly thanks to the lighter boards.

It is claimed that surfing was first observed being enjoyed by native Tahitians in 1767 by European explorers. Later travellers also reported seeing naked locals, both men and women, amusing themselves in the surf off the coast of Hawaii. Perhaps this is one of the reasons why the sport is synonymous with the South Pacific and Hawaii in particular. Today, however, the popularity of surfing is such that surf clubs have popped up almost everywhere, from the windy West Coast of Ireland, to the ultra-chic Californian beaches. Indeed, it is in Northern California where perhaps the most famous and glamorous surfing takes place.

The prospective surfer would be well-advised to consider the dangers associated with the sport before he takes to the waves. Like all water sports, surfing carries with it the inherent danger of drowning. Although the board itself offers buoyancy, it can also be a hindrance, and a deadly one at that if its leash becomes entangled in a reef, holding the surfer underwater. Ideal water conditions for surfing can be extremely demanding on the body, too, and require the surfer to be an extremely competent swimmer.

JUSTIFICATIONS OF THE ANSWERS
Reading Passage 2

14. The correct answer is **D**; "Nowadays, they are more commonly constructed out of polyurethane foam making them much lighter...." A and B are incorrect because they were true in the past; not today. C is true only for long boards.

15. The correct answer is **D**; "surfing was first observed being enjoyed by native Tahitians … Later travellers also reported seeing naked locals … amusing themselves in the surf off the coast of Hawaii. Perhaps this is one of the reasons why the sport is synonymous with the South Pacific and Hawaii in particular. " The two first locations are both in the south pacific.

16. The correct answer is **D**; "Today, however, the popularity of surfing is such that surf clubs have popped up almost everywhere, from the windy West Coast of Ireland, to the ultra-chic Californian beaches."

17. The correct answer is **D**; "The prospective surfer would be well-advised to consider the dangers associated with the sport before he takes to the waves."

18. The correct answer is **A**; "Although the board itself offers buoyancy, it can also be a hindrance, and a deadly one at that if its leash becomes entangled in a reef, holding the surfer underwater."

19. The correct answer is **C**; "Collisions … can also be extremely hazardous and can lead to concussion – a death sentence if the surfer is not rescued from the water quickly."

20-21. The correct answers are **B** and **D**; "Ideal water conditions for surfing can be extremely demanding on the body," and "Although more rare, attacks by marine animals are not uncommon, with sharks, rays, seals and jellyfish posing the greatest threats". A is incorrect because technically it is the leash holding surfers underwater, and C is incorrect because the encounters are rare.

22-23. The correct answers are **B** and **C**. For B - "it can also… be extremely rewarding, and there are few feelings to compare with the exhilaration of riding out your first wave", and for C - "So for those of you daredevil adrenalin junkies who fancy having a go…"

24. "surfing carries with it the inherent danger of **drowning**…"
25. "Five-day courses start from as little as **£100**…"
26. all inclusive means that everything is included - "there are **all-inclusive camps**, too, which cover accommodation, meals, lessons and equipment."

Collisions with sandbanks, reefs, surfboards and other surfers can also be extremely hazardous and can lead to concussion – a death sentence if the surfer is not rescued from the water quickly. Although rarer, attacks by marine animals are not uncommon, with sharks, rays, seals and jellyfish posing the greatest threats. You certainly need to be a courageous soul to brave the waves in this sport.

But for those who insist on giving it a go, the rewards can be very gratifying, and it isn't too expensive to get up and running either. Surf schools in popular destinations offer multi-day beginner and intermediate courses that focus on the basic fundamentals. Five-day courses start from as little as £100 and there are all-inclusive camps, too, which cover accommodation, meals, lessons and equipment. Longboards, given their superior paddling speed and stability, are usually preferred by coaches for use with beginners. Typically, the courses break down the technique into separate skills: the first one being how to get into position to catch a wave, the second one being how to ride the wave and not fall off. Balance, of course, plays a crucial role, so a lot of time is dedicated to balance training exercises as well.

Difficult though it may be to master the art of surfing, it can also be extremely rewarding, and there are few feelings to compare with the exhilaration of riding out your first wave. So, for those of you daredevil adrenalin junkies who fancy having a go, details of a surf club near you can be found on the British Surfing Association's website, britsurf.co.uk.

And try to remember as your feet are dangling over the side of the board, *Jaws* was just a film; it ALMOST certainly won't happen to you.

Reading

Questions 14 - 19

Choose the correct letter **A, B, C** *or* **D**.

14 Longboards and shortboards

   A often weigh more than 100 pounds today.

   B are usually made out of solid wood.

   C require surfers to perform difficult walking manoeuvres.

   D are lighter and more manoeuvrable today.

15 The sport of surfing

   A was invented by a group of European explorers.

   B was first observed by native Tahitians.

   C is commonly performed naked by both men and women.

   D was first practised in the South Pacific.

16 Surfing has become very popular

   A in windy coastal areas.

   B on the fashionable west coast of Ireland.

   C in Tahiti in recent years.

   D all around the world.

17 Before a novice surfer takes to the water, he should

   A check the latest weather report.

   B avoid big waves.

   C have good buoyancy.

   D be aware of the risks involved.

18 Although a surfboard can help you stay buoyant, it can also

   A get in the way of your safety in some cases.

   B help you escape from dangerous sea life.

   C be a very dangerous weapon.

   D prevent concussion or death.

19 Unless you are pulled from the water quickly, a bad collision can prove

   A hard to escape.

   B life-saving.

   C fatal.

   D rare.

Questions 20 - 21

Choose **TWO** *letters, A - E.*

Which **TWO** of the following are hazards that surfers face?

   A being held underwater by reefs.

   B the potential for shark attacks.

   C frequent encounters with jellyfish.

   D demanding water conditions.

   E hazardous rescue attempts.

Question 22 - 23

Choose TWO letters, A - E.

Which **TWO** of the following are true about surfing?

A It can become a rewarding career.

(B) It can be very rewarding as you see yourself improve.

(C) It can be an adrenalin rush.

D It can be expensive to start.

E It can be dangerous for swimmers around you.

Questions 24 - 26

Complete the table below.

Write **NO MORE THAN TWO WORDS AND/OR A NUMBER** *for each answer.*

Subdivisions of surfing:	Longboarding	Shortboarding			
Surfing originated in:	The South Pacific				
Common dangers include:	24 drowning	if the board's leash becomes entangled in a reef, can be deadly	difficult water conditions	collision & concussion	attacks from local sealife
Starting cost of five-day courses:	25 £100				
26 All-inclusive camps **include:**	accommodation	meals	lessons	equipment	

JUSTIFICATIONS OF THE ANSWERS
Reading Passage 3

27. "As investors tire of **stock market instability**..."
28. "Here are some tips from successful **real estate** mogul, Janet Anderson..."
29. "According to Janet, one of the best ways to identify a bargain is to **hunt for foreclosures**."
30. "Foreclosures are properties banks have repossessed because their owners were unable to meet the **mortgage repayments**."
31. "Banks want a quick sell ... They want to cut their losses and get **their money back** as quickly as possible."
32. "Developing a network... can be an excellent way to identify such **bargains**."
33. "the biggest mistake you can make is to **borrow too much** or **over-borrow**"
34. The correct answer is **Yes**; "For first-time investors, lenders usually demand bigger down payments"
35. The correct answer is **No**; it is the opposite - "That's

more of your money on the table and, therefore, should anything go wrong you're in for a big financial hit."
36. The correct answer is **Yes**; "mortgage payments and deposits are only part of the long-term cost of buying a rental property. There is also the cost of repairs, administration and maintenance, rental manager's fees, insurance... "
37. The correct answer is **No**; "...all of which require you to hold a significant amount of money in reserve" so it is implied that it is necessary, but banks do not require it.
38. The correct answer is **Yes**; "One of the biggest traps for first time investors ... is the temptation to pay over the odds to get the property you desire."
39. The correct answer is **No**; "... the housing market is not very hot at the moment, which means the danger of overpaying is not so great"
40. The correct answer is **Not Given**; the areas earmarked by the government are a separate idea from the areas of urban renewal. We know nothing about the relationship, if any, of these two ideas.

Reading   READING PASSAGE 3

You should spend about 20 minutes on Questions 27 - 40, which are based on Reading Passage 3 below.

Making a sound Investment Decision

As investors tire of stock market instability, the idea of owning a piece of real estate is gaining in popularity. Now, not everyone has what it takes to become a landlord, but if you can make a go of it, it certainly has the potential to become a good money-earner. Here are some tips from successful real estate mogul, Janet Anderson, on how to start building up your property portfolio.

According to Janet, one of the best ways to identify a bargain is to hunt for foreclosures. Foreclosures are properties banks have repossessed because their owners were unable to meet the mortgage repayments. Banks want a quick sell on these places, Janet says. They want to cut their losses and get their money back as quickly as possible. Developing a network – making connections with city clerks and bank employees who know which properties are about to be sold – can be an excellent way to identify such bargains. And bargains they certainly can prove to be; in a recent firesale auction ('firesale auction' is the phrase that has been coined to describe auction-room events dedicated entirely to the disposal of repossessed assets) a house with a market value nearing $1,000,000, but with a low reserve price designed to encourage bidders and secure a quick sale, went for $450,000; that's a whopping 55% discount.

It's also important to be realistic though and not stretch yourself too far financially. Janet says the biggest mistake you can make is to borrow too much or over-borrow. For first-time investors, lenders usually demand bigger down payments because you haven't got a proven track record. That's more of your money on the table and, therefore, should anything go wrong, you're in for a big financial hit.

Her business partner, James Nylles, is in complete agreement on this point. He also highlights the fact that the mortgage payments and deposits are only part of the long-term cost of buying a rental property. There is also the cost of repairs, administration and maintenance, rental manager's fees, insurance and so on, all of which require you to hold a significant amount of money in reserve. Failure to factor this in when calculating how much you can afford to part with in mortgage repayments can lead to disaster.

One of the biggest traps for first time investors, according to Nylles, is the temptation to pay over the odds to get the property you desire. Buyers often get carried away, especially in the auction-room setting, which can get quite competitive and even descend into a racket of one-upmanship. They end up paying top-dollar and landing themselves in a financial situation they can ill afford to be in. Remember, you are in the property game to make money, so the more money you have to pay upfront for a property, the less likely you are to recoup your investment in the long run. The good news, however, is that the housing market is not very hot at the moment, which means the danger of overpaying is not so great. Always set emotions to one side and think from a purely business perspective. The question of your liking or disliking the property is irrelevant. As Nylles points out: "you will not be living there." Business decisions are made in the cold hard light of day; your objective is to minimise your outlay and maximise your return. Whether you secure a huge home in pristine condition or a tiny flat with barely room to stretch in is irrelevant – if the tiny flat gets you a better return on your investment then the choice is a no-brainer.

And last of all, do your homework. You've got to get to know the location in which you are going to invest. Look out for areas which are earmarked for government investment. Urban renewal areas are often very attractive since house and rental prices in such places are low right now but can be expected to rise in the not too distant future. The range of local amenities, safety and the state of the local economy are all important factors to consider, too. As the old saying goes; 'location, location, location'. Invest in a good location and you will maximise your rental income.

Questions 27 – 33

Answer the questions below using **NO MORE THAN THREE WORDS** *for each answer.*

27   What are investors getting fed up with?
stock market instability

28   Janet Anderson is involved in the sale of property. What is another phrase used in paragraph 1 to describe this type of business?   real estate

29   What is one of the best ways to identify a bargain in the property market?
hunt for foreclosures

30   Failure to meet your what, can cause your home to be repossessed?
mortgage repayments

31   What do banks want to get back quickly on foreclosed properties?
their money

32   Developing networks is an excellent way to find what?
bargains / bargain properties

33   What is the biggest error of judgement first-time investors can make, according to Anderson?
borrow too much / over-borrow

Questions 34 - 40

Do the following statements agree with the information given in Reading Passage 3?
In spaces 34 - 40 below, write

> **YES**   *if the statement agrees with the information*
> **NO**   *if the statement contradicts the information*
> **NOT GIVEN** *if there is no information on this*

34	Banks demand larger deposits from first-time property investors.	YES
35	By making a larger deposit, investors can limit their personal financial risk.	NO
36	There are a lot of long-term costs to take into consideration before purchasing a rental property.	YES
37	Banks require you to hold a lot of money in reserve to meet your long-term property maintenance costs.	NO
38	Many investors are tempted to pay more than they should for their investment properties.	YES
39	At the moment, house prices are extremely high in general.	NO
40	There are a lot of urban renewal projects that have been earmarked by the government.	NOT GIVEN

Writing

WRITING TASK 1

You should spend about 20 minutes on this task.

> *The chart below shows the percentage of Irish language speakers by province (Leinster, Munster, Connacht and Ulster) in the Republic of Ireland (State) in five different years.*
>
> *Summarise the information by selecting and reporting the main features, and make comparisons where relevant.*

Write at least 150 words.

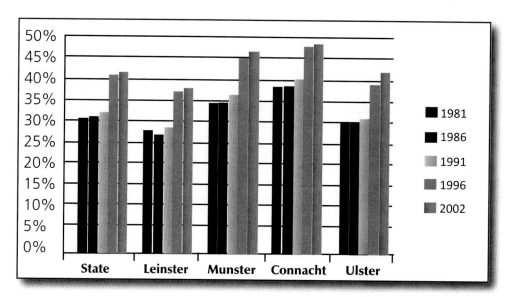

WRITING TASK 2

You should spend about 40 minutes on this task.

Write about the following topic:

> *Nuclear power is a necessary evil. Despite the potential human and environmental consequences of radioactive fallout, nuclear energy is a genuine alternative to non-renewable energy sources like oil and coal, which are quickly running out. In short, the benefits of nuclear power far outweigh the risks of using it.*
>
> *To what extent do you agree or disagree?*

Give reasons for your answer and include any relevant examples from your own knowledge or experience.

Write at least 250 words.

Speaking

PART 1   (4-5 minutes)

The examiner asks the candidate about him/herself, his/her home, work or studies and other familiar topics.

Music

- Do you like listening to music?
- Is music an important part of your life? Why?/Why not?
- For what occasions is music important in your culture?
- Do you think people will always enjoy listening to music? Why?/Why not?

PART 2   (2 minutes)

You will have to talk about the topic for one to two minutes. You have one minute to think about what you are going to say. You can make some notes to help you if you wish.

> **Describe a habit that is good for your health.**
> **You should say:**
> - **why you do it**
> - **whether it is difficult or easy to do**
> - **whether it requires self-discipline or not**
>   **and finally explain why this habit is**
>   **good for your health.**

PART 3   (4-5 minutes)

Discussion topics:

Eating healthily

- What do you think of fast-food restaurants?
- "Ninety per cent of the diseases known to man are caused by cheap foodstuffs. You are what you eat."
  Do you agree with that statement?
- Do you eat a lot of red meat or you prefer healthy alternative foods such as fish, vegetables etc.?
- A lot of young people are presently suffering from eating disorders, such as anorexia, because they want
  to look thin and beautiful. What are the reasons for this obsession with weight?

Health issues

- Why do you think some people turn to drugs?
- What do you think of the health service in your country?
- How would you try to persuade a friend of yours not to smoke cigarettes?
- Do you believe the day will come when we will be able to cure all diseases?

IELTS Scoring

IELTS is scored on a **9-band scale**. Candidates will be given a score for overall language ability as well as another score for each of the four skills (Listening, Reading, Writing and Speaking).

IELTS 9-band scale

9 Expert User	Has full command of the language.
8 Very Good User	Has full command of the language with occasional inaccuracies.
7 Good User	Has operational command of the language, although occasional inaccuracies do occur.
6 Competent User	Has generally effective command of the language despite some inaccuracies.
5 Modest User	Has partial command of the language and understands the overall meaning in most situations. Can handle basic communication in own field.
4 Limited User	Basic competence in familiar situations. Frequent problems in understanding; no use of complex language.
3 Extremely Limited User	Only understands general meaning in familiar situations. Has many problems communicating in English.
2 Intermittent User	No real communication is possible except for the most basic information. Has difficulty understanding spoken and written English.
1 Non User	Has no real ability to use the language beyond a few words.
0 Did not attempt the test	His performance cannot be assessed.